Modern Women Modernizing Men

Ruth Compton Brouwer

Modern Women Modernizing Men: The Changing Missions of Three Professional Women in Asia and Africa, 1902-69

UBCPress · Vancouver · Toronto

09 08 07 06 05 04 03 02   5 4 3 2 1

Printed in Canada on acid-free paper ∞

National Library of Canada Cataloguing in Publication Data

Brouwer, Ruth Compton (date)
  Modern women modernizing men

  Includes bibliographical references and index.
  ISBN 0-7748-0952-3 (bound); ISBN 0-7748-0953-1 (pbk.)

  1. Oliver, Belle Choné, 1875-1947. 2. Murray, Florence J., 1894-1975. 3. Wrong, Margaret, 1887-1948. 4. Women missionaries – Canada – Biography. I. Title.
BV2610.B76 2002   266'.0092'271   C2002-910487-4

Canadä

UBC Press gratefully acknowledges the financial support for our publishing program of the Government of Canada through the Book Publishing Industry Development Program (BPIDP), and of the Canada Council for the Arts, and the British Columbia Arts Council.

This book has been published with the help of a grant from the Humanities and Social Sciences Federation of Canada, using funds provided by the Social Sciences and Humanities Research Council of Canada.

Printed and bound in Canada by Friesens
Set in Stone by Artegraphica Design Co. Ltd.
Copy editor: Jacqueline Larson
Proofreader: Craig Wilson
Indexer: Christine Jacobs
Cartographer: Eric Leinberger

UBC Press
The University of British Columbia
2029 West Mall
Vancouver, BC V6T 1Z2
(604) 822-5959 / Fax: (604) 822-6083
www.ubcpress.ca

In memory of John, 1945-98

Contents

Illustrations / viii

Preface and Acknowledgments / x

Introduction / 3

1 "A Life Lived and Not a Message Delivered":
Challenge and Change in Interwar Missions / 11

2 "Colleagues and Eventually Successors":
Dr. Choné Oliver and the Struggle to Establish a Christian
Medical College in Late Colonial India / 34

3 The Triumph of "Standards" over "Sisterhood":
Florence Murray's Approach to the Practice and Teaching
of Western Medicine in Korea, 1921-69 / 66

4 Books for Africa: Margaret Wrong and the Gendering of
African Literature, 1929-63 / 96

5 Women in a Transitional Era: Links and Legacies / 120

Appendices / 132

Notes / 136

Select Bibliography / 178

Index / 194

Illustrations

44 Map of colonial India in Dr. Choné Oliver's time, showing places where she toured or worked

45 Dr. Choné Oliver in 1900, the year she graduated from the Woman's Medical College, Toronto, and in 1945, the year before her final retirement as secretary of the Christian Medical Association of India

46 Members of the CMAI medical college and executive committee meet in Allahabad in 1931

46 Dr. T.J. Joseph

47 Medical delegates and conference medical staff at the International Missionary Conference, Tambaram, India, December 1938

47 Dr. Hilda Lazarus, the first Indian woman appointed to the Women's Medical Service in colonial India

77 Map of Korea showing places where Dr. Florence Murray worked

78 Florence Murray in 1919

78 Dr. Murray and Dr. T.S. Lee holding babies and with the entire team of doctors at the mission hospital, Hamhung

79 Dr. P.K. Koh, who replaced Murray as superintendent of the mission hospital, Hamhung, in 1941

79 Dr. Helen Kim, president of Ewha Womans University

79 Murray with Korean war orphan Soon-Kile

80 Murray and unidentified friends stand before the monument erected at "Murray Village" to recognize her multifaceted work with families affected by leprosy

102 Map of continental Africa showing countries/colonies, cities, and some mission sites visited by Margaret Wrong

104 Margaret Wrong (Marga) with her father near Murray Bay, Quebec, 1906

104 Marga, probably as a teenager, at the Wrongs' country home near Whitby, Ontario, and in the 1930s

105 Margaret Wrong and Margaret Read with friend Elsie Gordon in front of a village hut, possibly the one Wrong and Read lived in in 1936 during their three-week stay in a Nyasaland (Malawi) village

105 Wrong displaying pictures and books at a makeshift stall in a village market, Nyasaland, 1936

106 Wrong and others at the Dick-Whittaker Dairy Parlour, Mason County, Alabama, 1947

106 Dr. Christian G. Baëta

106 Joseph H. Oldham some four decades after he had become the first general secretary of the International Missionary Council in 1921

Preface and Acknowledgments

Dr. T.Y. Whang, who liked to describe himself as Canada's first permanent Korean immigrant, consented readily when I asked to interview him about medical missionary Florence Murray in December 1998. He suggested his local Swiss Chalet as a meeting place and, on the appointed day, urged me to order the Christmas Special and resisted my efforts to pick up the cheque. "She taught me how to hold a scalpel," he said, by way of beginning his reminiscences about Dr. Murray and the mission hospital in northern Korea to which he had gone as a young intern in the late 1930s. Had he objected to Dr. Murray's teaching, I asked, mindful of the fact that men of his time and place had not been accustomed to mentoring by women and that Murray had been, by her own admission, a demanding taskmaster. Although Dr. Whang responded politely to my question, it was clear that he found it inane: having received little in the way of clinical training in the Japanese-run medical school in Seoul where he had been a student, he had gone to the mission hospital to get hands-on training, and Murray was eager to provide it. It was as simple as that. And yet, surely, not at all simple, given the cross-race, cross-gender dynamics that underlay their professional relationship and the fact that it developed in a Christian hospital under the ultimate control of a non-Western, non-Christian colonial power. The situation called for a kind of all-round wariness, and yet it did not preclude professional growth on the part of pupil and teacher. Surgery was Dr. Whang's main lesson, but with the medical journals that Murray lent him, he also began acquiring an English-language medical vocabulary and a window on the larger world of Western medicine.

There was much else that was fascinating about Dr. Whang's life as related over that lunchtime interview and in subsequent telephone and written contacts: the mission arrangements that brought him to Canada for further medical training in 1948; two decades of practice in northern Ontario following the painful decision not to return to war-torn Korea and his people in the communist-controlled North; two further decades in Toronto, where, ironically, he learned acupuncture and, in retirement, worked for the establishment of a permanent Korean gallery at the Royal Ontario Museum. Inevitably, given the central theme of this book, what interested me most about Dr. Whang's life was that period in a mission hospital in 1930s Hamhung when, as a young man, he had interned under a strong-minded Western woman. She, rather than he, is one of the subjects of the book. And yet it could not have been written without the help of people like Dr. Whang. He was just one of a large number of men and women who agreed to talk or write to me about Drs. Oliver, Murray, and Wrong, and the places and conditions of their work. The names of many interviewees and informants are listed in Appendix 1. But the list is not exhaustive, and it cannot begin to convey the usefulness and the sheer pleasure of talking to and hearing from men and women generous with their time and their memories. They have, quite simply, enriched my life as well as my research. One of my regrets about not having finished this book sooner is that several elderly informants died before I could thank them in print.

Since the book deals with religion, a controversial topic, and particularly with missions, an even more controversial topic, it may be of interest to my readers – as it certainly was to people like Dr. Whang – to know something about my personal relationship to the subject matter of my research. The book is written from a scholar's perspective rather than a faith position, but it takes seriously, and I hope treats respectfully, the religious beliefs of my three subjects and of the women and men, Christian and non-Christian, among whom they worked. I would like to think that if they were alive to read it they would not consider it demeaning of their lives and values, even if they found particular conclusions wrong-headed. Similarly, I hope that scholars of missions whose approach is less "respectful" than mine will nonetheless find plausible alternative interpretations in the pages that follow and that colleagues who share my interest in the history of women and the professions will enjoy seeing how three Western professional women responded to the particular challenges facing them in twentieth-century colonial settings.

It is a pleasure to acknowledge the debt I owe to scholars in these and other areas of research. The endnotes list books and articles cited directly, but numerous other works opened windows into the cultural and physical worlds of Choné Oliver, Florence Murray, and Margaret Wrong. In planning for and carrying out an all too brief research trip to east and west Africa in 1993, I had generous help from Nakanike Musisi of Kampala and the University of Toronto, from Nina Mba of the University of Lagos, and from Canon John Rye, in Toronto and Accra, among many others. For assistance in arranging and conducting research in South Korea in 1997, I am particularly indebted to my King's College colleague J.D. Han, to Nan Hudson, East Asia Area Secretary, Division of World Outreach, United Church of

Canada, and, in Seoul, to Lori Crocker, Helen Shepherd, and Margaret Storey. From her new home in Toronto Marion Current put me in touch with former Korea colleagues and friends and introduced me to Dr. Whang. Among those who helped with my India research in 1999, I want especially to thank Dr. Cherian Thomas, then president of the Christian Medical Association of India, and his associates, and Maina Singh, an enthusiastic colleague in mission studies and a generous host in New Delhi. Dozens of administrators, academics, and medical personnel in Nagpur, Bangalore, and Vellore also went out of their way to be helpful.

The families of Choné Oliver, Florence Murray, and Margaret Wrong gave ready access to personal papers. For this access and much anecdotal information I happily acknowledge Glenna Jamieson, Heather Murray, the late Agnes Wrong Armstrong, and Jo LaPierre. Archivists and librarians in Asia, Africa, and the West provided invaluable assistance in person and/or by mail. For their patience with return visits and follow-up requests, I am especially grateful to Joan Duffy and Martha Lund Smalley at the Yale Divinity School Library; to Rosemary Seton at the University of London School of Oriental and African Studies library; and to Alex Thomson and other staff at the United Church of Canada/Victoria University Archives, Toronto. For the financial help that made this protracted research project possible, I am happy to thank several institutions: the Social Sciences and Humanities Research Council of Canada for a Canada Research Fellowship, held at York University, 1990-93; Associated Medical Services, Incorporated, for grants-in-aid from the Hannah Institute for the History of Medicine for my research on Drs. Choné Oliver and Florence Murray; and King's College, University of Western Ontario, for grants for research on Oliver, Murray, and Margaret Wrong.

Portions of Chapters 3 and 4 of this book draw on previously published material. I am grateful to the publishers of the following journals and books for allowing me to use it in altered form here:

- "Margaret Wrong's Literacy Work and the 'Remaking of Woman' in Africa, 1920-48," *The Journal of Imperial and Commonwealth History* 23, 3 (1995): 427-52.
- "Books for Africans: Margaret Wrong and the Gendering of African Writing, 1929-63," *International Journal of African Historical Studies* 31, 1 (1998): 53-71.
- "Beyond 'Women's Work for Women': Dr. Florence Murray and the Practice and Teaching of Western Medicine in Korea, 1921-1942," in *Challenging Professions: Historical and Contemporary Perspectives on Women's Professional Work*, ed. Elizabeth Smyth, Sandra Acker, Paula Bourne, and Alison Prentice (Toronto: University of Toronto Press, 1999), 65-95.

- "Standards versus Sisterhood: Dr. Murray, President Kim, and the Introduction of Medical Education at Ewha Womans University, Seoul, 1947-1950," in *Nation, Ideas, Identities: Essays in Honour of Ramsay Cook*, ed. Michael D. Behiels and Marcel Martel (Toronto: Oxford University Press, 2000), 161-79.

For permission to quote from unpublished correspondence I gratefully acknowledge the following:

- Dalhousie University Archives for an excerpt from Dr. Florence Murray to "Dear Folks," 4 August 1967, in Robert Murray and Family Papers, MS-2/535, file G-2.
- Nova Scotia Archives and Records Management for excerpts from the following letters by Dr. Florence Murray, held in vol. 2276 of Maritime Missionaries to Korea Collection, Public Archives of Nova Scotia: file 1, 21 September 1921 to Foster; file 3, 15 August 1922 to Family, 20 August 1922, 2 October 1922 to "Dear Folks," 27 December 1922 to Father; file 8, 24 August 1925 to Father; and file 13, 15 September 1930 to "Dear Friends."
- United Church of Canada/Victoria University Archives for excerpts from the following letters by Dr. Florence Murray held in United Church of Canada, Woman's Missionary Society, Overseas Missions, Korea Correspondence: box 2, file 25, 20 August 1947 to Mrs. Taylor; box 83, file 51a, 28 November 1946 to Mr. Thomas Hobbs (copy).
- Yale Divinity School Library (YDL), for an excerpt from Dr. Florence Murray to Dr. William P. Fenn, 19 August 1954, in YDL, Special Collections, United Board for Christian Higher Education in Asia, Addendum A (UBCHEA-A), RG11A, box 181, folder 2578, Yonsei/Murray, Florence J./July-December 1954. (See page 93 of this book for the excerpt.)

Katherine Ridout and Marguerite Van Die generously read an earlier draft of the manuscript and provided sound advice, as did anonymous readers for the Aid to Scholarly Publications Programme funded by the SSHRC. Those who read and commented on portions of the manuscript, or on the published articles on which I have drawn for parts of Chapters 3 and 4, include Marion Current, Pat Dirks, Elizabeth Elbourne, Nina Mba, Jean McKenzie Leiper, Wyn Millar, and Cherian Thomas. Like other scholars who present work in progress at conferences and workshops, I have also benefited from informal as well as formal comments, shared anecdotes, and research tips. During the last half of the 1990s I was able to link up with congenial colleagues with overlapping research interests through a trans-Atlantic network, NAMP (the North Atlantic Missiology Project, which evolved into the Currents in World Christianity project), and a Canadian network for research on women and the professions (succeeded by the Research Group on Women and Professional Education). It is a pleasure to acknowledge the support I have received from UBC Press, first from Associate Director, Editorial, Jean Wilson and, more recently, from Managing Editor Holly Keller-Brohman. With the technical assistance of copy editor Jacqueline Larson, they have done a great deal to improve this book and shown convincingly that a long-distance relationship with a publisher can work. Problems of fact and questionable interpretations undoubtedly remain in the book, but neither UBC staff nor any of the people named in the preceding pages bears any responsibility for them.

My last words of thanks are to family and friends for enduring a decade's worth of missionary stories and for providing unfaltering support.

Modern Women Modernizing Men

Introduction

In the period between the two world wars, the phrase "women's work for women" increasingly fell into disuse as a way of representing women's work in overseas missions. Departing from the separate spheres approach of an earlier generation, some women in the mainstream Protestant missionary enterprise entered work worlds where their colleagues and clients were mainly men. This book is about three such women: Canadians Belle Choné Oliver (1875-1947), Florence Jessie Murray (1894-1975), and Margaret Christian Wrong (1887-1948). In calling them "modern," I am using the term neither in a strictly literal nor a mainly ironic sense, as the pages that follow will show. As for the "modernizing men" in the title, it refers to those Western men whose response to changing times and whose commitment to efficiency in interwar missions enabled them to work in more or less collegial – if not fully egalitarian – relationships with women like Oliver, Murray, and Wrong, either in foreign "fields" or from office desks in Britain and North America. It also refers to Asians and Africans who were colleagues or protegés of these women, associating with them from motives that reflected shared religious and professional commitments, personal or nationalist ambitions, or some combination thereof. Regarding Asian and African men, it is perhaps unnecessary to point out that, at the same time that Christianity was being jettisoned by many self-conscious moderns in the West, it was serving as a modernizing vehicle among various colonized and non-Western people.

Choné Oliver, the daughter of a small-town Ontario businessman, and Florence Murray, a minister's daughter from Atlantic Canada, began their medical missionary careers in overseas missions of the Presbyterian Church in Canada (after 1925, missions of the United Church of Canada). Arriving in India in 1902, Oliver left hospital work in 1929 for the world of missions bureaucracy, becoming the first full-time secretary of the Christian Medical Association of India (CMAI) and undertaking as her chief project the upgrading of Christian medical education. Its timing influenced by

Indian nationalism and a new theology of medical missions, that project became a crusade for the remainder of her life, as Chapter 2 explains. In Japanese-ruled Korea from 1921, following a period of professional preparation much different from Oliver's, Murray, too, fostered the upgrading of missionary medicine but in a direct and "hands-on" way as the superintendent of a general mission hospital. That stage of her career, which came to an end in 1942, is the main focus of Chapter 3. Margaret Wrong, the most privileged of the three by background and education, came from a Toronto Anglican family with important links to church, state, and university. Like Oliver, she entered the world of missionary ecumenism in 1929. Working out of London, England, she travelled tens of thousands of miles through sub-Saharan Africa as secretary of the International Committee on Christian Literature for Africa (ICCLA), a subcommittee of the International Missionary Council (IMC). Under Wrong, "Christian Literature" came to include a wide range of literary materials, secular as well as religious, and Africans came to be envisaged as writers as well as readers, as Chapter 4 demonstrates.

Although in taking up these careers they entered work worlds that privileged men, and did so as "modern" women, Oliver, Murray, and Wrong demonstrated what we would now call a feminist consciousness and also a strong Christian faith.[1] They were in sympathy with causes such as female suffrage and ordination at home, and they were moved by the plight of marginalized groups of women in their fields of work. Yet they eschewed careers that would have had them labouring for causes exclusively related to their own sex. In this respect they were part of a larger contemporary pattern in the West, one especially evident among professional women. One scholar has identified it as a hallmark of "modern feminism."[2] Other aspects of these women's relationship with interwar modernity were characterized by the uneven, unstable quality that one would expect of well-educated women in their line of work: too worldly wise to retain all the old certainties, too faithful and conventional and morally engaged for the new skepticism and smartness.[3] Beyond these generalizations, the patterns of social behaviour and religious expression in the three women's lives were strikingly different – and non-linear. Indeed, such patterns seem to have been functions of temperament, background, and working environment to a greater degree than of age and chronological timing.

Only twelve years younger than Oliver and seven years older than Murray, Wrong had a more modern sensibility in all the ways that are most easily perceptible. Where Oliver, for instance, spoke reverentially of "Mr. Oldham," the first secretary of the IMC (to which both her organization and Wrong's were linked), Wrong spoke casually of "Joe" and saw nothing untoward in sharing dinner and wine with him when both were at meetings in Germany.[4] Likewise, she had no taste for the intense religious language that seems to have been as natural for Oliver as comments about the weather. As for Murray, while she outgrew her youthful uncompromising disapproval of drinking and dancing as grievous sins, she seems never to have been tempted to try such behaviours herself.[5] And if, unlike Oliver, she did not wear her faith on her sleeve, the evidence in private correspondence and from colleagues who remember her nonetheless bespeaks serene religious convictions. Wrong did not become cynical about religion even after the death of one brother in wartime France and another at Oxford in 1928, but she moved in a social world where religious cynicism was becoming a new norm, and these family tragedies were severe tests. Yet if the three women were dissimilar in their familiarity with and ability to accommodate the social and intellectual challenges of modernity, they nonetheless shared a broad commitment to the modernizing of missions in ways that would incorporate both new techniques and technologies from the West and the special gifts and goals of indigenous Christianity.

The segments of the three women's careers featured in this book may be read as case studies of a missionary world in transition. Their work reflected changes taking place in the mainstream missionary enterprise, which, in turn, reflected larger changes in the West and in Asia and Africa. The reality – and the perception – of secularization and materialism, and the increased importance attached to professional training in the West, had a significant impact on the international missions community, as did the demands of nationalizing and Westernizing young men in mission settings. These broad patterns of stimulus and response in the missionary enterprise are discussed in Chapter 1 in order to provide the necessary context for subsequent chapters on Oliver, Murray, and Wrong.

Missions in Asia and Africa were generally located in formal colonies; their relationships with their colonial hosts ranged over time and according to circumstances from symbiotic to ambiguous to hostile. During the last few decades, postcolonial studies and scholarly studies of missions have flourished. Regrettably, they have developed largely as separate spheres. Dane Kennedy's 1996 injunction to conventional imperial historians to broaden their "methodological horizons" by taking account of postcolonial scholarship, notwithstanding its empirical shortcomings and "theoretical excesses," is equally apt for missions historians.[6] In the realm of women and missions, for instance, we have sometimes been too inclined to read the discourse of missions-minded women uncritically, interpreting a progressive language of sisterhood as proof of egalitarian practice while minimizing their personal investment in stereotyping and dramatizing the "plight" of "Oriental womanhood."[7] Andrew Porter's interrogation of the concept of "cultural imperialism" illustrates the benefits to be derived when an imperial historian with an interest in missions responds methodically to issues raised in postcolonial critiques. Brian Stanley's *The Bible and the Flag* is also attuned to such critiques, at once a rigorous work of scholarship and a forthright statement of a faith position. Written from yet another angle, the introduction and some of the essays in a recent collection edited by Mary Taylor Huber and Nancy Lutkehaus suggest that valuable insights may be drawn from a cross-fertilization of missions, gender, and postcolonial scholarship.[8]

If historians of missions have been slow to draw on the insights of postcolonial scholars, postcolonialists have been even less inclined to undertake, or engage with, research on missions. Neither the most seminal works of postcolonial scholarship nor those that have followed in their wake have devoted much attention to close-grained, discrete studies of missions, or of indigenous Christian groups and their relations to colonialism.[9] Among postcolonial scholars who have taken women and missions as their subject matter, a few seem almost embarrassed about having done so, given what Susan Thorne calls "the missionary project['s] ... present state of postcolonial disgrace," and hence are at pains not to appear as apologists for women missionaries' activities.[10] One also finds a widespread assumption that mission Christianity was just another expression of colonialism's praxis, the missionary perhaps nicer than the local colonial authority in his or her relations with "the native" but with the same ultimate goals in view.[11] Missionaries often emerge from such studies as men and women incapable of change, too rigid or obtuse to learn from new circumstances.[12] That some of them *were* like that is unlikely to be disputed by anyone who has spent much time in mission archives. But the same records also reveal individuals who changed considerably in the course of their careers and provide evidence of significant generational differences in missionaries' attitudes to their cultural environment. Fortunately, studies of missionaries and their relationships to colonialism and indigenous culture that allow for complexity and change are beginning to emerge in postcolonial scholarship.[13] Meanwhile, much valuable and relevant research defies any neat historiographic label. By the breadth of its range and sympathies, Terence Ranger's work on Africa, for instance, serves all scholars with an interest in interactions between indigenous people and colonial and missionary interveners.[14]

Even if it is increasingly recognized that missions had an agenda distinct from formal colonialism, the question remains: was missionary activity imperialism in a cultural dress? Missionaries, it could be argued, were cultural imperialists par excellence, seeking as their ultimate goal nothing less than to win the souls of another people, a change more fundamental than anything envisioned by colonial lawmakers or Western profiteers. As a result of constraining circumstances and their own increasing diffidence, missionaries often stopped short of that ultimate goal, or quietly abandoned it, especially in the period featured in this book, and confined themselves on a daily basis to working for specific social and material changes. Did that make them less "imperialistic"? The paradoxical nature of their endeavours is highlighted in an argument made by Brian Stanley and William Hutchison, among others: that as liberal missionaries became increasingly involved in trying to improve here-and-now conditions for the missionized rather than "saving" them for the hereafter, it was they, rather than more narrowly focused proselytizers, who were closer, in practice, to "cultural imperialism."[15] Andrew Porter, on the other hand, finds "cultural imperialism" unhelpful as a label for what Protestant missionaries sought to do in the high imperial era. Following the logic that applies the concept to all missionary interventions, he argues, all "externally induced reform ... can be seen as part of cultural imperialism ... Only if it can somehow be shown that change involved no external ingredients and occurred in the absence of imbalances of material or social power, could we perhaps presume otherwise."[16] If the concept is to be useful for the interwar era it must, at a minimum, take account of the fact that by that time many participants in the missionary movement were seeking to function as cultural gatekeepers. In that self-appointed role, they sought to sustain and even vivify various aspects of "tradition" rather than to substitute Western culture wholesale. Meanwhile, many of the missionized were showing considerable agency in adopting only what they wanted from the menu of missionary offerings, and a few were agitating vigorously for deletions and additions.

The tendency in scholarship dealing with missions (from whatever "school" it comes) has been to focus on those missions located in colonies of the European powers and especially the British Empire. There have been few attempts at systematic comparisons of differences in broad aims, strategies, and outcomes in locations where the missionaries and the colonial power were, and were not, united by their cultural and religious backgrounds, although T.O. Beidelman long ago pointed to the need for these and analogous types of comparisons.[17] *Good Citizens: British Missionaries and Imperial States, 1870-1918* provides this sort of perspective by looking at the relations of British missionary societies with French, Belgian, German, and British colonial administrators and their policies.[18] But what was the nature of the relationship between missions and the colonial power when the colonizer was neither Western nor Christian? *Good Citizens* deals only briefly with this question; the present work makes no pretense of answering it fully. Yet the research on which Chapter 3 is based suggests that missionaries in Japanese-ruled Korea pursued essentially the same kinds of goals and institutional strategies as their counterparts in British colonial settings, while necessarily working under particular constraints.[19] What is striking, however, is that there could also be significant advantages and opportunities for missionaries who worked in a setting where the colonizers were not cultural kin.

The relationship between missions and colonialism is an important subtheme in this book, but its central concern is changing gender roles and relationships. Mine is not the first book on women and the overseas missionary movement to note the waning of the separate spheres phenomenon.[20] To my knowledge, however, it is the first to foreground that phenomenon and explore its significance in specific mission settings. How representative was the experience of my three subjects in this respect? So few case studies of interwar missionary activity have been undertaken to date that other accounts of shifts in gender roles and professional responsibilities are largely unavailable. Margaret Prang's biography of Caroline Macdonald, a YWCA secretary turned prison and labour reformer in Japan, seems to illustrate the "modern women modernizing men" phenomenon, but Prang does not speculate on the possible representativeness of Macdonald's career evolution.[21] An in-house account of the establishment and functioning of the IMC and its ancillary bodies showed women enthusiastically and successfully taking on non-gendered roles, and as I will explain in Chapter 1, some missionary modernizers advocated coeducation at advanced levels.[22] (As studies of gender and interwar imperialism appear, instances of secular women working with, and mentoring, men are also emerging, Margery Perham being the outstanding example.)[23] It is certainly too soon to say that these kinds of developments signalled wholesale change across mission sites. However, what cannot be denied is that the once-dominant paradigm of separate spheres lost its salience as changing Western and colonial contexts, and new personal and professional ambitions, coalesced in a modernizing project that allowed (indeed, bade) women like Oliver, Murray, and Wrong to enter work worlds where their colleagues and clients were mainly men.

It is important to emphasize that the chapters on Oliver, Murray, and Wrong are not intended to serve as biographies. In introducing each chapter, I have tried to provide sufficient biographical information to make sense of what follows. But by choosing to focus on a particular aspect of the career of each of the women, I have necessarily omitted or given short shrift to topics worthy of further attention: Oliver's social hygiene work, for instance; Wrong's involvement in the early 1920s with the European Student Relief branch of the World Student Christian Federation; Murray's event-filled years in postcolonial Korea; and the private lives of all three women. Nor are their Canadian origins and ties given much attention. While their nationality seems to have made Oliver and Wrong attractive candidates for their respective positions in missions bureaucracies by virtue of Canada's unexceptionable role in the mission version of the North Atlantic triangle, neither woman made much of her Canadianness on the job or was controlled by made-in-Canada funding or policy decisions. Wrong's Canadian identity was obscured by her long residence in England and her ties with organizations based there. Significantly, when in 1942 she attended the eighth conference of the Institute of Pacific Relations, held in Quebec, she was part of the United Kingdom rather than the Canadian delegation. Murray's Canadian identity – and also, in her early years, her Maritime regional identity – were certainly important to her and frequently expressed in acerbic anti-American comments, even in the Cold War era. Yet she, too, was a product of an era when international "brotherhood" and Christian internationalism were concepts as salient for mainstream Protestant missionaries and their supporters, as they were for many of their counterparts in the nascent world of Canadian diplomacy and international relations.[24] Ecumenism took all three women beyond nationalism as well as beyond denominationalism. Nothing, perhaps, illustrates the ecumenical and cosmopolitan nature of their working lives more tellingly than the fact that although Oliver and Wrong seem to have known each other only in passing or by reputation, they had many international contacts in common, among them prominent spokesmen for Asian and African Christianity.

As aware as they were of the growth of secularization in the West in their own era, and of the enthusiasm for evangelism among many indigenous Christians, Oliver, Murray, and Wrong could scarcely have imagined the changed patterns that would have emerged by the end of the twentieth century. The numerical strength and the vitality of Christianity have shifted decisively from Europe and North America to the Southern Hemisphere, and the typical "missionary" both comes from and evangelizes there. In spite of restrictions or outright bans on European missionaries in many newly independent countries in the postcolonial era, Christianity was able to spread "as a people's movement."[25] To be sure, missionaries are still going from the North to the South, and in surprisingly large numbers. But they are mainly American evangelicals, committed not to the causes featured in this book, but rather to meeting what some of them call "the unreached people's challenge."[26] As for the United Church of Canada, the Canadian denomination with which all three of my subjects had their most significant professional links, its Board of World Missions has long since been transformed into the Division of World Outreach; it works on development issues with overseas "partners," religious and secular, much like other nongovernmental organizations.[27] The chapters that follow are part of the history of that transformation writ large and, perhaps in a small way, provide insights into ongoing challenges in global good works and gender issues in development.

1
"A Life Lived and Not a Message Delivered": Challenge and Change in Interwar Missions

In 1934 an article called "Ideals of the Missionary Enterprise" appeared in the *Indian Social Reformer*, a nationalist weekly whose editor provided considerable space for exponents of Christian missions even as he subjected them to his critical gaze. The text of a sermon preached at Cambridge by former missionary Paul Gibson, the article dealt with the challenges that had confronted the enterprise since the First World War. The war, Gibson wrote, had exposed to the rest of the world the lack of real Christianity in the so-called Christian nations. The Jerusalem Conference of the International Missionary Council a decade later had rightly acknowledged "that the imminent danger lay not in non-Christian religions but in the rapid spread of secularism." With nationalism also on the rise, missionaries could no longer afford to arrive from the West with a complacent sense of superiority. Instead, they must demonstrate a willingness to be co-workers with increasingly vigorous indigenous churches. As for the non-Christian religions, now that the sophistication of their texts was known, their adherents could no longer be regarded as benighted victims, dependent for salvation on missionary preaching. The central challenge of missionary work had passed "from enunciation of doctrine to the compelling power of the Christian life." Yes, Christ offered something unique and "universally needed" in the personal link He provided between God and man. Nonetheless, what was required of the modern missionary was a "life lived and not a message delivered."[1]

As anyone familiar with this period in the history of the mainstream Protestant missionary movement can attest, observations such as those made by Gibson were the stock in trade of missions-minded men and women of a moderate to liberal bent at the "home base" and in many "foreign fields." (Even these once-routine geographic signifiers were now under scrutiny.) The one point raised by Gibson that was perhaps not as routinely made was that governments were now taking up the kinds of educational, medical, and agricultural work that missions had pioneered. Although he did not elaborate, the implication was that missions would need to improve their performance in these areas in order to avoid redundancy.

Like Gibson's article, this chapter deals with changes taking place in the world of missions in the period after the First World War. Inevitably subjective and necessarily selective, it focuses on developments that had broad significance for the careers of Oliver, Murray, and Wrong, and makes frequent use of representative individuals and illustrative anecdotes. Although I have taken challenge and change as the broad theme for this chapter, I have tried not to lose sight of the fact that this was very much a transitional era, both within and beyond the world of missions. Alongside new institutions and the "ideals" and threats that Gibson identified, there were continuities with an earlier time, unevennesses in the shifts taking place, even in individual lives, and sometimes reversions to old norms and attitudes. For the moderates and liberals of the mainstream Protestant missionary movement with which this chapter is concerned, the old certainties were undeniably gone, and there was a new sense of a need for circumspection and humility in living out a missionary calling. But the new approach did not automatically foster healthier relationships with the missionaries' Other. An exemplary "life lived" could breed its own kind of arrogance; zeal in applying Christianity through social reforms and the application of Western techniques and technologies could, in practice, be even more culturally invasive than a narrowly focused zeal for conversions; and it always proved easier to "talk the talk" of devolution than to put it into effect.

These risks and conundrums confronted missionaries of both sexes. Many professional women in the movement experienced them while also moving away from the "women's work for women" paradigm that had defined the role expectations – if not always the practices – of their predecessors.[2] Neither Gibson nor other contemporary commentators on the interwar mission enterprise were attentive to that particular change. Nonetheless, it had a significance that reached well beyond the women most directly concerned.

Ecumenical Superstructures

Some major structural features of the interwar foreign missionary movement had begun taking shape prior to the First World War. The establishment of a permanent international and ecumenical organization to facilitate the achievement of shared mission goals was perhaps the most important such development. American dominance in the movement, in terms of broad approach and values as well as volume of personnel and financing, was increasingly evident (and here, too, there were pre-war roots).[3] Nonetheless, the international missions bureaucracy would have its base and key actors in Britain. The historic international missionary conference at Edinburgh in 1910 was chaired by the dynamic American layman John R. Mott, but another layman, Joseph H. Oldham (who was India-born of Scottish parents), was responsible for conference preparations, and it was he who became editor of the *International Review of Missions (IRM)*, established in 1912, and salaried secretary of the Continuation Committee that worked after Edinburgh to establish a permanent organization. The outcome of the latter effort, delayed by the First World War, was the establishment of the International Missionary Council (IMC). The stages in its creation reflected the attempt to have British, continental, and North American involvement in organizing international mission structures. The groundwork meeting was held in Crans, Switzerland, in 1920. The official founding took place at Lake Mohonk, New York, a year later, and "head office" was Edinburgh House, London, where the Conference of British Missionary Societies (CBMS) also had its headquarters. John Mott became the IMC's first chairman, and another American, A.L. Warnshuis, was Oldham's associate secretary, based in New York from 1924. Still, Oldham remained the key figure in IMC planning and networking, even for some years after he had persuaded the peripatetic Mott to make the chairmanship his main commitment and after William Paton (a fellow Scot) had joined him at Edinburgh House in 1927 as associate secretary.[4]

IMC "members" were national or regional organizations of mission boards or churches rather than individual institutions, the CBMS and the Foreign Missions Conference of North America (FMCNA) being the largest of these. Canada's leading Protestant denominations were members of the FMCNA. The United Church of Canada, the home church after 1925 of Choné Oliver and Florence Murray, and the chief Canadian supporter of Margaret Wrong's work, was affiliated with the FMCNA through its Board of Foreign Missions and its Woman's Missionary Society. Created as a result of the union of Methodist, Congregationalist, and most Presbyterian churches, the new United Church – now the largest Protestant denomination in the country – was a vibrant expression of practical ecumenism and as such a good fit within the IMC family of member organizations.[5]

The IMC did not interfere with the doctrines and faith practices of the denominations in its member organizations or with their particular missionary policies. But its ecumenism and its focus on institutional and social service work nonetheless made it an unacceptable umbrella body for some conservatives and fundamentalists. Large numbers of fundamentalists, strongest in the US, withdrew from mainline denominations in the 1920s (more would leave in the 1930s) and went on to establish their own mission organizations. The British and Canadian member-organizations, having experienced less dramatic ruptures from modernist-fundamentalist controversies, perhaps had a greater diversity of theological views to bring to their participation in the IMC, but overall the dominant tone was moderate.[6]

The IMC functioned as a coordinating and central planning body and, in theory at least, only in an advisory capacity, pursuing its goals through the extensive travels of its senior officers and the routine work of their permanent staff, the activities of ad hoc and permanent committees, and periodic administrative and international conferences. Margaret Wrong would come to be part of the IMC fold in 1929 as secretary of one of its specialized committees. What looms largest in contemporary and later accounts of the IMC, though, is not its routine work or specialized committees but rather its international missionary conferences. In these accounts, the words "Jerusalem" and "Tambaram" are immediately understood to refer to the conferences and to have momentous significance. The first, held in 1928, and, to an even greater degree, the second, held in 1938 at Tambaram, near Madras, brought together delegates from the "older" and "younger" churches. Following a pattern begun in preparation for the Edinburgh conference, these men – and some women – were expected to have done much advance preparation by reading position papers and printed agendas that were previously circulated and to return to their own region as publicists and promoters of what they had seen and learned.[7] As will be seen later in this chapter, the conferences could be dramatically effective as sources of inspiration and empowerment. The first IMC conference held after the Second World War, at Whitby, Ontario, in 1947, is presented as a smaller and less noteworthy event in the history of the organization, its significance undoubtedly overshadowed by the formal establishment a year later of a long-sought goal of many IMC leaders: the World Council of Churches.[8]

Between 1921 and 1948, member organizations of the IMC in the non-Western world increased from just four, out of a total of seventeen, to eighteen out of thirty.[9] Mott and Oldham had made it an early priority to establish such organizations and to encourage a strong indigenous presence in them rather than a mere token representation of nationals in mission-dominated bodies. The national Christian councils established in the early 1920s in China, Japan, and India were notably successful in this respect. For instance, the constitution of the National Christian Council of India, Burma, and Ceylon (the NCC), which replaced the National Missionary Council in 1923, required the council to have a governing body that was at least 50 percent Indian. Its structure and function replicated that of the IMC, with representatives drawn from provincial and regional councils, a periodical to further its goals, salaried executive secretaries, and others employed in specialized roles, the number of whom inevitably grew. Choné Oliver was responsible for the NCC's medical committee in her capacity as secretary of the Christian Medical Association of India, and, for much of the period, for its social hygiene work as well. National or regional Christian councils were slower to be established in sub-Saharan Africa, and indigenous Christians had more limited roles. The 1920s saw the establishment of a national Christian council in Korea, but its successful functioning hinged uneasily on the participation of Presbyterians, the leading Christian denomination, and in

1938 it was dissolved by Japanese colonial authorities, to be reborn only after the Second World War.[10]

Unlike Oliver and Wrong, Florence Murray had no direct link to these ecumenical structures until after the Second World War. Nonetheless, her work world was also affected by them, even if only indirectly. Ecumenical initiatives, especially in higher education and medical work, had, of course, preceded the establishment of the IMC and the national mission organizations and Christian councils that came under its umbrella. Severance Union Medical College and Hospital in Seoul, where Murray worked from the late 1940s, was a good example. But the new ecumenical organizations could assist – and occasionally disrupt – even pioneer institutions through their capacity to facilitate coordination and rationalization and to discourage duplication, all in the interest of "modernizing" and "efficiency." For all that its role on paper was that of an advisory body, the IMC, especially under the leadership of men like Mott, Oldham, and Paton, had access to the corridors of political power, and this, as well as its ability to influence the spending priorities of mission boards, could significantly affect the circumstances of missionaries' work.

Challenges and Responses

As Brian Stanley has observed, "Missions in the twentieth century ... had to relate, both to the mature forces of Western imperialism which enveloped them, and to the emergent forces of indigenous nationalism which they helped to bring to birth."[11] Necessarily, they also had to relate to changes in Western society. This section deals with the impact on missions of interacting challenges from both worlds, beginning with the most worrisome phenomenon in the West.

Secularism: The Home-Grown Enemy

The IMC officials who organized the Jerusalem conference identified secularism and materialism rather than non-Christian religions as the greatest foe of Christianity. A preparatory paper written by an American Quaker, Rufus M. Jones, at the request of Mott and Oldham, urged delegates to go to Jerusalem

> not as members of a Christian nation to convert other nations which are not Christian, but as Christians within a nation far too largely non-Christian, who face within their own borders the competition of a rival movement as powerful, as dangerous, as insidious as any of the great historic religions. We meet our fellow Christians in these other countries, therefore, on terms of equality, as fellow workers engaged in a common task. More than this, we go as those who find in the other religions which secularism attacks, as it attacks Christianity, witnesses of man's need of God and allies in our quest of perfection.[12]

The new challenges in the West were evident on a number of levels. The most directly felt impact was in the decline in the prestige of missions and their power to attract new personnel. Numbers generally held firm in most mainstream sending societies in Britain and North America until the late 1920s (in fact, they increased in the first decade after the war), but significant groups like university students were beginning to criticize past missionary methods and to show less interest in volunteering.[13] Veteran Canadian evangelist Louise McCully, home on furlough in 1923, typified a certain kind of reaction among older missionaries when she lamented "the declension in spiritual things in our own land" and longed to return to Korea, where "the atmosphere is so much purer in every way."[14] To people like the planners of the Jerusalem conference, a skipped Sunday service or a cigarette-smoking woman (the kinds of "declension[s]" that troubled McCully) were less of a concern than the fact that in the most advanced societies the natural and social sciences were distancing themselves from religion. Far from allowing the transcendent assumptions and social policy values of elite Protestant Christianity to frame its questions and shape its agenda as it had done in its early days, social science in 1920s America was, in the words of R. Laurence Moore, "moving away from transcendent references into the realm of the rational and secular" and coming to regard religion "as a cultural artifact to be placed for purposes of objective study alongside all the other cultural artifacts that determined or circumscribed human conduct in any time and place."[15] Faced with this new context, mission reformers like Oldham did not react by attacking the sciences, for they were themselves intellectuals who recognized the power of scientific thought to reduce physical suffering and improve many facets of everyday life. But neither were they prepared to accept the view that a belief in transcendence, however labelled, could be abandoned without loss to human relationships and individual lives.[16]

It was, then, hardly surprising that, far from continuing to regard the great religions as their main enemy, many moderates and liberals in the missionary movement began to emphasize their value in the shared project of resisting a secular explanation of life. Especially in Hinduism's greatest living guru, M.K. Gandhi, they recognized a religious leader whom they, too, could revere. Certainly, conservatives and moderates never ceased to hope that Gandhi would "graduate" from recognizing Jesus as a great prophet to accepting him as God incarnate, and they grumbled privately (and sometimes publicly) when he challenged missionaries' goals and their methods of seeking converts. But given the common enemy they shared with him, their praise was genuine as well as (in India at least) pragmatic.[17]

Enthusiasm for Gandhi extended to the West and probably in most cases – and undoubtedly in Protestant Canada – owed more to his spirituality than his nationalist views.[18] In its own way, this enthusiasm provided evidence that secularism had not yet won the day. There was, of course, much more to show that Protestant Christianity's reaction to postwar skepticism and materialist explanations of life extended beyond support for religious conservatism. On both sides of the Atlantic, the Oxford Group movement appealed to middle-class people seeking a religious experience that was at once based on "sharing" (small groups were the favoured venue) and personally enriching, while neo-orthodox theology attracted those who wanted an intellectually rigorous, faith-based theology rather than a social-gospel-type understanding of the problem of evil and the Kingdom of God.[19] The social-gospel approach remained evident at the institutional level in Canada, perhaps most notably in the efforts of the United Church to make the social sciences vehicles for vivifying social Christianity rather than substitutes for it.[20]

In Britain, profoundly disturbed by the extent to which a Christian outlook was disappearing from his country's institutions and popular consciousness, Oldham turned his primary attention in the 1930s from missions and race issues in Africa to a many-faceted effort to promote a Christian understanding in his own society of such problems as totalitarianism. For many years he was joined in one facet of this struggle by a remarkable group of intellectuals collectively called "the Moot," its membership including such diverse figures as modernist literary icon T.S. Eliot and social scientist Karl Mannheim, a German Jewish refugee. The Moot's existence was testimony to the desire of individuals, vastly different in other respects, to reflect seriously on ethical and spiritual issues in a society apparently indifferent to them.[21] Few of Oldham's colleagues in the upper echelons of missions bureaucracy chose, like him, to devote their mature years to a mission to their own society, however necessary they believed it to be. Many, however, did share the concern he had expressed to Mott in 1924 that missions must effectively reinvent themselves if they were to be "adequate to the demands of the hour."[22]

Social Activism on Mission Ground
Mainstream Protestant missionaries in Asia and Africa encountered the Oxford Group movement, Barthianism, and other new religious tendencies in the course of their reading and when they were home on furlough. As Choné Oliver's diaries make clear, such encounters could have a significant impact on their private faith lives.[23] In their working lives, however, it was characteristically in terms of increased institutional and social service activity that they responded to "the demands of the hour." For fundamentalists, this was proof positive of the triumph of theological liberalism and the retreat from conventional evangelism. Some fundamentalists who had visited overseas missions insisted that liberal missionaries should frankly acknowledge what they were doing there: steeped in social gospel and

modernist teachings, they had given themselves over to "physical and social agencies, to the detriment of simple gospel preaching," though they
dared not admit that fact to their constituencies at home for fear of losing
financial support.[24] Missionaries who favoured an activist approach did not,
of course, understand or present their work as a retreat from their historic
faith but rather as an attempt to make Christianity relevant and attractive
through practical demonstrations of Christian values.

It has been commonplace for historians as well as contemporary critics to
link mainstream Protestants' social activism in their missions to the influence of the social gospel.[25] Yet it is important to remind ourselves that educational and medical work had been an important part of Anglo-Saxon
missions in the nineteenth century, particularly where women and
unordained men were participants, and that other factors in addition to the
spirit of the social gospel were also at play in the interwar era. What was
new was not social activism in itself but rather its role and rationale, its
volume and quality. With regard to all of these factors but perhaps especially the issue of quality, it is essential to take the values and assumptions
associated with professionalism into consideration. Increasingly, men and
women trained in Britain and North America in education, medicine, agriculture, social work, and other fields were unwilling to have their expertise
used amateurishly or as bait in proselytization when they took it abroad.
They wanted opportunities and facilities to do solid professional work.

The readiest examples come from the field of medicine. In the nineteenth
century, medical missionaries had understood that they were expected to use
their skills to "open doors for the gospel." Many went abroad with incom-
plete training and without any clinical experience in order to get on with this
task in settings where, it was assumed, "good enough" would be good enough
for people unfamiliar with anything better. When personal inclination or the
immediate priorities of the mission required it, medical missionaries sometimes devoted themselves wholly or mainly to evangelism or other work for
extended periods of time. Thus, in Central India, Choné Oliver was temporarily put in charge of an orphanage in 1909 when she returned from furlough,
an experience that still produced painful memories decades later.[26] The author of *The Way of a Doctor*, published in the last half of the 1920s, offered an
enthusiastic picture of the new era in missionary medicine:

> Medical Missionaries are not only urged to prepare themselves in the most
> thorough manner on the medical side, but in most instances Societies insist
> upon a high professional standard ... And intending Medical Missionaries
> are counselled to become familiar with the latest advances in Medical Sci-
> ence. The enthusiasm of the young Missionary Doctor is not damped but
> encouraged, and his plea for the best Hospital provision that can be given
> to him is viewed sympathetically.

Medical missionaries' journals and conferences, he wrote, also signalled their new desire to be active participants in the larger world of medical science.[27]

That this new approach was still far from being the norm was shown when *Re-Thinking Missions* was published in 1932, following a critical examination of mission fields in Asia by a team of American laymen. The book's depiction of veteran missionary doctors as jacks of all medical trades, used to running one-man shows, out of touch with new knowledge and standards and thus unacceptable colleagues for the new breed of professionals, gave great offence, but it was not declared to be wholly inaccurate. Acknowledging that the professional standards of "the medical pioneer in the jungle" could not be the same as those of the university professor of medicine, *Re-Thinking Missions* nonetheless insisted that "the work of the medical missionary in the jungle should be the best available in that jungle."[28] Georgina Gollock, associate editor of the *IRM*, made a similar point about professional qualifications in a paper written for the founding meeting of the IMC in 1921 and subsequently published in journal and pamphlet form. Whether preparing for ministry, educational work, or medicine, she maintained, missionary candidates should have the same standard of training as those preparing to work in their own country.[29]

As concerns about the quality and efficiency of missions' institutional work increased, it seemed to many mission modernizers, both on the ground and in the West, that union institutions supported by various denominations and, where feasible, modification of the earlier pattern of gender segregation, especially in higher education and medical work, offered appropriate routes to achieving these goals. Consolidation of effort in the fields, it was argued, would mean fewer but better institutions. Of course, for those whose institutional ox was to be gored, this was not an attractive proposition.

Pressure for the development and improvement of mission institutions for advanced education did not come only, or perhaps even mainly, from Westerners themselves. Modernizing young men with personal and/or nationalist ambitions looked to such institutions to further their goals. But, even if they were Christians, they were often quite ready to turn to state-run or other educational institutions if these promised better training and greater opportunities for advance. In early twentieth-century China, as historian Lian Xi has explained, competition from government colleges was an added incentive to move towards union education work in missions.[30] In the case of colonial Korea, state facilities for advanced education provided far too few places to meet the demand from upwardly mobile Koreans. Nevertheless, Korean students were anything but docile when it came to putting pressure on missions to improve the quality of their educational offerings.[31] In India, missions recognized that they were under particular pressure to provide high-quality educational, medical, and social services in the interwar era in order to demonstrate that they were worthy of having an ongoing place in a future, independent India.

Such pressures also contributed to the tendency in mainstream missions to sever the link between social services and proselytization. Conservative critics of this tendency associated it with modernist teaching and the new cultural milieu in the West. The missionary products of this milieu, they charged, were quite prepared to confine their efforts to good works, to live in peace with the non-Christian religions, and even to promote "syncretism." Yet as the title of Lian Xi's monograph, *The Conversion of Missionaries: Liberalism in American Protestant Missions in China, 1907-1932*, suggests for the China context, increased social activism and openness to other faiths were also responses to pressures on the ground. The old-style confrontational approach in preaching, and the linking of medical treatment and schooling to compulsory sermons and Bible lessons, was increasingly less likely to be tolerated by educated Asians as nationalism brought resentment and resistance into the open. What Gandhi called "the double purpose" in the social service work of missions, that is, helping the vulnerable with a view to weaning them from their native faith, was an aspect of missionary practice of which he was particularly critical.[32] In 1933 an unidentified but presumably Christian writer in the *Indian Social Reformer* gave a critical definition of proselytization in order to denounce it and to counter the editor's claim that Christian missions "are primarily proselytizing agencies." Proselytization, he wrote, was the practice of trying to win converts "by deprecating the faith of others, by any kind of pressure, or any kind of bribery, however subtle; anything, in a word, that does violence to the personality of others." It was the "ideal" of Christian missions, he added, to avoid any of these tactics, "though individuals may occasionally fail in achieving the ideal."[33]

The writer's claim that hearing the Christian message was entirely voluntary in normal circumstances was certainly wide of the mark when it came to mission schooling in India. Under the terms of imperial legislation dating from the mid-nineteenth century, privately operated schools had been entitled to receive government grants-in-aid without being subject to interference with their religious teaching. Mission schools had proliferated under that legislation, but in the interwar era their compulsory classes in Christianity became a subject of increasing controversy and much missionary soul-searching. Even before the Government of India Act of 1919 (the so-called Montagu-Chelmsford Reforms) made education a "transferred subject" and thus a matter for Indian-controlled provincial legislatures, there was much talk about the likely introduction of a "conscience clause" that would allow students to opt out of a religion class whose teachings conflicted with their own faith. Only one province introduced such a clause in the immediate wake of the Government of India Act, but many

missionaries saw it as only a matter of time before more provincial governments would legislate against compulsory religious teaching in grant-aided
schools, and some believed that mission educators should take the initiative and end compulsion voluntarily. Especially as nationalism increased,
non-Christian young men in the upper ranks of the mission educational
system expressed resentment about compulsory religious education.[34]

"Native" Evangelists and "Young Churches"

Full-time evangelism among non-Christians as well as much basic education was, in any case, increasingly in the hands of indigenous Christians.
Like the work of the national Christian councils, much of the routine work
of mature missions was with, and for, established Christian communities, a
matter of supervisory roles and institutional or social service activities. Ordained Western missionaries and women evangelists who went out from
their stations to the urban or rural "unreached" typically did so as a break
from their routine work. Thus, when Lesslie Newbigin (a future architect of
the merger of the IMC and the World Council of Churches) arrived in Tamil
Nadu in the late 1930s with his Cambridge theological training, and when
Hilda Johnson returned to the Central India mission from furlough in 1945
as one of the first women ordained by the United Church of Canada, neither was deployed in full-time work among non-Christians, and not only
because of language barriers.[35] In India, as in East Asia and sub-Saharan
Africa, white missionaries, whether ordained or unordained, generally
worked in supervisory or teaching or other professional roles. In the case of
Africa, historians Lammin Sanneh, Richard Gray, and Adrian Hastings have
all argued that virtually from the outset of missionary activity, African Christians themselves played the leading role in presenting the gospel and "translating" it into the cultural idioms as well as the vernaculars of its new
audiences.[36] As "missionary work" came increasingly to include such varied
matters as organizing YMCAs and YWCAs, and teaching Western agricultural techniques and social hygiene, as well as the kinds of tasks already
mentioned, there was correspondingly less opportunity for old-style
proselytization even if the inclination lingered.[37] Perhaps the most dramatic
instance of the torch being passed was in Japan in the early 1930s, where
Kagawa Toyohiko's Kingdom of God Movement with its goal of "a million
souls for Christ" was regarded as a source of leadership as well as inspiration
for Western missionaries, some of whom hoped that his evangelistic tours
of North America could also spark revivals there.[38]

Indigenous Christians were also increasingly in charge of their own
churches, which, in turn, were increasingly entities outside the direct purview of the missions, operating parallel to rather than "under" them. Here
again, perhaps the most dramatic case was in Japan, where the small but
able middle-class Christian community directed its own affairs and was

encouraged by the imperial government during the late 1930s to distance itself further from Western missions and to undertake its own missionary work in the Japanese empire. Yet even in Korea, where the Christian community was poorer and less sophisticated than in Japan (being drawn, as in many other parts of Asia, from marginalized groups), missionaries took delight in reporting that the churches there had moved rapidly towards financial independence and responsibly handled self-government, becoming "truly indigenous to an extent perhaps unique among mission fields."[39]

In India and sub-Saharan Africa, the churches remained financially dependent on Western funds to a greater degree and for longer, but especially as they gained advanced Western education and the confidence that came with it, their pastors were anything but "yes men" to their erstwhile mentors. The African independent churches (AICs) that began to appear in the late nineteenth century were the ultimate expression of this assertive spirit, but they were neither the norm nor necessary to its further growth (as is shown in Terence Ranger's riveting account of Thompson Samkange's Christian and nationalist leadership in what is now Zimbabwe).[40] Missions in British colonial Africa were slow to advance African churchmen to positions of senior leadership. They became much more reluctant to do so after Church Missionary Society (CMS) missionaries in Nigeria determinedly undermined Samuel Ajayi Crowther, who had been appointed Bishop in 1864 at Henry Venn's insistence in an early effort to establish an indigenous African church. A different time and place allowed for a much more successful outcome following the appointment in 1912 of V.S. Azariah as the first Indian bishop within the Anglican communion. Indeed, Azariah went on to great success, becoming, in the words of his recent biographer, "the leading Christian statesman of India and the most successful Christian evangelist among the untouchables."[41]

The desire of the so-called younger churches to move beyond being treated as junior partners was evident at the IMC conferences of 1928 and 1938. At Jerusalem, C.Y. Cheng concluded a session he had chaired on relations between the younger and older churches by calling for missions and churches "at least to begin to look forward to the day when the work will be truly church-centric rather than mission-centric."[42] The numbers and participation of indigenous Christians at the conference showed how much things had changed in the preceding two decades. At Edinburgh in 1910, the few non-Westerners present had attended under the auspices of their missions, and as Azariah had learned from the shocked response to his address, they were expected by most to be grateful and tractable, rather than even mildly critical of mission policies and practices. At Jerusalem, about one-quarter of the delegates were non-Western, chosen through the national Christian councils. Ten years later, at Tambaram, their number had increased to about half the total number of delegates, and, according to the IMC's chief historian, they "shared full equality ... in initiative, leadership, and responsibility."[43] Not only could the subaltern now speak; their collective tone was a good deal more forceful than Cheng's had been at Jerusalem just ten years earlier, and for Western delegates there was a certain *cachet* to being associated with them and their views. Samkange, representing the Methodist Church and the Native Missionary Conference of Southern Rhodesia, did not give an address as his sophisticated fellow African C.G. Baëta of the Gold Coast (Ghana) did (calling for a reconsideration of the ban on polygamy in the Christian church), but he was greatly impressed by the confidence with which Baëta and the Asian delegates spoke and by the seemingly natural and easy relations between Western and non-Western delegates. Ranger considers that Samkange was re-made by this conference. Back home, he named his new farm "Tambaram" and was more than ever determined not to be a "yes man" for his white mentors.[44]

Evangelism and church work were the areas of responsibility that were yielded soonest to indigenous Christians. YMCA and YWCA secretaries from the West also seem to have had Asian counterparts and successors at an early date, and from this source would come a significant number of indigenous Christian leaders in the national Christian councils and delegates to the Jerusalem and Tambaram conferences.[45] Although there was much talk about devolution in other areas, it was a good deal slower in coming, especially in higher educational and medical work, and in supervisory roles generally. But in these areas, too, there was pressure for change, and it met with varying responses. For example, nationalist student movements in 1920s China challenged, among other things, foreign control of mission higher educational institutions and compulsory religious instruction. American medical missionary Edward Hicks Hume, responsible for the Yale-in-China medical education program, was one who responded positively to the new mood, but others had more difficulty in yielding.[46] As will be shown in Chapter 2, medical missions in India were particularly slow to practise devolution.

Beyond Paternalism: "Give us FRIENDS"
As more indigenous Christians achieved high levels of education and attained leadership positions in churches and mission institutions, the possibilities for cross-race collegiality in workplaces and for friendships in social situations increased.[47] Near the end of her more than four decades in India, Choné Oliver observed that it was not until she had come to live and work in Nagpur in 1929 that she had known educated Indians.[48] This was probably something of an exaggeration: her church's Central India mission was proud, for instance, to claim the Rev. Yohan Masih, a nationally known Christian leader, as one of its own. Still, the nature and locations of her work in the Central India mission had limited her opportunities for such contacts, while her new life as a missions bureaucrat meant routine interaction with Indians who were her

professional equals or superiors, and with whom workday encounters could evolve into social relationships.[49] To a much greater degree than Victorian-era missionaries could perhaps have imagined, friendships were developing based on shared interests and mutual regard rather than kindly condescension on the missionary's part and real or feigned acceptance of the status quo on the part of the "native Christian."

Nonetheless, the road to the new type of relationship was often rocky. Dr. P.V. Benjamin, whose interwar career flourished in a union mission sanatorium in South India, memorialized his white mentor as his colleague and friend at the time of the mentor's death in 1943. Yet Benjamin's son remembers hearing of a tension-filled event early in that relationship: the white mentor's refusal to let his new assistant borrow the station car on the grounds that it was exclusively for the use of missionaries. A professional friendship developed in this case because the self-respecting young Indian doctor, aware that he had other options, challenged rather than accepted the status quo.[50] But many of his fellow Indian Christians still did not – could not – do so. Lesslie Newbigin's diary recorded his reaction to the huge gap that still separated "the missionaries and the people" when he arrived in South India a few years after the incident involving Dr. Benjamin and his mentor. Here again an automobile figures in the memory of racial distance, this time as Newbigin accompanies some veteran missionaries in supervisory mode: "We drive up like lords in a car, soaking everybody else with mud on the way, and then carry on a sort of inspection, finding all the faults we can, putting everyone else through their paces. They all sort of stand at attention and say 'Sir.' It's *awful*." Newbigin recognized how much he himself depended on the car and all the other artifacts of white privilege in his new environment, and that as a newcomer he should avoid making self-righteous judgments. But he was nonetheless horrified: "surely they won't stand this sort of thing from the white man much longer."[51]

Just how much genuine friendships – as well as opportunities for collegial exchanges and career advances – mattered to educated indigenous Christians in professional relationships with missionaries is evident when we return to their presence at the international missionary conferences. At Edinburgh in 1910, Azariah called not only for workplace changes but also for missionaries to stop being "fathers" and become "friends." Indeed, it was on this note that he ended his address: "Give us FRIENDS." It was the easy friendship that seemed to prevail between Western and non-Western delegates even more than the addresses and deliberations that impressed Samkange at Tambaram in 1938. "We sat at meals anyhow and anywhere," he recalled. "It was a wonderful sight, there was no colour or nationality, all were one in Christ." It was this sense of camaraderie that made it impossible to accept the old indignities and gratuitous insults back in Southern Rhodesia. Samkange had always chafed. Now, increasingly, he would speak out, though with a strong residue of respect for the father figures of his youth, who had led him into literacy with all its promise, as well as into the Christian faith that he had made his own.[52]

The increasing possibilities for friendship across race lines may have reflected changing scientific ideas in the West about the significance of "race"[53] as well as a sense that if Christians truly were "all one in Christ," that conviction should be manifested in daily interactions. Nonetheless, increased exposure to the educated Other in a context that began with, but moved beyond, work relationships was probably the most significant factor. For example, Choné Oliver first referred in her diary to meeting Dr. Hilda Lazarus in the mid-1930s when she was seeking the eminent Indian doctor's support for her medical college project. As the contacts continued, a personal as well as a professional element entered the relationship. Lazarus became more than a valuable potential ally: she was an admirable Christian, a highly qualified doctor (with credentials and specialities superior to Oliver's), and, like Oliver, an enthusiastic gardener. There were, in short, bases for personal bonds.[54]

Florence Murray's career in Korea was marked by a similar evolution. During her first term in Hamhung, northern Korea, writing to her parents as their "dutiful daughter," Murray tended to describe social gatherings with Korean co-workers as affairs in which she participated only for the good of the missionary cause. But decades later in Seoul, where many of them had come as refugees, she was united to those same co-workers by shared memories of the loss of the Christian and medical work that they had helped build together in the north, and full of sympathy and admiration for their resilience in the face of great hardship. Now, Murray herself took the initiative in organizing social get-togethers. With Hyo-Soon Kim, the Korean woman doctor who had put herself at risk to help Murray when she was under house arrest in Hamhung following the outbreak of hostilities with Japan in 1941, and who later became a refugee from the Communist north and, in turn, in need of Murray's help, the bond was particularly strong, surviving time and distance after Murray's retirement.[55] Of such shared experiences were friendships made. But lest this paragraph end with too rosy a glow, it is important to reiterate that there were many painful episodes along the road to such friendships and many instances where a speaking subaltern was perceived as a threat and held to a higher standard for failures and shortcomings than his or her white counterparts. *That* was the experience of Thompson Samkange in the Southern Rhodesia of his old age, as he experienced the rigid regulations and professional standards of a new generation of colonial and missionary educators and looked back with nostalgia on the days when his own most important missionary mentor had practised a kindly if classic paternalism.[56] Tambaram, then, was an inspiration, but it was not the real world.[57] Moreover, there may have been a number of "native Christians" who, like Edward Said's great-aunt Melia, a teacher in the mission-founded American College for Girls in Cairo, were members of elite and close-knit families and communities that were sufficient unto themselves. As such, they would have had little interest in social interaction with their Western co-workers, especially when those co-workers seemed incapable of moving beyond the condescending workplace attitudes of an earlier era.[58]

Taking Stock and Re-Thinking Missions: Formal Investigations

If the interwar era was an era of halting steps towards cross-race friendships in the changing world of missions, it was also, as has already been suggested, a period of re-evaluating the strategies and even the basic aims of Christian missions in response to changed conditions. What should be done differently? Were there some strategies that should be altogether abandoned? To what extent could missions collaborate with colonial governments, foundations, anthropologists, and other interested actors to obtain assistance without being diverted from or sacrificing essential principles and goals? What sorts of attached "strings" would be tolerable? Such stock-taking took place in numerous informal conversations and group discussions at home and abroad, but it was also undertaken in a good many formal studies and commissions.

Education received a good deal of attention in these studies. After the First World War, an initiative that began with US mission boards (and that subsequently won support from British missions officials) led to a survey of education, broadly understood, in west, southern, and equatorial Africa. Financed by the Phelps-Stokes Fund, the 1921 commission was headed by the Fund's director, Thomas Jesse Jones, a Welsh-born American with strong preconceptions that the "right" sort of education for African Americans would also suit Africans. In undertaking such a study, the mission boards were, as Oldham's recent biographer, Keith Clements, notes, undertaking "an exercise in self-criticism." They recognized their need for a more coherent educational policy for their work in Africa based on a sound knowledge of their current practices. At the same time, British colonial officials were taking a new and pragmatic interest in missions' educational work in Africa on the basis of their own needs and concerns and in response to growing African demand. The key figure in bringing these constituencies together was Oldham. The report of the commission was published in 1922. A year later, following discussions Oldham had initiated with Colonial Office officials and a memorandum he had prepared, the Colonial Office established the Advisory Committee on Native Education in Tropical Africa, made up of government and missionary representatives and educational experts. At Oldham's urging, one of the Advisory Committee's first acts was to call for a second commission, this one mainly directed to East Africa. Like the earlier one, it was headed by Jones and included the American-educated

African doctoral student J.E. Kwegyir Aggrey, who, until his untimely death, would briefly serve as assistant vice-principal of the Gold Coast's newly created and much celebrated Achimota College.[59] Following these investigations and new arrangements for collaboration, missions remained by far the most important agents for providing Western-style schooling in British colonial Africa, but they now had more reliable access to government educational grants, came under government inspection, and shared with government officials in the development of broad lines of policy.

While mission officials like Oldham were in general agreement with Jones's view that education for Africans should relate to their overwhelmingly rural environment and provide mainly vocational rather than academic training (the so-called Tuskegee model), they by no means shared his assumptions about Africans' general inability to benefit from a different sort of education. Nor were they prepared to be merely the educational agents for meeting colonial economic and manpower needs. However paternalistic their approach may seem in retrospect – and the paternalism is palpable – they were anxious to make schooling more readily available and more directly useful to Africans in the face of the growing demand. They also wanted to foster respect for "worthy" indigenous "traditions," to screen out "inappropriate" aspects of Western culture and technology, and to identify, mould, and encourage future social leaders by giving them advanced education informed by Christian beliefs and values.[60] In these circumstances, the challenge for mission leaders was how to work in partnership with colonial officials and with the new, mainly American, philanthropists and foundations without losing control of their own agenda. Some studies largely fail to recognize that the mission enterprise *had* a separate agenda and that Africans themselves had some agency in determining what happened after groups like the Phelps-Stokes commissioners had filed their reports and gone home.[61] In appointing Aggrey to his commissions, Jones may have wanted him to serve as a particular kind of object lesson, but as Richard Gray has pointed out, the message to be read from Aggrey's success was not in Jones's hands:

> Dr. Aggrey ... might advocate rural adaptation and racial moderation, but, quoting Latin tags at Fourah Bay, feted by [Gold Coast governor] Guggisberg, welcomed as an equal by missionaries and liberals throughout the continent, he symbolised for his countrymen in the Gold Coast and for the thousands of Africans who saw and heard him elsewhere, the successful seizure from the whites of the advantages of their classical education.[62]

An educational investigation of a quite different sort took place in India and resulted in 1931 in the publication of the *Report of the Commission on Christian Higher Education in India*. Constituted by the IMC following a 1929

request for such an investigation by Indian Christian and missionary educators in India, it was known as the Lindsay Commission for its chairman,
the Master of Balliol College, Oxford. The request from India had asked for
a commission that would deal with the decline in the influence and quality
of Christian colleges resulting from such changed conditions as the growth
in number and resources of government and private non-Christian colleges.
The Commission was asked to set in motion a policy of coordination and
concentration, even at the cost of closing down some existing Christian
colleges.[63] Once established, it undertook an enquiry broader than that called
for by the India group. At least in theory, it was prepared to consider the
possibility of having missions altogether abandon the field of higher education to government and other agencies, or, alternatively, the establishing of
a full-fledged Christian university. Ultimately, however, what it recommended was a new, unified, approach to the task of Christian higher education within the existing educational system in India, with permanent,
ecumenical committees to facilitate its objectives. A central committee within
the NCC, working with responsible persons in provincial Christian councils, would serve as a liaison among existing colleges and as a united voice
for them in dealing with the national and provincial governments, the universities, and the general public. At the same time, a "Joint Committee on
Christian Higher Education in Britain and America," composed of persons
with expertise in the field, would be appointed by the mission boards and
have as its priority a unified appeal for men and funds for all the Christian
colleges.[64]

A central board for Christian higher education was in fact constituted as
part of the NCC in the wake of the Commission's report, and unified
fundraising was undertaken in Britain and North America under the IMC's
William Paton, who had played a leading role in getting the Commission
established.[65] The Depression, however, had a dampening effect on efforts
to finance the upgrading of the Christian colleges on the scale envisioned.
Meanwhile, by drawing high-ranking colonial officials into its orbit at
fundraising meetings in London, by taking a less conciliatory approach to
Hinduism than the Jerusalem conference had done, and by stating that the
long-term goal of such colleges should remain the making of converts as
well as educating the Christian community, the Commission raised the ire
of nationalists such as the editor of the *Indian Social Reformer*. Declaring an
ongoing interest in making converts may have seemed necessary to reassure
those who thought the colleges needed to recover their original sense of
purpose. But it was both unrealistic and out of keeping with what had been
happening on the ground, where mission colleges often seem to have had a
better record of producing nationalists than converts to Christianity.[66]

The commissions to Africa and India had focused on education and dealt
with what were essentially questions of strategy. Reporting a year after the

Lindsay Commission, the American Laymen's Foreign Missions Inquiry had a much broader geographic focus and asked much more fundamental questions: should foreign missions continue to exist in the changed conditions of the modern world, and, if so, what should their role be? Instigated and funded by John D. Rockefeller Jr., the inquiry idea won acceptance from Rockefeller's Baptist denomination and went on to have the support of seven US Protestant denominations. The actual Commission of Appraisal contained no clergy. Its members were university presidents and professors, lawyers, businessmen, physicians, and others, including three women. Its fields of inquiry were India, Burma, China, and Japan. Prior to its visit to these countries, the commission, chaired by Harvard philosophy professor William Ernest Hocking, sent out an advance guard of data gatherers and research workers under the supervision of the Institute of Social and Religious Research (also a Rockefeller-funded institution). Their reports were published only after the 1932 publication of Hocking's controversial summary volume, *Re-Thinking Missions: A Laymen's Inquiry after One Hundred Years*, seemingly as an exercise in damage control.[67]

While it depended on the cooperation of organizations like the IMC and the national Christian councils, and individual mission boards and their personnel in numerous mission sites, the Laymen's Inquiry was in no sense a mouthpiece for any of these bodies. Indeed, its consultations extended well beyond the world of missions and indigenous Christians in the countries visited. Several aspects of its report were troubling to the missions-minded public and some gave great offence – especially its criticism of mission personnel. After paying a formulaic tribute to the "saintliness" of some missionaries, *Re-Thinking Missions* went on to say that the "greater number" seemed to be "of limited outlook and capacity" and that there were "not a few whose vision of the inner meaning of the mission has become obscured by the intricacies, divisions, frictions and details of a task too great for their powers and their hearts." This, followed by the suggestion that missionaries often deliberately exaggerated the flaws in the cultures and religions of their field of work out of "a sort of professional interest in deprecation," would have come as an especially painful piece of revisionism to veteran workers accustomed to the reverential regard of those at home, who in turn had been accustomed to regard missionaries' accounts of "the field" as beyond doubt.[68] More generally disturbing to fundamentalists and, for different reasons, to missions supporters influenced by Continental neo-orthodoxy (more numerous in Britain than in North America) was the apparent willingness of the Laymen's Report to interpret "mission" in the modern world primarily as a matter of social service and to take a sympathetic, even a syncretic, approach to other world religions.[69]

Among the developments following from the publication of *Re-Thinking Missions* was a fundamentalist breakaway from mainstream American

Presbyterianism. The acclaimed writer Pearl Buck, who had spent much of her life in China mission circles (the daughter of one Presbyterian missionary and the wife of another), created shock waves when she gave the book a glowing review and then used the occasion of a large gathering of Presbyterian women and Board officials in New York to present her own critique of the conduct and personnel of the missionary enterprise, not sparing those at the home base.[70] Although it was a pronouncement by US laymen on (mainly) US work, *Re-Thinking Missions* inevitably aroused interest among the Americans' partners in mission. At Edinburgh House, Paton, whose commitment to evangelism was intense, sought to contain its effects and worried that it would "jeopardize the implementation of the Lindsay Report." Oldham, a friend and admirer of Hocking, had himself for years called for many of the specific changes recommended by the book, perhaps most strikingly the concentration of effort as a route to improved mission social services. Having recently come under the influence of Barth, he was, however, troubled by what he saw as the lack of theological rigour in *Re-Thinking Missions*.[71] Yet despite the controversies it aroused, the book's findings and recommendations were not officially condemned by most mainstream boards, for as Hutchison writes of the American context, "the incursions of liberal thinking had been substantial." The United Church of Canada's *The New Outlook* contained several discussions of *Re-Thinking Missions*, including a generally favourable assessment by Choné Oliver, who had served as a resource person for the medical personnel on the Inquiry. In the foreword to the book, Hocking had declared that its proposals lay "in well recognized directions of advance" and "call[ed] far less for innovations than for the emphasis and encouragement of tendencies already present in the field and at home."[72] While the controversies it stirred up have received most of the attention from historians of missions, Hocking's statement was not wholly wide of the mark.

Mission Change and Gender

The implications of the changes in this era for gender roles and relationships in the mission enterprise were considerable, both in the new ecumenical bureaucracies and on the ground. In his history of the IMC, Hogg documented (but evidently did not feel a need to account for) a pattern whereby women came to play important roles in the new structures. One can speculate that the combination of the lower salaries for which they worked (a few were volunteers) and the extraordinary educational background and talents that they brought to their tasks made this group of women attractive to cash-starved organizations such as the IMC. Hogg acknowledges the women's skills and education in a matter-of-fact way when introducing IMC staff. While the chairman and the three secretaries appointed in the 1920s were men, women held important secondary roles. Thus,

Georgina Gollock was from 1921 to 1927 Oldham's co-editor at the *IRM*, while Betty Gibson was associated with him as a translator, researcher, and, later, author, officially receiving the title of assistant IMC secretary in 1925. Four years later, Wrong and Oliver were appointed to their specialized committee work within the IMC and the NCC, in London and India respectively. For many years Alice Van Doren was Oliver's colleague within the NCC, with broad responsibilities for facilitating rural education.[73] All these women seem to have maintained a strong interest in developments affecting their own sex, and yet all seem to have found great satisfaction in roles that took them beyond the separate-spheres approach of an earlier era. Some would work mainly with and for men, and eventually be succeeded by men.

The working relationships in these ecumenical organizations could not be described as egalitarian. Even in 1936, in the context of discussing an impending new secretarial appointment, which they wanted to go to a woman, some of Oliver's women colleagues spoke of Oldham as having a problem in remembering that "half the people in the world are women."[74] Yet over time, the relationships in the ecumenical bureaucracies do seem to have evolved in the direction of greater formal acknowledgment of women colleagues' contributions. It was Oldham himself who suggested in 1921 that Gollock's position at the *IRM* should be upgraded from assistant editor to co-editor. As for Gibson, in a self-mocking letter to her family written the same year, she declared that at work she sat "like a mouse and listen[ed] to the words of wisdom" of her seniors. In the course of the 1920s, though, as Oldham took on ever more tasks, he came to rely more heavily on her expertise, particularly on African matters, and he acknowledged that fact. It was he who recommended in 1925 that she be officially appointed to the IMC secretariat, and when *The Remaking of Man in Africa* was published in 1931, both Oldham and Gibson were credited, and recognized by colleagues, as its co-authors.[75] Paton was evidently somewhat less ready to acknowledge publicly the contributions of female colleagues: even Eleanor Jackson's seldom-critical biography of him reports that Margaret Sinclair, his able associate at the *IRM*, was "annoyed ... that he would pirate her ideas without acknowledging them."[76] Yet there was no denying that the new ecumenical structures had given rise to a need and opportunity for able men and women to work collegially.

Changes in the gender organization of mission work also took place in mission sites, of course, although by no means evenly or easily. As mission institutions strove to be more efficient and up-to-date, there was a growing tendency to favour coeducation for higher academic and professional education wherever local circumstances made it feasible, especially in the face of the greater need for economies brought about by the Depression. In China the majority of the Christian colleges were already coeducational by 1932. The same trend was emerging in India's Christian arts colleges by the end of the decade. Nationwide, higher education still affected only a tiny minority of India's women, but those with such schooling had an influential voice, and by the 1930s many saw coeducation as a route to higher quality training at advanced levels. Thus, the 1934 meeting of the All-India Women's Conference called for Allahabad and Benares Hindu universities to become coeducational and for other institutions to consider the same move. In its brief discussion of female colleges, the Lindsay Commission took note of this sentiment in the new India and observed that, especially for women planning to enter professional life, coeducation was good preparation. Although it declared the women's Christian colleges to be far superior to the men's in terms of their spiritual life and influence (having a far larger proportion of Christians among staff and students), it nonetheless recommended experiments in coeducation, while warning that, if implemented, "it must be real co-education with women members on the teaching staff alongside of men, and with such facilities for the women students as will enable them to have a real college life and not be merely appendages of a men's college."[77]

When they turned to the issue of how best to teach and practise the ideals of Western scientific medicine in postwar Asia, many missionary and secular modernizers were even more strongly drawn to the possibility of institutions that somehow integrated work for both sexes in the same facility. In view of the costs involved in medicine, the economic arguments were compelling. Given the existence of purdah traditions, the Laymen's Inquiry was doubtful that integration of women's and "general" hospitals was as feasible in India as in China, where the celebrated Peking Union Medical College and other important medical institutions were coeducational.[78] But it recognized that some government hospitals in India and a few mission medical reformers wanted indigenous women nurses to be trained in the care of both sexes as a way of modernizing hospitals.[79] With regard to the training of indigenous doctors, as Chapter 3 will show in the case of Korea, young men eager to acquire Western expertise and professional qualifications were prepared, if necessary – although it often came as a struggle – to put aside the patriarchal assumptions in which they had been raised and accept women medical missionaries as instructors and colleagues in general hospitals. As such, these young men were a good fit with doctors like Murray who, as part of the new, postwar, generation of women missionaries, often understood their calling in a more expansive way than their predecessors had.

Not surprisingly, in both academic education and medicine, there were women missionaries who resisted such changes. Those, especially, who were part of an earlier generation often clung to the separate-spheres approach, insisting on the necessity of distinctively female institutions for the respectability, security, and access to opportunities of their female clients. Probably, too, they recognized in the new approach a threat to the niches they had carved out as powerful, influential figures in settings where local indigenous women were their particular – and often devoted and subservient – constituency. In the late nineteenth and early twentieth centuries, when few other agencies and individuals had been in a position to do so, they had provided small islands of opportunity for indigenous women, Christian and non-Christian, through the training and the examples of independent female initiative they offered. By the interwar period, much had changed: home-grown mentors had come forward to challenge gender-based restrictions and inequalities and to serve as role models.[80] Yet many old-style missionaries continued to generate universalizing discourses about downtrodden Indian womanhood and to resist restructuring in their institutions, whether in the direction of gender integration or the devolution of responsibilities to indigenous female co-workers. By comparison with their male counterparts in mission institutions, they had a smaller pool of well-educated, confident professionals to draw upon as indigenous colleagues and successors, and within that small pool there were few who were militant in pressing for devolution. Meanwhile, in the West, the mission public, and particularly the women's societies that funded their work, had some difficulty in moving beyond familiar images of benighted Eastern women dependent on their Western "sisters" for leadership and protection from abuses. In these circumstances, many of those Western "sisters" were inclined to allow old patterns to continue.[81]

Missions certainly remained gendered spaces in the interwar era, notwithstanding specific changes in work roles and institutional organization. Both as mission personnel and as the missionized, women remained the second sex. Given missions' origins in patriarchal Western societies, and the deeply patriarchal cultures in which they were planted in Asia and Africa, it could scarcely have been otherwise. The debates about the merits of sex-segregated versus integrated mission work that took place in this era intersected with and reflected other forces for change, discussed above. Modernizers who favoured a gender-integrated approach to mission institutional work were typically concerned with questions of efficiency and economy. But they also maintained that the interests of indigenous women would be well served by coeducation and "general" institutions. Those who argued otherwise were not free of personal and institutional self-interest in predicting dire outcomes, but neither would history always prove their predictions to be wrong. While the modernizing of missions was essentially a project initiated by men, it enlisted the enthusiastic cooperation of some able professional women, among them Oliver, Murray, and Wrong. It is time to consider their respective projects.

2

"Colleagues and Eventually Successors": Dr. Choné Oliver and the Struggle to Establish a Christian Medical College in Late Colonial India

> It is, no doubt, impossible to prevent his praying for his mother, but we have means of rendering the prayers innocuous. Make sure that they are always very "spiritual," that he is always concerned with the state of her soul and never with her rheumatism.
>
> – Advice from Screwtape to Wormwood
> in C.S. Lewis's *The Screwtape Letters*

In 1943 Belle Choné Oliver (1875-1947) used the fictional Screwtape's advice to his nephew, a "Junior Tempter" in "Satan's Kingdom," to introduce one of her numerous contributions to the *Journal of the Christian Medical Association of India, Burma and Ceylon*.[1] It was not typical of Oliver to use humour in the interwar crusade to reform the understanding and practice of Christian medicine in India. But it *was* very much like her to argue that a concern about rheumatism, or any other physical limitation on human well-being, was, in itself, an expression of Christian spirituality. It had not always been that way. As a young, first-term medical missionary, she had regarded healing as a means to an evangelistic end and believed that real spirituality in her own life should manifest itself in winning souls. This chapter briefly outlines Oliver's background and her years in mission service in west-central India before turning to the 1920s, when she became involved in the task of re-evaluating medical missions on an India-wide basis. That task, in turn, led her into missions bureaucracy and a leadership role in the crusade to upgrade Christian medical education in late colonial India, the aspect of her career that is the main focus of this chapter. The outcome of that decades-long struggle was the transformation of the women's Christian medical school in Vellore, South India, into Christian Medical College, Vellore, a modern, coeducational medical complex that would gain an international reputation in the last half of the twentieth century.[2] If a new theology of medical missions combined with challenges arising from Indian nationalism account for the timing of the move to create a Christian medical college, competing agendas, gender politics, and the constraints created by the Depression were responsible for the protracted nature of the process. Like her critics in this struggle, Oliver and her fellow crusaders were uneasy with "merely" humanistic social reform. Like her critics, too, her colleagues included Indians as well as Westerners, usually, in both cases, men. Studies of Victorian-era missions have generally not prepared us for such patterns. Yet as scholarly work takes us into the largely unexplored territory of late-colonial missions history, the inadequacy of theoretical formulations that insist on bifurcation – spirituality *versus* social concern, "the imperial West" *versus* the "colonized Other," women's sphere *versus* men's – becomes increasingly clear. Oliver's career as a missionary modernizer illustrates the flux of her era.

The Background of a Calling

Choné Oliver was born in Oxford County, Ontario, a part of Canada where Protestant farm and village families seemed to have a bent for producing preachers and missionaries. The spectacular Pentecostal evangelist Aimee Semple McPherson came from there.[3] Yet like Aimee's family, Choné's was scarcely representative of the type that sent forth missionaries. Her businessman father, Adam Oliver, the first mayor of the town of Ingersoll and a Liberal member of the provincial legislature, was unseated after his 1875 re-election, following charges of illegal election practices by supporters, and later named in a royal commission in connection with conflict of interest in a land deal.[4] Choné (she was named for a Jesuit who had saved her father from drowning) was the third of four surviving children of his second marriage and half-sister to six siblings from his first. Stricken with paralysis in 1880, Adam Oliver died two years later. His young widow and former housekeeper, Helen Rintoul Oliver, who had come to Canada as a lone Scottish immigrant, developed a serious drinking problem. As a result, Choné and two brothers were removed from the family home to the community of Chesterfield, where they lived for some years with the Presbyterian minister and his wife. One of Choné's sisters divorced; another joined Divine Science, a sect that, while smaller and more esoteric than Christian Science, shared its reliance on faith as a route to health.[5]

Despite this unconventional background – or perhaps because of it – Choné Oliver developed into an intensely religious person, one in whose girlhood missionary enthusiasms figured prominently. She evinced a particular interest in becoming a medical missionary after attending the designation service for fellow Presbyterian Margaret MacKellar, a local woman who had returned to public school in adulthood and then attended the Women's Medical College, Kingston, to prepare for foreign missionary service. Because the large estate left by her father was gone, Choné taught school before moving to Toronto to study medicine. For a time she and her brother Ed, also a medical student, boarded together. But when their mother became fatally ill, it was, inevitably, Choné who interrupted her studies to care for her. Like MacKellar and most of her other predecessors, she studied in a women's college. After attending the Woman's Medical College affiliated with the University of Toronto and Trinity College and graduating in 1900 with an MB, BS from the former and an MD, MC from Trinity, she interned for some ten months at the Woman's Hospital of Philadelphia. The hospital had been founded in 1861, chiefly to provide clinical experience for the Woman's Medical College of Pennsylvania (WMC), an institution that claimed, and celebrated, a large number of medical missionaries among its alumnae.[6] Although sex-segregated institutions such as the ones with which Oliver was associated would largely disappear in the decades to follow (WMC would be a rare exception) as new standards of professionalism came to the fore,[7] they produced a generation of medical women whose sense of shared identity and moral vocation was strong even when they entered diverse fields of work.[8] Meanwhile, having successfully passed examinations to qualify as a practitioner in the province of Ontario and the state of Pennsylvania, Oliver sailed for India. Arriving in January 1902, she began her career in princely Central India, where the Presbyterian Church had established its mission in 1877.[9]

From the first year of its existence, the Central India mission had a majority of women on its staff. Partly for this reason, it had developed a strong emphasis on social service and institutional activities, particularly the "rescue" of widows and orphans, and educational and medical work. Home-base supporters had great expectations about the evangelistic possibilities in these lines of work, and perhaps especially in medicine. For a time in the 1890s, more than one-third of the mission's single women workers were doctors. Within the mission itself, a strong evangelistic ethos prevailed. Coming into this environment as a sensitive first-term missionary, Oliver felt a strong obligation to look for opportunities for proselytizing both within and beyond her medical work. Diary entries from this period of her life reveal moments of personal anguish and self-reproach over occasions when she felt that she ought to have seized, or created, opportunities for presenting the claims of Christianity but was, at the same time, uneasy about that task. The tension between her personal discomfort with proselytizing and her longing "for souls" during a period of revival in the mission in 1906-7, along with the guilt that she experienced over such stolen pleasures as secular reading, led Oliver into a period of depression about her own spiritual state so intense that it occasionally left her incapable of routine work.[10]

A furlough in 1907-8 restored her to better physical and mental heath. And through reading, reflection, and contact with other medical missionaries, she gradually developed a new understanding of the place of medical work in modern Christian missions that gave her both greater personal peace of mind and the ability to play a leadership role in formulating a new theology and praxis for medical missions. This new understanding, in turn, informed and energized the crusade to upgrade Christian medical education in India that dominated the last two decades of her missionary career. Yet as the diaries reveal, Oliver remained immensely concerned about her personal spiritual life and thus, as noted in Chapter 1, was responsive to religious phenomena such as the Oxford Group movement, which, for a time in the early 1930s, provided a congenial outlet for like-minded, usually middle-class, men and women who found it helpful to talk about their faith and their frailties in small-group settings.[11] She was also attracted by the concept of the Christian ashram, which a few missionaries such as E. Stanley Jones had adapted from Hindu practice with a view to establishing simple and egalitarian religious communities as sources of spiritual nurturing and renewal, and by Gandhi's combination of personal asceticism and social concern. Notwithstanding his denunciations of Western medicine and his much publicized criticism of medical missions in 1931 (to which she wrote a reply), Oliver found Gandhi's spirituality compelling and in 1935 welcomed the opportunity for a personal interview.[12]

But all this still lay ahead in 1902. Between the year of her arrival in India and her new role from the mid-1920s as a reformer and modernizer of medical missions, the career path that Oliver followed took her to several different stations in her church's Central India mission (from 1925 a mission of the United Church of Canada). It also took her beyond the "women's work for women" model that had framed the career understanding of missions-minded girls of her generation. Serving first in Indore in a hospital for women carefully designed to respect caste distinctions, she was later in charge of the mission's smaller women's hospitals in Neemuch and Dhar. After her 1915 furlough, she began pioneer medical work in Banswara, South Rajputana, the station that would be her official home for the next fourteen years. In contrast to her previous postings, at Banswara she was in charge of a general hospital. Although it served women and men of all backgrounds, the hospital was intended primarily for outreach to the region's large – and largely un-Hinduized – tribal Bhil population.[13] The lack of rigid sex segregation in the work at Banswara was a pragmatic reflection of what was locally feasible. But it was also a good fit with Oliver's approach to matters of gender in mission work. A feminist when it came to asserting women's abilities and forwarding women's interests when they appeared to be neglected, she had no taste for perpetuating unnecessary gender separatism in "the work."[14] Fractious gender politics during the first decades of the Canadian mission's existence had led to the creation of separate men's and women's mission councils. To Oliver's regret, these councils continued to exist, undermining effective consultation and cooperation, well after larger mission bodies such as the all-India Medical Missionary Association were open to both sexes. As a 1913 letter to the secretary of her church's Foreign Missions

Committee makes clear, Oliver found the more inclusive gatherings congenial as well as useful.[15] Indeed, they contributed directly to the larger
missionary life that opened up to her in the third decade of her career.

Changing Missions

Despite Banswara's isolation[16] – it was sixty miles from the nearest railway –
Oliver managed to keep in touch with new currents of thinking about mission work generally and medical missions in particular. It was as a result of
this effort at remaining connected that she ultimately moved on from
Banswara to national and ecumenical mission involvement. She would later
recall that a reprinted address by J.H. Oldham came to her attention "about
1923" stressing "the need for missions to survey their work, deal ruthlessly
with what was ineffective, and plan for at least ten years ahead." A conversation on this subject with William Paton, then secretary of the National
Christian Council (NCC), specifically with regard to medical missions, led
to her paper in 1924 before the Medical Missionary Association conference
in Calcutta on the subject "Do we need a Survey of Medical Missions?"
During the next two years, with American Presbyterian medical missionary
R.H.H. Goheen, she became the key figure on the Association's Survey, Efficiency, and Cooperation Committee. The committee's report, published in
1928 as *Survey of Medical Missions in India*, reflected its investigation of medical
mission work in Ceylon as well as India.[17]

By the time the *Survey* was issued, the Medical Missionary Association
had transformed itself into the Christian Medical Association of India
(CMAI). Through this transformation, it opened its doors to Indian Christian doctors and other practitioners who had "a recognised, registrable quali-
fication or its equivalent" and who were in sympathy with its aims.[18] It was
as a member of this organization and as a co-author of the *Survey* that Oliver
was sent from India to the IMC's conference in Jerusalem in 1928, along
with Danish medical missionary Christian Frimodt-Möller. As two of only
three medical delegates to the Jerusalem conference (there had been no
plan to include medical work on its agenda), Oliver and Frimodt-Möller not
only drew insights from the *Survey* to the attention of an international audience; they also presented a rationale for Christian medical work that officially moved beyond the old view that its function was simply to open
doors for the preaching of Christianity.

Strict adherence to the "old view" had long since been abandoned in
everyday practice by many medical missionaries.[19] But the argument that
medical work in a mission was "a spiritual service in itself" and "not a mere
pioneer agency or only an instrument for evangelism" had not previously
been presented as a basis for policy.[20] Frimodt-Möller, who was permitted to
present the medical delegates' views to a plenary session of the Jerusalem
conference, featured Christ as the "Great Physician," one who had healed

frequently and out of compassion rather than occasionally and "with the sole object of getting hold of people." The ministry of healing, he stressed, should be regarded as "an essential part of the work of the Church" irrespective of a larger future medical role by the state, and both Western and indigenous Christian practitioners should be better prepared than ever before and able to work in settings where consolidation of technical and human resources made for maximum efficiency.[21]

These arguments were developed more fully in *The Ministry of Healing in India*, compiled and largely written by Oliver as an updated and expanded adaptation of the *Survey*.[22] The new work continued the task of re-educating those (including some medical missionaries) who

> still retain the view that the ministry of healing is an evangelistic agency, to be abandoned when the Church is established or when Government or other agencies care for the sick ... Some people [also] seem to fear that by our emphasis on the care of the sick as an essential part of the Christian testimony, we are omitting evangelism. Not at all. Service of the sick, when inspired by Christlike compassion is the gospel message in action.[23]

As these lines suggest, some missionaries were uncomfortable with the new rationale for medical missions, interpreting it as a disavowal of the religious aspect of medical missionaries' work and a sign of concern exclusively with technical and professional matters.[24]

This was far from being the case. Although in his speeches and writings Frimodt-Möller was more outspoken than Oliver about the inappropriateness of imposing prayers and sermons on a captive audience of sick people, he shared with her (and probably most of their colleagues) the view that it *was* appropriate to speak to patients about the faith that motivated medical missionaries' lives when appropriate opportunities presented themselves. In the years ahead, Oliver would write frequently and passionately about the links between body, mind, and spirit in health and healing. Nonetheless, in developing this new theology of medical missions, Oliver and her reform-minded colleagues had taken the position that they could be true disciples of "the Great Physician" without proselytizing. Instructions to medical missionaries that stressed "the importance of giving constant attention to the spiritual part of their work, and not allowing their medical duties unduly to absorb their time and energies" – still in at least one society's regulations in the 1920s – could now be recognized for what they were: professionally insulting and potentially dangerous.[25]

For Oliver personally, the working out of this new position was clearly a liberating experience.[26] Meanwhile, through her role on the medical missions survey and at the Jerusalem Conference, she had become associated in a public way with the task of rethinking Christian medical work in India in order to make it viable in a rapidly changing political and professional environment.[27] It was this background that the NCC and the CMAI were drawing upon when in 1929, the same year that Frimodt-Möller was chosen as CMAI president, they asked the United Church of Canada for her services. The arrangement was initially an interim one, and Oliver was to act simultaneously as the NCC's secretary for medical work and as secretary-treasurer of the CMAI. In 1933, when her role with the CMAI became permanent, she remained on the NCC as its honorary secretary for medical work, sharing office space at its headquarters in Nagpur, the bureaucratic centre of Christian ecumenism in India. In one or both of these roles, she would initiate or advance such diverse undertakings as a nurses' auxiliary linked to the CMAI, a hospital supplies agency to coordinate purchasing for medical missions, social hygiene work, and a prayer cycle for medical personnel. Although she was not the editor of the CMAI's *Journal*, a bi-monthly containing an eclectic mix of scientific, inspirational, and news material, Oliver wrote several columns for each issue, provided frequent special articles, and generally oversaw its preparation. She also represented and publicized the CMAI's causes in her frequent travels throughout India to inspect medical work and attend regional gatherings. As past-president Sir Henry Holland would aptly observe when she was about to retire in 1944, "To all intents and purposes ... Dr. Oliver is and has been the C.M.A.I."[28] While Oliver threw herself into all the Association's projects, the one that most fully absorbed her was the struggle to create a Christian medical college.

The Long Crusade for a Medical College

Making the Case
The re-evaluation of Christian medical work that took place in 1920s India pointed to the desirability of establishing a Christian medical college. To understand the connection it is necessary to take the history of Christian medical missions and the contemporary political situation into account.

In the last half of the nineteenth and early twentieth centuries, mission hospitals and dispensaries had been the best, and indeed often the only, sources of Western-style medical treatment in many parts of India. The medical services provided by the imperial state were intended primarily for the military and other colonial state servants even in the late nineteenth century, and they existed mainly in urban areas.[29] Missionary physicians had rejoiced in the recognition and assistance their work received from British and "native" officials. Home-base mission societies had likewise thrilled to stories of medical mission "firsts" and to accounts of princely rulers offering land and/or funds to missionaries to open medical work in their state. Women's work was particularly encouraged. Even after the

National Association for Supplying Female Medical Aid to the Women of India (the Dufferin Fund) had been established under the aegis of the imperial state in 1885, the "lady physicians" on mission staffs had continued to rejoice in a disproportionate share of Kaiser-i-Hind medals and other tokens of imperial recognition.[30]

Yet by the mid-1920s, and especially with the 1928 publication of the *Survey of Medical Missions in India,* missions were forced to face the fact that, overall, their medical work did not bear comparison with the best of what the Government of India and some provincial governments were providing, or aiming to achieve.[31] Thanks in part to the financial support they received from cooperating mission societies, a few union institutions such as Frimodt-Möller's tuberculosis sanatorium at Arogyavaram, and the hospital and medical school for women at Vellore, established by the dynamic American Ida Sophia Scudder, enjoyed good reputations. Frimodt-Möller hired able and fully qualified Indian doctors who, like him, contributed to respected medical journals and helped to establish Arogyavaram as the best sanatorium in India.[32] Vellore's mobile rural dispensary and the expansion of its physical plant in the 1920s attracted widespread attention; even Gandhi seemed to approve, providing Scudder with an invaluable photo opportunity when he visited in 1928.[33] A few denominational institutions such as the American Presbyterians' hospital at Miraj in the Bombay Presidency, established by the Canadian-born William Wanless, enjoyed a reputation for excellence in particular specialities. (Wanless, a surgeon whose patients had reportedly included Gandhi, was knighted at the time of his retirement in 1928.)[34] But these were exceptional places. Many mission hospitals had only one Western doctor, sometimes with one or more Indian assistants. Ill-equipped and inefficient, they were run by men and women who were often out of touch with current Western medical thinking and with the larger professional and political changes taking place around them. It was left to the Laymen's Foreign Missions Inquiry in the early 1930s to make the harshest of these criticisms, but the point was clear even in the milder language of the *Survey:* not good enough.[35] Meanwhile, government hospitals and clinics with access to richer funding were increasing, as were private practitioners with full professional training in Western medicine.

The same unease prevailed with regard to Christian medical education. While three medical schools had been established to train Indian Christian doctors – the Women's Christian Medical College at Ludhiana in the Punjab and the Miraj Medical School for men, both begun in the 1890s, and Scudder's Missionary Medical School for Women, established in 1918 – they provided only licentiate-level training. Such training was inferior to the baccalaureate degree in medicine and science (MB, BS) both in terms of the advance preparation required and the quality of courses offered.[36] The graduates of these schools were not promoted to leadership roles in mission hospitals, much less in a position to become medical educators themselves.

Few people would have suggested that medical missionaries were more prone to racist attitudes than their non-medical colleagues. Yet there was no denying that less devolution had taken place in medical work than in any other aspect of mission or church work in India. In theory, Indian Christian doctors with full professional qualifications were available for hiring. But they had typically obtained their training in government medical colleges, and only those who were most dedicated – or least likely to find jobs elsewhere – subsequently went into mission service, given the low salaries.[37] Like their non-Christian counterparts, many of them sought to enter government medical service, an area that had opened up to Indians more than many other areas of colonial government service by the early twentieth century. By that time, nationalist-minded Indian professional elites were increasingly advocating the highest standards of Western medicine for their country.[38] With the passage of the Government of India Act of 1919, which devolved responsibility for such matters as public health and education to popularly elected provincial governments, such elites could work for their goals at the provincial level.[39] In these circumstances, and with Britain's General Medical Council policing medical training in India more rigorously as a condition of recognizing degrees granted there, standards for medical training outside mission settings would rise, especially in the 1930s as a drive developed to abolish licentiate-level training,[40] and more job opportunities would exist for Indian doctors with recognized Western-type degrees. Meanwhile, Indian Christian medical practitioners associated with mission and church work, and already suffering from an image of being de-nationalized because of their "foreign" religion, risked being further marginalized in the new India of the future if their professional training was also deemed substandard.[41] As was the case for the Western medical missionaries themselves, their place in an evolving India was very much in question.[42]

Faced with daunting problems with the quality and reputation of their medical work, and simultaneously the likelihood of a growing medical role for the state, missions in India could simply have opted out of institutionalized medical work, as had largely happened in metropolitan Japan.[43] Some Christians, both Indians and Westerners, did think this should happen, especially given the huge financial costs involved in maintaining up-to-date institutions and training indigenous personnel to full professional standards. There was also a related and long-standing concern that Christian training institutions tended to turn out "hothouse plants" (that is, Christian graduates whose faith and morals could not withstand the challenges of the outside world). But those who, like Oliver, were passionately in favour of upgrading the medical training of indigenous Christian practitioners so that they could become medical missionaries' colleagues and successors, put forward several arguments. These arguments reflected both religious and pragmatic perspectives.

There was, to begin with, the position taken in *The Ministry of Healing* and at Jerusalem: that Jesus had healed not to gain a hearing for his verbal messages but because, as an expression of love and compassion, healing was an essential part of his ministry and should, therefore, also be regarded as an essential part of the Indian Christian church of the future, not something that it could jettison. It followed from this position that there had to be Indian Christian practitioners in sufficiently large numbers and of sufficiently high professional and ethical standards to meet the needs of Christian medical institutions. Oliver and her supporters doubted that state-run medical colleges could produce such doctors, both because there would be few places for Christian medical students in any future entrance system based (however informally) on communal allocation of spaces, and because state colleges could not be expected to instill the ethic of selflessness required of those who would be labouring in mission institutions at salaries far lower than what was available in the secular world.[44]

Advocates of the establishment of a high-grade Christian medical college drew attention to the fact that such colleges already existed in China and Korea. They also argued that, irrespective of a larger role for state medicine in the future, missions and churches should be prepared to play an ongoing role in areas of health care in which they had already become dominant or influential contributors – leprosy and tuberculosis work especially – and in areas in which private and state practitioners seemed unlikely to invest significant effort: the treatment of mental illnesses, for instance, and rural and preventive work. An analogous argument was that *well-trained* doctors in Christian institutions could and should give a lead, both technically and ethically, to the profession as a whole by reaching out to establish creative working relationships with colleagues in state and private practice and by contributing to medical research. Including a percentage of non-Christian students in a Christian medical college was also perceived as a useful form of bridge-building (and would at the same time be a way to avoid the hothouse-plants phenomenon).[45] Especially dear to Oliver's heart was the argument that even "modern science" now recognized the links between body, mind, and spirit in the promotion of health and healing, and that Christian practitioners thus had unique opportunities and obligations to contribute to a therapeutic holistic medical environment. Hers was not, obviously, an argument for "faith healing" but rather for faith as a contributing factor to health and healing in conjunction with modern preventive and curing techniques.[46]

The arguments just outlined would be repeated, along with others of a more ad hoc nature, in various forums in the two decades after 1929 as CMAI leaders and Indian Christian medical personnel who shared their fear of an impending beleaguered status sought to solve their dilemma by

creating a medical training institution so strong that even its Christian identity would not be a barrier to acceptance in a postcolonial India.

Early Days and Easy Optimism

When a resolution in favour of establishing a union medical college was
first presented to the CMAI membership, at its biennial conference at
Allahabad in January 1929, Miraj was identified as the likely site of such a
college. Soon after, however, the executive acknowledged that it was premature to settle on a location. Instead, Oliver was authorized to look into
the whole matter following a six-month leave of absence to consult with
medical and mission officials in England and North America, after which,
in October 1929, she would officially take up her dual secretarial roles with
the NCC and the CMAI. By the end of the year, she was writing to inform
William Paton, who was by now in London as associate IMC secretary, that

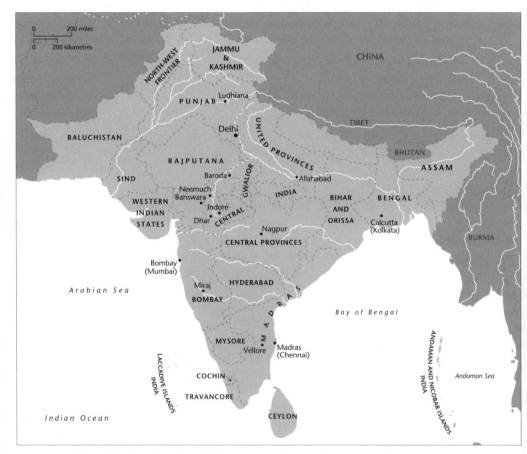

Colonial India in Dr. Choné Oliver's time, showing places where she toured or
worked.

Dr. Choné Oliver in 1900, the year she graduated from the Woman's Medical College, Toronto, and in 1945, the year before her final retirement as secretary of the Christian Medical Association of India (CMAI). Photos courtesy United Church/Victoria University Archives, Toronto (UCA).

Miraj was not, after all, considered to be the most suitable site.[47] At its fourth biennial conference, the CMAI membership again supported the idea of a college and authorized the establishment of a College Committee to look into matters such as a site and financial needs. By May 1931, with the desirability of a rural hinterland in mind, the committee had recommended Allahabad as the best site and prepared tentative estimates. It had also elaborated on the anticipated functions and governance for the proposed college and prepared draft promotional material for use in cultivating moral and financial support. The cultivation of support was to begin (for largely symbolic reasons) among Christians in India and then to be directed to "men of large means" in the West.[48]

The project at this stage was being planned and publicized as a college for men. But given the fact that there were more mission hospitals operated by and for women than for men, and that there were reportedly no fully qualified Indian women doctors on the staffs of the women's hospitals,[49] it is important to consider why the project as initially conceived was exclusively for training men. The easy answer is that plans were already under consideration at the medical schools at Ludhiana and Vellore to upgrade to MB, BS status, and that meantime Lady Hardinge Medical College in New Delhi, the only medical institution in the country offering full professional training exclusively for women, produced a significant number of Christian graduates. The proportion of Christian women enrolled in India's coeducational medical colleges was also high.[50] There was, furthermore, disturbingly little indication that the mission hospitals for women were anxious to alter the status quo by hiring and promoting fully trained Indian women doctors, especially since their qualifications entitled them to the higher salaries available in the Women's Medical Service (WMS), administered by the Countess of Dufferin Fund.[51]

Members of the CMAI medical college and executive committee meet in Allahabad, 30-31 December 1931. Joining them from the visiting Laymen's Foreign Missions Inquiry is Dr. Henry S. Houghton, dean of the medical college, University of Iowa (front row, centre). Oliver is second from left, front row. Anna Martin, her friend and personal physician and the CMAI treasurer, is second from right, front row. Standing behind and to the left of Dr. Martin is Dr. Christian Frimodt-Möller. Reproduced from CMAI *Journal* (March 1932), courtesy Yale Divinity Library (YDL).

Dr. T.J. Joseph. A strong supporter of the CMAI's controversial plan for building a Christian medical college, Joseph saw no reason why a Christian college could not be "as nationalistic as any other college." A protegé of Frimodt-Möller, he later became superintendent of the Lady Linlithgow Sanatorium, Kasauli. Reproduced from *Tales from the Inns of Healing*, courtesy UCA.

Medical delegates and conference medical staff at the International Missionary Conference, Tambaram, India, December 1938. Included in the front row are Hilda Lazarus, far left, and Sir Henry Holland, centre. Standing behind and to the left of Lazarus is P.V. Benjamin, who became the first Indian president of the CMAI. R.H.H Goheen, second row, far right, is beside Dr. Oliver. The two conducted the investigation that resulted in the 1928 *Survey of Medical Missions in India*. Reproduced from *Tales from the Inns of Healing*, courtesy UCA.

Dr. Hilda Lazarus was the first Indian woman appointed to the Women's Medical Service in colonial India. In 1948, a year after her retirement as chief medical officer of the service, she became the principal of Christian Medical College, Vellore. Reproduced from CMAI *Journal* (January 1952), courtesy YDL.

These factors aside, the nationalist climate in interwar India supplied a powerful logic of its own for the initial CMAI decision to make Indian Christian men the beneficiaries of superior medical training, for it was they, much more than Indian Christian women, who suffered, as Christians, from an "image problem" and who needed the leverage that proper professional training could give. At this stage, women's professional attributes, or lack thereof, still appeared to be of little account in matters related to a particular community's public image.[52] And in regard to gaining access to scarce spots for training in state-run medical schools, Christian women applicants still had proportionately less competition (because of the lower numbers of qualified female applicants from the non-Christian communities) than their male counterparts.[53]

Yet if factors related to the nationalist climate in India suggested the logic of concentrating on training men, the politics of fundraising in the West meant that asking for a large sum of money exclusively for a men's medical college would be unwise, given all the dramatic things that had been said in the past about India's need for "lady doctors," and given the new tendency in the interwar era in the upper echelons of missionary planning to emphasize coeducation and the consolidation of missions' institutional work as routes to modernization and efficiency. Following a meeting with the two medical representatives on the Laymen's Foreign Missions Inquiry, the CMAI executive decided at the beginning of 1932 to drop "for men" from the title of the proposed medical college. The decision was confirmed in an important joint meeting of the executive committees of the NCC and the CMAI in March of that year.[54] As will be seen in what follows, however, gender issues related to planning for a Christian medical college were far from being resolved.

Up to this point, the general idea of establishing a medical college had enjoyed a comparatively warm reception, not only from the CMAI's own constituency but also from the NCC and its constituent regional and provincial councils and from the various missions, church bodies, and conferences to which it had been presented. The bureaucratic support that was most crucial to the project was that of NCC secretary J.Z. Hodge and, to an even greater degree, that of his predecessor, William Paton, now, as the IMC secretary with special responsibility for India matters, a crucial figure in promoting it in the West.

It probably helped that Hodge was a self-described liberal in sympathy with the aspirations of moderate nationalists in the early 1930s. He was optimistic about the outcome of the Round Table conferences being held in London to discuss constitutional changes for India and entertained the hope that leading Christian nationalists like Round Table delegate S.K. Datta (whom the NCC had hoped to obtain for its first secretariat) could forge friendly links with Gandhi.[55] Hodge seems to have regarded the establishment of a

Christian medical college as the kind of step that would be in keeping with India's national aspirations and with what he foresaw as its peaceful and evolutionary advance to national autonomy.[56] He was also inclined to be sympathetic to the project because of his close working relationship with and personal regard for Oliver. The regard would last even when, in later years, he proved less than resolute about defending the project as it came under attack.

As for Paton, he was present in India for the CMAI's 1931 biennial conference and took a lead in stimulating the discussion of difficult issues regarding the establishment of a medical college. En route back to London, he wrote to inform Oliver that his own early skepticism about the project had been overcome and authorized her to use the arguments in his letter to respond to other skeptics. Back in England, he seems to have presented the college plan in a positive light to the India Committee of the Conference of British Missionary Societies (CBMS) and subsequently reported to Hodge that the response had been surprisingly positive considering that it was "an entirely new and rather formidable proposal."[57] In the same year, in an article in the *Journal* dealing with Gandhi's recent charge that medical missions engaged in their work only for subversive religious ends, Paton used the Mahatma's attack as an occasion to argue for the vital importance of a Christian medical college for training the practitioners needed by Christian institutions.[58] Both because Paton's support was so crucial to her project, and because of her regard for him and other gurus of the international missionary movement, Oliver had good reason to be dismayed when that support began to evaporate in the context of the worsening Depression.

Reservations and Resistance

Evidence of Paton's waning enthusiasm surfaced in his response to the joint resolutions on the college project passed by the NCC and CMAI executive committees in March 1932. In addition to outlining the rationale and administrative structure for the proposed college, the resolutions had reiterated that the fundraising approach in the West would be to "a few individual donors and not by a public appeal which would be likely to divert funds from Missions and Churches."[59] The resolutions also contained a tentative budget – $5,500,000 – for the establishment and maintenance of a 400-bed hospital and a medical college for 125 students, and a request that the IMC form committees in Britain and America to help recruit staff and promote interest in the college. Names were provided of appropriate people to serve on such committees. In forwarding these resolutions to Paton, Hodge asked that, if possible, he establish the British committee in time for a June meeting with Oliver, who would then be on furlough. "But," he added, "you will know best."[60]

Paton *did* think he knew best. The resolutions came with the NCC's endorsement, and they provided for ongoing NCC representation on the College Committee. This provision might have been expected to reassure him about the decision-making process. (He had, from the outset, seemed unconvinced that medical personnel on their own had the ability to make sound financial judgments and keep the larger mission picture in perspective.) Nonetheless, he responded by recommending that the committee "go very gently and slowing in this matter of the big Medical College scheme. I am frankly nervous about the size of the whole plan, and as we have not yet been able to launch any combined appeal for Christian education in India I am most unwilling to frighten people by the mention of a colossal sum for a medical college, even though it is hoped to get it largely from Dr. Firor and his group of millionaires." Oliver should meet only with him and a few others to talk over the college plans, he wrote Hodge, rather than with a formal committee. "I am sure I am right in this and not merely timorous."[61]

In 1935 Paton's private reservations about the college scheme hardened into official resistance. In March he declined Oliver's request that he write an introduction to a promotional pamphlet, saying that "any kind of public appeal" for the huge sum now requested – it had increased significantly following Oliver's consultations with experts in the US while on furlough – would serve only "to make the missionary enterprise [look] ridiculous" and "hopelessly out of touch with reality."[62] At the end of the year, in India once again for the CMAI's biennial conference, he declared the college plan "Utopian" and launched a personal attack on Dr. Frimodt-Möller, one of its strongest advocates.[63] The following summer, in the wake of a private meeting in New York to discuss fundraising for the college, he and S.K. Datta were described as "strongly dissenting voices." In the same period he charged Drs. Firor and Goheen, two of Oliver's American colleagues, with being naïvely optimistic about fundraising possibilities. He seemed to regard them as partly responsible for the same tendency in Oliver, whom he now described as living in "a green world." His IMC counterpart in the US, A.L. Warnshuis, echoed his view that the existing college plan was unrealistic and should be sharply scaled back.[64]

Before turning to Oliver's response to these and other mid-1930s challenges, it will be useful to review her role up to that point and to enlarge on the context for Paton's hardening position. As the only doctor working full-time for the CMAI and its college plan, Oliver had the greatest investment of time and emotional energy in the plan. In addition to being the person chiefly responsible for procuring information and preparing estimates and promotional material, she presented the plan in person to regional and provincial Christian councils and to many missions and regional medical mission conferences in different parts of India. When she was not travelling within India on behalf of the college scheme and other CMAI business, she used her regular columns in the Association's *Journal* as well as feature articles to press home the college's importance to the future of Christianity in India. On furlough in 1932-33, she worked quietly on behalf of the plan in Britain and North America and participated in the establishment of a small New-York-based committee to facilitate planning for the college.[65] En route back from furlough, she inspected medical colleges in metropolitan Japan, China, and Korea, visiting not only mission institutions but also the Peking Union Medical College (PUMC). Founded as a mission institution in 1906, PUMC was supported by the Rockefeller Foundation's China Medical Board from 1915 and with that aid became East Asia's "medical mecca." Following her return to India, Oliver used a series of articles in the *Journal* to draw attention to the value and importance of the Christian medical colleges for Christian work in East Asia, commenting in each case on specific administrative and technical aspects to be emulated or avoided. She reported approvingly on the increasing trend to coeducation in medical training (and higher education generally) in the East. Coeducation was one of PUMC's many strengths, but she argued that despite its professional excellence, something vital had been lost when mission control had been surrendered. And, in the case of Japan, where mission-sponsored medical work had been all but abandoned in the face of the state's large role, the loss to the Christian cause was now recognized and lamented.[66]

Oliver drew on her familiarity with the East Asian colleges in a May 1934 fundraising letter to a man "of large means," in this case, the attorney for a recently established Detroit estate valued at more than $16 million. The letter is of interest not only for what it shows about how plans for the college had grown and the way that the appeal was framed but also because the letter was destined to be both the first and last of its kind. The college plan, she explained to the attorney, called for some $2 million for land, buildings, and equipment for a medical college and a hospital to serve some seven hundred patients, and an additional $7 million for endowment. By comparison, the establishment of PUMC had cost $10 million with an additional $7 million for endowment. Given the size and the medical needs of India's population and its potential to contribute to the cause of world health as a kind of tropical research laboratory, the plan for a high-grade medical college there, she argued, was very much in keeping with the expressed wish of the late Mr. Rackham "to improve the conditions of mankind everywhere." Eschewing any attempt at providing a theological rationale for the plan of the sort normally deemed appropriate for missions supporters (and such as was important to her personally), Oliver stressed the project's ecumenical and cooperative character and the sense of vocation that would inspire its staff, who "would stand pre-eminently for training in character and for the directing of attention to the places where the need for medical service is greatest." In addition to the mission boards and churches who were in favour of the scheme, Oliver explained, it had the "sympathy" of the recent Lindsay Commission on Christian Higher Education in India and of the Laymen's Foreign Missions Inquiry (though she acknowledged that the Laymen's endorsement was linked to some questions that they wished to see answered).[67] As for the College Committee itself, it included some of the best-known Western doctors in India. In her broad list of supporters of the scheme, she included two names that were sure to be recognized approvingly by any American with a modicum of interest in missions: the late Sir William Wanless and IMC chairman John R. Mott, the revered elder statesman of the international missionary movement. She concluded her letter by asking those responsible for the Rackham estate to recognize her request as a great opportunity, "the opportunity of financing a project that may have in India as great an influence as certain great colleges in America and Europe which were connected with religious movements at their foundation."[68]

Oliver was strongly supported in all these efforts by CMAI activists who shared her view on the importance of establishing a Christian medical college in India. Frimodt-Möller used the *Journal*'s pages in January 1932 to argue for the special importance of converting the temporary CMAI secretaryship into a full-time position following Oliver's furlough so that she could continue her work on the college plan. Goheen, her partner on the 1920s survey of medical missions, echoed this point in a 1934 *Journal* editorial, when she was permanently established in the position.[69] Goheen was active in promoting the cause in the US, along with Johns Hopkins surgery professor W.F. Firor, whose claims to having access to a cadre of sympathetic American millionaires Paton were more than once derided.[70] Other strong American supporters and frequent confidants included Galen Scudder, who took over the secretaryship while Oliver was on furlough, and Douglas Forman, who, during his tenure as *Journal* editor, used the position to promote the interests of the college and to suggest the kinds of "ancillary" functions it could serve beyond those most directly tied to Christian interests.[71]

Among Indian doctors who were strong advocates of the plan, two who stood out were T.J. Joseph and P.V. Benjamin, both protégés of Frimodt-Möller in the sanatorium at Arogyavaram. An early appointee to the College Committee, Joseph had written a letter publicly endorsing the project in 1931. In it he presented himself as a spokesman "on behalf of Indian Christian young men" and addressed concerns related to the nationalist context. It was true, he said, that in the past "mission and exclusively Christian institutions" *had* had the effect of "denationalising Indian Christians," but given the "general awakening" there was no reason "why a Christian College cannot be as nationalistic as any other college." Indeed, far from turning out denationalized Indians or "hot house plants," a Christian medical college of the highest professional standard would produce doctors who could give a lead to their non-Christian colleagues both professionally and ethically, and at the same time be proud Indians.[72] P.V. Benjamin, the young Indian doctor whose enthusiasm for the cause of a medical college Oliver had commented upon as early as 1930, was back from overseas postgraduate study by mid-decade and poised to become an important advocate.[73] In the 1940s he would be recruited, like his mentor Frimodt-Möller, for the central government's tuberculosis work and in the same decade become the CMAI's first Indian president.

The commitment and solidarity of Oliver and her colleagues notwithstanding, Paton was undoubtedly correct in perceiving a certain vagueness in the early stages of planning for a Christian medical college and a naïveté in their ongoing optimism about obtaining large sums for its development from a few wealthy donors, especially in the context of the Depression and the apparent tendency of major philanthropists like John D. Rockefeller Jr. to move away from supporting large ventures that were narrowly linked to missions.[74] Further, there can be no question but that Paton's on-the-spot experience of the dampening impact of the Depression on Western philanthropy generally was the central factor behind his growing resistance to a medical college. Nevertheless, his new, tough-minded approach has to be seen in a broader perspective.

As IMC secretary, Paton was anxious to use his role to exert an influence on political as well as missionary matters, especially where India was concerned.[75] Like Hodge, he wanted to encourage colonial officials to pursue a policy of liberalism and sympathy towards moderate nationalist leaders, but from his London base he developed a different perspective on how particular mission projects might affect this agenda. Any plan likely to make the international missions bureaucracy look "ridiculous," as he thought the expensive medical college scheme would, had to be avoided. Yet after moving cautiously at the beginning, and frequently seeking his advice, Oliver and her colleagues had enlarged the proposed project and agreed on a new location for it without first consulting him. The choice of Allahabad had even been reported in the Indian press as a fait accompli after Forman, whose medical work was located there, had investigated the purchase of possible sites.[76] Furthermore, as far as the future of Christian India and its financial needs were concerned, Paton's priorities at this time were, on the one hand, with efforts to aid higher Christian arts education as a follow-up to the Report of the Lindsay Commission, and, on the other, with mass movement evangelism.[77] He shared both these priorities with S.K. Datta, who, as noted, opposed the medical college plan; with Bishop V.S. Azariah, who also opposed the college plan, he certainly shared a commitment to evangelism.

Given their position as strong Indian nationalists, Datta and Azariah might have been expected to support an endeavour that would improve the professional training and hence the image, and opportunities for advancement, of their fellow Christians. Yet a project as expensive as building *and maintaining* a strong Christian medical college would make heavy demands on mission resources in their own day and on the Indian Church of the future, demands that would necessarily divert funds from the projects they favoured. Although Datta had himself studied medicine in Edinburgh in the first decade of the twentieth century, he seems never to have practised. Instead, after years of involvement in YMCA work in India and Europe, and a brief period as a member of the Indian Legislative Assembly, he became involved in the cause of higher Christian arts education in India. He was appointed principal of Forman Christian College in 1934 and may have looked forward to a similar role in an all-India Christian university when that project was briefly under consideration by the Lindsay Commission, on which he served.[78] As for Bishop Azariah, his commitment in the 1930s to mass movement evangelism among the depressed classes of village India was so strong that it brought him into sharp conflict with Gandhi. Having himself left Madras Christian College without obtaining a degree, he was unconvinced of the value of higher education in village ministry and believed (like Gandhi) that the West's culture of professionalism was influencing India's professional classes to the detriment of spiritual values.[79] Thus, while the medical college project had the potential to facilitate more egalitarian relationships between Indians and Westerners within the Christian medical community, he opposed it even at the early, "optimistic" stage of NCC deliberations on the subject. It was this attitude that he brought to the CMAI's College Committee, to which he was appointed in 1932. Nor would his feelings about the project have been made less hostile by the experience of his doctor son, who about this time was refused a place on the staff of a Church Missionary Society (CMS) medical mission in northern India on the grounds that for its higher-grade positions it hired only Europeans.[80]

Datta and Azariah were influential figures within the Indian Christian community, but they were also men whose voices commanded attention in the West (where committee work frequently took them), especially as liberal mission bureaucrats sought to be more attentive than in the Edinburgh-conference era to the perspectives of indigenous Christian leaders. Paton was certainly an exemplar of this new attitude of openness, but he was also being pragmatic when he cited the views of such leaders to support his own reservations about the medical college project.[81]

Oliver's close association with American activists on the college project may also have lessened Paton's willingness to support it. CMAI men like Firor and Goheen were, he thought, unduly sanguine about getting the "colossal" sum in the estimates and unduly focused on a big medical facility as a route to providing Indian Christian doctors with the nationwide "influence" to be derived from "the prestige of superior training." His unease with their approach reflected a more general discomfort with the growth of "American" values and influence in the mainstream Protestant missionary movement. (His reference to the project as the "American College" in one letter to Oliver was, she recognized, not merely an absent-minded slip.)[82] In the same way, Oliver's role as a key informant for the medical personnel on the Fact-Finding and Appraisal teams of the wholly American Laymen's Foreign Missions Inquiry in India-Burma, and her later review of *Re-Thinking Missions* in the CMAI's *Journal,* may also have inflicted some indirect damage on the college project.[83] In addition to Paton, there were those like Datta and Azariah and Dr. Edith Brown, the founder of the mission medical school at Ludhiana, who objected to the Inquiry's syncretist approach to other world religions and its seeming preoccupation with technical expertise in mission institutional work.[84] If Oliver's association with the Inquiry *did* hurt the college project, it was a deeply ironic outcome: not only had its medical experts expressed some reservations about the feasibility of the project; Oliver's review of *Re-Thinking Missions*, while generally favourable, was by no means a blanket endorsement of the Inquiry's findings. As well, she would later criticize its failure to recognize "the tendency of modern medicine ... to stress the inter-relation of the physical, mental and spiritual."[85] Indeed, while she shared the broad view of the Laymen's Inquiry that "to serve men in the spirit of Christ *is* to preach Christ,"[86] she was far more inclined than those who wrote its medical sections to focus on issues related to religion in health and healing. Her feature articles and reviews for the *Journal* were much more likely to deal with this theme than with scientific and technical medical matters.[87]

While there were, then, a number of factors in the resistance that had developed to the college project by the mid-1930s, the impact of the Depression on Western philanthropic and religious giving and Paton's role as gatekeeper were crucial. A senior missions bureaucrat with a strong sense of the rightness of his own judgments and with many irons in the fire, Paton drew back from the scheme, which was at once the most expensive of the many mission projects that came across his desk and by no means the one closest to his heart. He would later maintain that he had always supported the "principle" of a Christian medical college (and that seems to have been true) but from the perspective of Oliver, whose life work it had become, his stand in the mid-1930s clearly did not seem supportive. Without his aid, Oliver and the College Committee were unable to win the assistance and endorsement of the two crucial umbrella organizations in the West, the CBMS and the FMCNA, and were thus unable to systematically identify and approach potential private donors.

As her diaries make clear, Oliver was deeply hurt by Paton's withdrawal of support in 1935, perhaps the more so because his encouragement had been an important factor in her mid-1920s move from clinical work to the medical missions survey and thereafter the world of missions bureaucracy.[88] She also had to deal with opposition to the project while her own health was fragile: she had suffered a heart attack while on furlough in 1932, some ten years after her brother Ed had died from the same cause, and she was frequently very ill in the years that followed. There was fragility, too, in her level of confidence as she faced complex issues for which the years of medical practice in Central India had not prepared her. In these circumstances, as the diaries show, she turned for reassurance to prayer, to her Bible and other inspirational works, and to a few close women friends.[89] Yet at a public and day-to-day level, she dealt with the challenges facing her with a good deal of practicality and aplomb, defending the college scheme with considerable spirit when she thought it had been misrepresented or misunderstood, while at the same time being amenable to the need to consider some changes. As the previous pages will have made clear, at this public and tactical level, her colleagues and confidants were usually men.

In responding to Paton's new toughness, Oliver explained why the cost of medical training was necessarily much greater than for higher academic education, corrected errors in the figures he cited, and reminded him that her committee had never contemplated a public appeal that would draw funds away from other mission schemes. Nor could they be said to have failed in targeted appeals to the wealthy, since, on the advice of those like himself on the ground in the West, they had as yet made *no* targeted appeals except for the one to the Rackham Estate.[90]

As well as responding privately to Paton and other individual critics, Oliver used the CMAI *Journal* to restate the "principles" underlying the plan for a college, to draw attention to aspects not previously highlighted, and to respond to specific (sometimes contradictory) criticisms that had been raised by various groups or individuals.[91] She also repackaged these *Journal* arguments in a pamphlet for wider use. Its section on principles restated familiar themes, like the need for devolution and for Indian Christian doctors to be able to continue work in fields such as leprosy that missionaries had made their own;[92] it also contained her argument for the spiritual and psychological dimensions of healing, which, she insisted, Christian physicians were uniquely qualified to understand and provide. The pamphlet as a whole, and particularly the section dealing with the financial aspect, reflected Oliver's characteristic dual emphasis on specific practical problems to be addressed and the need for a faith-based response. Yes, the large sum asked for looked "ridiculous" and, yes, the appeals for the Arts Colleges had fallen short; but even in these hard times there was "still great wealth in the hands of Christians and humanitarians," some of whom had recently given larger sums to related or analogous undertakings. The college project was a "spiritual undertaking," and timely inspiration could be found in J.H. Oldham's advice that the "dead past must not be allowed to prevent us from fulfilling God's will in the living present. Plans must be made not only for the immediate future, but for some years ahead so that when increased funds become available they can be applied to well-considered and fully thought-out schemes."[93]

As well as continuing their efforts to publicize their project as both a practical and a godly undertaking, Oliver and her colleagues undertook the task of recasting it along more modest lines in order to meet the objections of those with the power to block it. At the CMAI's biennial conference at the end of 1935, where, as noted, Paton's opposition was dramatic and public, there was strong support from the membership for pursuing the project. Nonetheless, the members instructed the College Committee to revise its estimates to provide for the development of the project in stages and take them back to the NCC for approval. There, too, they faced resistance from Paton, and from Datta as well. Acting on instructions from the NCC executive meeting, Oliver and her committee undertook to cut the budget to an "irreducible minimum" and to deal with NCC concerns about such issues as the likely availability of academically and morally fit students for such a college. This done, they won formal if unenthusiastic approval from the NCC to launch a quiet appeal to wealthy individuals in the West assisted by the CBMS and the FMCNA.[94]

Predictably, there were still more obstacles. This time, however, they were destined to take Oliver and the college project in a wholly new direction. Although representatives of the FMCNA did authorize her committee to seek out sympathetic wealthy donors, they held out no encouragement that such persons would be found.[95] As for the CBMS's Advisory Board on Medical Missions, it declined outright to support the proposed fundraising appeal, declaring the college plan "impracticable as it stands." Instead, it counselled a new method of proceeding: calling in an outside authority, Dr. Edward Hicks Hume, to provide a disinterested and expert perspective. Although Oliver and her committee remained reluctant to abandon their own vision for the medical college and their long-favoured fundraising strategy, it was this new approach that the NCC effectively compelled them to adopt. The fact that medical personnel had almost no voice within the NCC (her own position was ex officio) and that it seldom gave extended attention to medical matters was an added source of frustration.[96]

An Outside Perspective and a New Direction

Born in India of American missionary parents and briefly employed there by the US government, Hume had made his name with the Yale-in-China university medical school, stepping down in 1927 in the face of rising nationalism to make way for a Chinese administrator. Back in the US, he had been in charge of the Post-Graduate Hospital in New York until it became part of Columbia University. His subsequent position as an acknowledged expert on medical missions and a sympathetic interpreter of Chinese culture, as well as his reputation as a moderate on theological issues, also marked him out as a suitable candidate for investigating and providing expertise on the protracted issue of a Christian medical college for India.[97]

Hume travelled in India for three months before submitting his report to the College Committee at the end of 1937. During that time he saw government medical officials and educators as well as their missionary counterparts. His contacts included the Minister of Health for the United Provinces, Mrs. R.S. Pandit, as well as her brother, Jawaharlal Nehru, as part of his effort to establish a sympathetic nationalist climate for Christian medical work and a basis for cooperative undertakings. In his report Hume expressed regret at the lack of past action to promote indigenous leaders in the Christian medical enterprise in India, and at the failure of missionary societies to facilitate the creation of the type of university-level Christian medical education that had existed in China for many years (setting the pace there for government institutions). He strongly supported the establishment of a Christian medical college, but only under certain conditions and only if, as urged by the IMC secretaries in London and New York, those planning for it abandoned "illusions that large sums of money are to be obtained" and concentrated on "the working out of a practical programme." He recommended a coeducational, union Christian medical college to be established in stages and as part of a larger strategy for a much more active program of rural and preventive work coordinated with provincial government goals. In keeping with his strong rural emphasis, he favoured Allahabad as the most appropriate site for establishing the college "if the field were free" and if the CMAI were not forced by financial constraints to confine their plans to "a progamme of reasonable dimensions, likely to be attained by gradual stages." Since the field was not free, however, and since the women's medical school at Vellore was in any case faced with the Madras Presidency's requirement to upgrade as soon as possible from licentiate- to college-level training, Hume recommended starting there. After briefly paying tribute to its record of service, he made it clear that major changes would be required at Vellore, including "new officers, a new staff, a new board of control ... [amounting to] a wholly new institution."[98]

As will be shown below, Oliver and her colleagues acted promptly on Hume's chief recommendation. Yet they had reason to be frustrated both with the circumstances of his coming to India and with various aspects of his report, in addition to its thinly veiled criticism of what he saw as their naïveté about fundraising prospects. From the early 1930s, they had shown that they valued his expertise; they identified him as the most desirable person to become the first director of a union Christian medical college and more than once requested that he visit India to assist them in their deliberations. Their own thinking and planning had anticipated many of his concerns, including the importance of a rural focus and institutional governance within India.[99] While Oliver seems not to have met Nehru and his sister personally, Forman had accompanied Hume to the interview with the two nationalist modernizers and probably arranged it (like Nehru, he lived in Allahabad). Meanwhile, John Mott had already spoken to Nehru on behalf of the project and evidently ascertained his goodwill.[100] Oliver had organized the financing and the broad itinerary for Hume's tour and had met with the Vice-Chancellor of the University of Madras and other government officials as part of the groundwork for it.[101] Yet for anyone unfamiliar with the previous years of struggle for a Christian medical college in India, it would have been natural to assume that the concerns raised in Hume's report had largely originated with him.

As for the report's most significant recommendation, a joint coeducational venture at Vellore, the College Committee had investigated that possibility almost two years earlier. Frimodt-Möller, who served on the local Vellore Council and who was aware of the financial difficulties facing Vellore in its struggle to upgrade, had raised the idea with Oliver early in 1936. The Vellore Council's response had been negative, as it was again when, early in 1938, acting on Hume's report, the College Committee renewed its proposal.[102] Understanding these negative responses requires some knowledge of Vellore's history, funding, and government and takes us into the complex missionary world of gender politics and institutional loyalties.

The first step towards creating the celebrated institution that came to be known simply as Vellore had been taken by Ida Sophia Scudder in 1900. The first woman doctor in a family of American medical missionaries whose India roots went back to the early nineteenth century, she had begun by treating female patients in a room in her parents' bungalow.[103] The Missionary Medical School for Women, Vellore, which she established in 1918, operated as a union institution from 1923. A decade later it had a greatly improved physical plant, mainly as a result of financial contributions from the US. The moving spirit behind this development was Mrs. Lucy W. Peabody, a wealthy widow who raised millions of dollars for seven women's colleges in Asia and who was for years the key figure on Vellore's powerful US Governing Board.[104] Thanks to her fundraising acumen and her part in mission controversies, Peabody's was a household name among missions-minded Americans. Scudder, meanwhile, came to be internationally known, honoured not only in the United States but also by the Government of India and its most important critic, M.K. Gandhi, who, as noted, visited her in 1928.[105] Scudder's personal life and the institutional life of Vellore came to be seen as inseparable. Indeed, a "personality cult" developed around "Aunt Ida," making her the head of an "extended family" that was dedicated to treating and training women.[106]

In North America in 1935, seeking funds to upgrade Vellore in a tour organized by Mrs. Peabody, Scudder was given access to wealthy potential donors and was even received in the White House. Yet in the face of the Depression, neither her charisma nor Mrs. Peabody's skill and experience was able to achieve the desired results. Although a handsome matching grant in memory of his mother had been provided during the 1920s colleges campaign by John D. Rockefeller Jr., a call on the Rockefeller Foundation was now unproductive. Following an eight-thousand-mile tour of the American West Coast, Mrs. Peabody lamented that "people no longer boast of wealth. Instead, they all brag of poverty."[107]

Yet even in the face of this new situation and the necessity of upgrading to meet Madras Presidency requirements (it was in the forefront of states moving to abolish licentiate-level medical training),[108] Scudder and her sponsors were determined to maintain Vellore's distinctive identity as a women's institution. A 1937 fundraising letter illustrates their competitive approach to the CMAI plans as well as their still-optimistic expectations: "Personally I am glad we can go on and become an MB, BS before this new Men's Medical College [sic] comes into being."[109] Mrs. Peabody commissioned Scudder's friend and former colleague Dr. Mary Jeffrey to write her biography as a spur to fundraising. Like other promotional literature developed by Vellore, the biography perpetuated old stereotypes about the benighted state of India's womanhood – what Pearl Buck in the China context called "sob-story propaganda"[110] – and stressed the need for single-sex facilities to train women doctors and treat women's ills. In making these arguments, it was out of step with a tendency among modernizing Indians of both sexes to emphasize changing social conditions and to advocate co-education as the best route to high-quality academic and professional education for women.[111] But given the pride in its past, and the professional and emotional investment of various stakeholders in its existing identity, Vellore's second "No" was scarcely surprising. The council secretary informed Oliver that while it did not wish irrevocably to "close the door" on the possibility of future cooperation, it could not recommend the College Committee's proposal to the home boards.[112]

Far from despairing over Vellore's negative response, Oliver and her colleagues seem to have been relieved, since it allowed them to proceed with plans for what they were now calling a "medical centre" at Allahabad, albeit along the lines for scaled-down, gradual development recommended by Hume.[113] With some important Indian critics in the NCC gradually being won over to the scheme, and warm expressions of confidence in her ongoing leadership from Hodge and the CMAI membership, Oliver felt buoyed to carry on, still hopeful of obtaining "large sums from a few donors." But this time she arranged for a medical missionary to act in Britain as a full-time fundraiser and sought support for endowed chairs in the proposed medical centre and for the loan of qualified medical staff from denominational boards.[114]

But it was not to be. Foreign missions officials in the West were unwilling to consider financing two medical colleges. At a special meeting of the CMAI's College Committee in December 1938, senior representatives of the overseas ecumenical organizations and of various denominational boards were present (they had come to India for the upcoming IMC conference at Tambaram), along with representatives of Vellore and the NCC. The entire history of efforts to upgrade Christian medical education in India was reviewed and the position of the overseas officials made clear: they would strongly support an appeal for funds for one coeducational medical college in India. Having heard first-hand from these officials, the College Committee and the Vellore representatives voted unanimously in favour of what was not the first choice of either: to ask the Vellore Council to reconsider the CMAI proposal for coeducation presented to it in February.[115]

That both Ida Scudder and Vellore Council Secretary C.R. Wierenga had participated in the unanimous vote did not, of course, mean that they were fully and permanently "on side" or in a position to ensure either the council's or the American Governing Board's agreement to establish coeducation at Vellore. Both seemed to recognize the practicality of a cooperative approach, but there were lingering reservations. And because Mrs. Peabody remained adamantly opposed, they were especially cautious about moving forward. Mrs. Peabody reportedly reproached Scudder for even considering coeducation for Vellore and accused her of serving as a mouthpiece for Frimodt-Möller and other *male* advocates of the plan.[116] Like Scudder's other wealthy benefactor, her long-time personal companion, Gertrude Dodd, Mrs. Peabody chose to ignore the fact that the key figure in the CMAI scheme had, from the outset, been a woman. Like Miss Dodd, too, she sometimes chose for propaganda purposes to represent its goal as a *men's college*, though it had ceased to be that almost ten years earlier.[117] Confronted by these pressures, Scudder agreed to leave for the US and campaign for funds for Vellore as a women's college. With the elderly Miss Dodd, who would not survive the fundraising campaign, she left India in 1941, returning only in 1945.

Meanwhile, with the University of Madras insisting that Vellore must meet its timetable to either upgrade to MB, BS level or terminate its teaching program, Oliver and her colleagues concluded that they had no choice but to assist it, even though no commitment to coeducation had yet been made and the American Governing Board remained opposed. Having taken a furlough following her participation as a delegate to the IMC conference,[118] Oliver was back at work in India in early 1940, although, like Scudder, she had reached retirement age. An editorial in the *Journal* in July 1940 declared that there was now "no greater emergency" than "the establishment of Vellore on a sound footing."[119] It was from this position that Oliver and her colleagues worked to assist in procuring the minimum funds and staff necessary for the first stage of upgrading Vellore's teaching standard.[120]

A year later, Vellore had developed sufficiently to obtain affiliation with the University of Madras for teaching the first two years of the MB, BS course to its women students. Faced with difficulties in recruiting teaching staff from outside India, especially under wartime conditions, Oliver wrote to boards within the country that had qualified staff (the University of Madras insisted on a minimum of three years' experience teaching at the MB level), asking them to donate salaries as well as personnel to the cause.[121] Yet as turf and gender struggles re-emerged in the early 1940s, it appeared that the plan to upgrade Vellore fully as a coeducational institution – or indeed to establish *any* Christian medical college – might still fail. Oliver's fellow Canadian on the CMAI executive, Dr. L.B. Carruthers, editor of the *Journal* from 1936, favoured once again re-opening the question of a site for the college so that his institution, Miraj, could be reconsidered. (For abusing his editorial position in this way and opposing his own Association's policy, he was asked to resign.)[122] Galen Scudder, a strong advocate of the CMAI's plans despite being Ida Scudder's cousin and a member of the Vellore Council, expressed private doubts that the existing staff at Vellore had a sufficient grasp of the needs of a modern medical college to upgrade adequately to meet full affiliation requirements. For his part, Frimodt-Möller was skeptical that the CMAI could place any faith in a commitment from Vellore to cooperate; "ladies change their minds!" he observed acidly to Oliver, evidently excluding her from that gender construct.[123]

What saved the project from further and perhaps fatal delays was the new sense of urgency about modernizing and Indianizing Christian medical education imparted by the Second World War. In this spirit, representatives of the Vellore Council and the CMAI College Committee came together in an effective joint committee to work for a single, coeducational Christian medical college "so strong and so distinctive in its contribution to the needs of India that its value cannot be questioned by any government or medical council of the future ... [able] not just to conform to the minimum standard for University affiliation but to develop a college that can give a lead in lines that need emphasis such as research, service in rural areas, [and] the moral and spiritual basis of healthful living."[124] The Vellore representatives behind this new position included Ida Scudder's niece and medical colleague, Ida B. Scudder, and the new secretary of the Vellore Council, who distanced himself from the recalcitrance of Mrs. Peabody and her supporters.[125] In reality, Mrs. Peabody no longer had unanimous support from her board because representatives of its constituent societies were becoming advocates of coeducation.[126] When even Ida S. Scudder bowed to the pressure for change at the institution she had founded and, in the words of her chief biographer, decided to take a stand "for the India of tomorrow," effective resistance was at an end. In January 1943 the American Governing

Board cabled its consent to proceed with plans for completing Vellore's upgrade on a coeducational basis.[127]

Oliver was able to spend the final two years before her formal retirement working for a cause that at last had the sanction of all the principal parties concerned. Shortly after receiving the American Board's cable, she wrote to Dr. Hilda Lazarus, the Indian Christian principal of Lady Hardinge Medical College, inviting her to become the first principal of Vellore as a college.[128] She also continued to seek teaching staff from the small pool of those with the requisite qualifications, ideally with salaries donated by their mission boards, or, in the case of Indian Christian doctors employed elsewhere, willing to work for mission-level salaries.[129] Before leaving India in 1944, she was able to preside over the official opening of the men's outpatient department at Vellore. Back in North America, she delayed her return to her native Ontario to promote the college cause in New York and Washington. She also made a special trip to Philadelphia to recruit Jacob Chandy, the young Indian doctor whose training under Wilder Penfield she would set in motion and who would later establish India's first neurosurgery department.[130]

At the time of her retirement and following her death three years later, her leadership in the long struggle for a Christian medical college was widely acknowledged, most warmly by her fellow warriors in the CMAI but also by the NCC and the Vellore Council.[131] Yet it would be misleading to feature Oliver's decades of struggle as terminating in a triumphal conclusion. Vellore was not in a position to admit its first class of male students until July 1947, a few months after her death. And ironically, because of her professional eminence, Dr. Lazarus was unable to take up her appointment as Vellore's principal until 1948.[132] As Lazarus explained in her first report as principal, inadequacies in the staffing and facilities for some mandatory medical departments and insecurity of finances resulted in the postponement of the original date for Vellore's full and permanent affiliation with the University of Madras. When affiliation was achieved at the beginning of 1950, the announcement was timed to coincide with the celebration of Ida S. Scudder's fifty years of service at Vellore.[133] It was, in fact, Scudder who would flourish in its institutional memory. To the extent that Oliver's legacy lived on at Vellore, it was in medical practitioners who had never heard her name,[134] but who combined Christian faith, professional skill, and Indian identity in ways that reflected her vision: "men and women capable of being colleagues and eventually successors."[135]

Conclusion

"In all the chief matters of life we are alone and our true history is never deciphered by others." Even without this warning from Oliver – a quotation appended to her first diary entry for 1935 – there would be no temptation to declare that one had "deciphered" her and could thus put her forward as either a representative or a unique female figure in the interwar missionary enterprise. Although the term "liminality" has become something of a postmodernist cliché, it does suggest the threshold nature of her modernity and her label-defying location on "women's issues."

Nationalism in India set the timetable for the crusade to establish a Christian medical college to produce medical missionaries' successors, but, especially in Oliver's case, religious belief was the fuel. No matter what became of missionary doctors and other Western practitioners in a future India, Western medicine itself had come to the subcontinent to stay – the Bhore Committee's 1946 report would make that clear.[136] Yet for Oliver it was not sufficient for transplanted Western medicine to be fully professional and humanistic. In Christian India it also had to be informed by the spirit of the "Great Physician" and as firmly a part of the Indian church of the future as worship and verbal forms of witness. Her CMAI colleagues shared that view, but not the intensity with which she held it. In the farewell tributes, and in numerous earlier acknowledgments of her leadership on the college issue, the single most common theme was the degree to which her leadership was rooted in her Christian faith. Nor was this merely the "right" thing to say. Indeed, it is clear from some of the public tributes as well as from private correspondence that Oliver "repelled a few by ... [her] ardour." And Paton was doubtless not alone in his impatience with her unyielding assumption that the college scheme was God's will.[137]

But if Oliver's religious discourse sometimes seemed fervent, even by the standards of Indian and mission Christianity, and if her private spirituality still led to moments of self-reproach, there was another, more "modern" and secular side to her personality. It emerged in the efficient, well-organized bureaucrat who was capable of dealing with conceptual planning as well as mundane tasks and resolute in tackling sensitive socio-medical issues like birth control despite some colleagues' unease. It emerged, too, in a private life that made room for pleasures both transient and transformative – the occasional movie, a fascinatingly eclectic range of reading, and rich female friendships.

If Oliver's private world was largely a world of women, her professional milieu from the mid-1920s consisted mainly of men. A few of these men, like Frimodt-Möller, may occasionally have forgotten her gender in the shared pursuit of a common cause, but others would doubtless have agreed with the unnamed – but probably male – author of the *Journal's* memorial tribute to her: he borrowed from the epitaph of an eighteenth-century Irish gentlewoman to speak of "her manly sense joined to her female tenderness."[138] Among such colleagues, Oliver escaped the charge of being unsexed that had long been used to denigrate women who had entered "men's worlds." Old-style social feminists like Peabody, however, had difficulty reconciling her leadership on the college project with a woman's consciousness. Rather than recognizing that a woman, and a feminist, could pursue an agenda that transcended exclusively women's concerns in response to larger societal changes, Peabody sometimes simply ignored the fact that leadership on the college issue came from Oliver.

In choosing to forsake the separate-spheres path in her professional life, Oliver was part of a larger pattern in the secular world. Scholarly studies have analyzed the change; biographies of prominent interwar women have demonstrated its complexity and unevenness.[139] If she was occasionally bruised in the largely male world of missions bureaucracy, where modernizing men like Paton and Hume could be condescending and unfair (and she too "womanly" to express her frustrations in other than polite and private ways), Oliver was nonetheless not inclined to withdraw, or return to the old world of "woman's sphere." What a later generation of feminist scholars would celebrate retrospectively as a world of women caring for women, she had come to experience in the context of missions as stifling and inefficient: a kind of missionary purdah. She would not be alone in choosing to leave that world behind.

3
The Triumph of "Standards" over "Sisterhood": Florence Murray's Approach to the Practice and Teaching of Western Medicine in Korea, 1921-69

At the end of 1946, fatally ill with Hodgkin's disease, Choné Oliver passed through Halifax, Nova Scotia, on the final leg of her homeward journey. Florence Murray went to the train station to see her and her companion, nurse Margaret Colthart, before they continued on to Toronto.[1] The poignancy of the moment was heightened by the fact that Murray herself was full of vitality and busily planning her return to the career in Korea that war with Japan had interrupted some four years earlier. Chapter 3 focuses on that interwar career, which, though quite unlike Oliver's in its particulars, illustrates the broad theme of this book. The chapter also deals with Murray's postwar career, albeit more briefly, in order to show the persistence of her commitment to "standards" rather than "sisterhood."[2]

Dr. Murray's practice in Korea was not confined to women and children. Nor were the Korean doctors with whom she worked mainly women. Her approach to the practice and teaching of Western medicine reflected changes taking place within North American society as well as her perception of what was most serviceable in the Korea of her day. More specifically, Murray's commitment to the model of Western medical professionalism that gained ascendancy in early twentieth-century North America, especially when reinforced by complementary values reflecting "modern" feminism and her understanding of class and gender relations in northern Korea, led her to eschew strict sexual segregation in the practice and teaching of Western medicine.[3]

In directly linking Murray's mode of practice in Korea to the culture of medical professionalism in the West, I have found few scholarly models to draw upon for comparisons. Like other aspects of women's missionary work, the experiences of women who were medical missionaries have so far been studied mainly in nineteenth- and early twentieth-century contexts, and the emphasis has been on their seeking opportunities and finding fulfilment by doing "women's work for women."[4] Their experience has also received some attention in critical studies that present the use of Western medicine as a colonial strategy for "the manufacture of consent" and in postcolonial scholarship employing discourse analysis, although such studies have generally featured male medical missionaries.[5] Overall, remarkably little attention has been paid to missionary medicine as an aspect of the social history of Western medicine, much less to the ways that the practice and teaching of medicine by Western women might have altered in mission contexts in the first half of the twentieth century as a result of their own grounding in the new ideals and technologies of scientific medicine.[6] As Chapter 2 has shown, Oliver was a product of an earlier, women-focused culture of professional preparation; the new ideals reached her only indirectly and in the last half of her career. In Murray's case however, the new professional ethos was there from the beginning.

Family and Professional Formation

Florence Jessie Murray (1894-1975) was the eldest of six children of a Presbyterian (later United Church) minister and his wife, a former schoolteacher. "Home" was the manse in several rural and village communities in Nova Scotia and Prince Edward Island. A strong work ethic, social concern, and the value of higher education were among the lessons taught there. Three of her siblings, Foster, Ed, and Anna, would also become doctors. The eldest brother, Alex, obtained a doctorate in theology in interwar Germany; the youngest, Charlie, a science graduate and the family's never-disowned red sheep, participated in Depression-era communist activism and union organizing and work in Maritime primary industries.[7] In her published memoir, Murray wrote that she had chosen medicine as a career only after learning that she could not enter the ministry. She also wrote that she had decided on overseas missionary work in part to fulfill one of her father's own dreams. (Family responsibilities had stood in the way of his being included in the small group of ordained men from the Maritime provinces who were chosen to establish the Presbyterian Church in Canada's mission to Korea in 1898.) There was, of course, more to her decision than an awareness of her father's thwarted ambition: a heritage of Maritime Presbyterians' mission involvement stretching back to the mid-nineteenth century; the stimulus of Student Volunteer Movement recruitment when she and Alex were students at Charlottetown's Prince of Wales College; and the attraction of a vocation that was also a route to a larger life than anything she could anticipate in Atlantic Canada.[8] A career in missionary medicine may not have been her girlhood choice, but once the decision had been made, she prepared rigorously.

Even before her five years of training (1914-19) had been completed at the Dalhousie University Faculty of Medicine in Halifax, Murray had acquired a rich fund of practical experience as a result of unique opportunities for female medical students created by the First World War and her own initiative in seeking out chances for professional development outside the classroom. The most dramatic such opening came in the immediate aftermath of the explosion of a munitions ship in Halifax Harbour in December 1917. She was called on to be the official anaesthetist at the YMCA's emergency hospital despite the fact that she had then had only one day's experience in giving anaesthetic. The following year she was sent to the fishing community of Lockeport, Nova Scotia, where twenty-five people had died of Spanish influenza, when the local doctor himself came down with the disease. Following her graduation in 1919, Murray served briefly as an intern in a Boston hospital, attracted by its offer of salary and room and board and the opportunity to attend lectures by well-known Harvard University medical specialists. But her dismay at the low level of medical care and personal attention given to the hospital's largely indigent patients prompted her to return to Halifax, where she was able to act as an assistant to a prominent surgeon, work as a demonstrator in the anatomy department at the medical college, and treat private patients in her spare time.[9]

By comparison with other Canadian medical graduates of her era, Murray was a seasoned practitioner.[10] In 1921 when her missionary career began, it was unusual for Canadian medical missionaries to begin their overseas service with *any* postgraduate experience.[11] Her years of experience as a student and new practitioner were especially important, since they coincided with a period when new ideas about how to teach and practise modern, scientific medicine were taking hold, although not without conflict with other traditions. Indeed, such conflicts had been working themselves out in the medical school in Halifax in the years just prior to her arrival.

In 1910 the proprietary Halifax Medical College had been one of several Canadian institutions indicted for their shortcomings in Abraham Flexner's influential report on medical education in the United States and Canada. Prepared for the Carnegie Foundation, the report had subsequently served as the foundation's blueprint in its continent-wide campaign for medical school reform. As well as insisting on a model of medical training linked to laboratory-based research and clinical experience, the foundation required that assisted schools be part of a university.[12] Although instructors at the Halifax Medical College had resented Flexner's report, Dalhousie acted promptly on its recommendations. Improved physical facilities and more endowed chairs had to wait until after 1920, when Rockefeller Foundation funding was provided, but within a year of the report's publication, the Halifax Medical College had formally become the Faculty of Medicine at Dalhousie, with upgraded standards and entrance requirements.[13]

Like many other centres of medical education in North America, the Halifax College was already considering reforms before Flexner's report was published (although not necessarily along the lines he envisaged). Hence the resentment of medical faculty who regarded Flexner's criticisms as sweeping and unfair.[14] At the same time, the report "had a galvanizing effect on public sentiment," making the achievement of advances in medical training both more compelling and more feasible.[15] This new mood undoubtedly contributed to Murray's zeal for high standards of professionalism in the practice and teaching of Western medicine, especially when combined with the powerful work ethic and sense of Christian duty instilled in her by her Presbyterian upbringing.[16]

The fact that Murray's medical training took place in a coeducational institution rather than a women's medical college was probably also significant for her future attitude towards missionary medicine and women's work for women. Only two women's medical colleges had been established in Canada in the late nineteenth century when professional medicine first opened to women, and both had ceased to exist by 1906, but like the more numerous women's medical colleges established in the United States in the last half of the nineteenth century, they had been vitally important in training the first generation of women medical missionaries, whose particular mandate was work among women.[17] Indeed, training medical missionaries had been one factor in the support given for the establishment of women's medical colleges.[18] Although many of these colleges had ceased to exist in the United States even before 1900, the Flexner Report was an important factor in all but finishing them off. Such schools had frequently been proprietary rather than university affiliated, and associated with "irregular" and holistic approaches to medicine, approaches increasingly considered unworthy of financial support in the early twentieth century. Dr. Mary Putnam Jacobi, a nationally prominent research- and publication-oriented American woman doctor, was already repudiating the notion of a distinct "female" vision of medicine and a separate-spheres approach to training and practice in the late nineteenth century, despite the fact that her career as a student and instructor had begun in a women's medical college.[19] In the same period, a small group of wealthy Baltimore women who wanted to give able female medical students access to the best possible training made their offer of funds to Johns Hopkins University conditional on its starting its elite medical school as a coeducational institution.[20] Predictably, the changes that took place around the turn of the century as "the practice of medicine became a science" led not only to the demise of the separate schools but also to a sharp falling off in the proportion of women taking up the study of medicine.[21] Florence Murray may not have known of this decline, and she may not have been personally familiar with Jacobi's career or that of other medical women who won respect and acceptance for their good fit with the new, scientific milieu. Nonetheless, she seems to have been part of the new breed of women doctors who valued "science" and "standards" over sisterly service and female mentorship.

The Context and Its Challenges

A primarily agricultural country that had been under Chinese cultural suzerainty for centuries, Korea was deemed a poor, ill-governed, and backward place even by comparison with other pre-modern societies in the late nineteenth century. Initially, this perception made modernizing Japan's increasing influence and its formal annexation of Korea in 1910 seem acceptable, even desirable, to the American Presbyterians who had pioneered Protestant missionary work in Korea in the 1880s.[22] In reality, Japanese rule increased the poverty of the rural masses, while the colonial administrative structure and educational system offered few opportunities for Koreans to advance.[23] In these circumstances and in the face of the colonial government's harsh responses to real or suspected dissident activity, missionaries sympathized with the plight of Koreans and were consequently suspected of disloyalty to the Japanese regime even before the March First Movement for national independence in 1919, in which Korean Christians played a prominent role.[24]

By comparison with their counterparts in other Asian countries, Protestant missionaries in Korea had enjoyed great success in winning converts, and, under the leadership of a vigorous indigenous church, Christianity would ultimately become the second largest religion in the country.[25] But in the decade following the March First Movement, mission Christianity experienced external and internal challenges. Communism was a powerful rival ideology for nationalist-minded Koreans.[26] Despite the failure of the independence movement, many Korean Christians demonstrated a new self-confidence and assertiveness, and as a result some grew impatient with missionary paternalism.[27] At the same time, missionary institutions providing higher education and professional training (and occasionally serving as gates to further opportunities abroad) attracted modernizing young men, non-Christian as well as Christian, who saw in them a route to upward personal mobility and national regeneration.[28] One group of Protestant nationalists, described by Kenneth Wells as "self-reconstruction nationalists," rejected any immediate and militant steps for ending Japanese rule and instead worked for "improvement of individual morality, knowledge and expertise" as steps that "would inevitably transform society and finally secure independent statehood."[29] Regarded by left- and right-wing nationalists at the time (and by some historians subsequently) as compromisers and collaborators,[30] these self-reconstruction Protestant nationalists seem to have been the Koreans with whom Murray had the closest affinity. Their values and pragmatic strategies were consonant with the way she practised and taught medicine in Korea.

Her biggest challenge during her first term (1921-27) was learning to adapt her medical values and modes of practice to the unpropitious environment of her church's mission in northern Korea. Like their American Presbyterian mentors, the Canadian missionaries had offered Western medical services from the time of their arrival (one of the three "founding fathers" had been a doctor as well as an ordained missionary). But their medical practice was sporadic, and, since they saw medicine as only a subordinate part of their evangelistic task, they did not attach much importance to acquiring suitable buildings or equipment.[31] Even in 1921 when Murray arrived, the facilities and professional standards that she had learned to regard as the minimum necessary for practising medicine were almost entirely absent in the mission's hospital in the city of Hamhung, northern Korea, to which she was posted. The opening chapter of her published memoir graphically described her first tour of the hospital and its grim conditions, both inside and out:

> Outside the back door I was horrified to see a bedpan with its contents setting on the ground together with a pail of bloodstained dressings and a pan full of pus. All were swarming with flies. My heart sank. How could I ever maintain decent standards under such conditions? There would be plenty to do all right, but conditions must be improved. *This would be a teaching job as well as a medical one.*[32]

Written in retirement and for publication, Murray's memoir avoided openly blaming Dr. Kate McMillan, the hospital superintendent and the mission's pioneer woman doctor, for the conditions Murray saw there. At the time however, her criticisms had been more forthright in private correspondence to her family. Indeed, within a month of her arrival in Korea, she was writing to her brother Foster, then a medical intern in Halifax, to express her dismay about conditions at the hospital. Even more disturbing than the lack of modern conveniences, professionally trained nurses, and sanitary standards was the easy tolerance of such conditions evident in the attitude of Dr. McMillan and her Korean assistant, Dr. Pak. "The way they do things horrifies me," she told Foster. "I feel like I did in Boston when I saw the patients experimented on and was helpless to prevent it or do anything better for them ... I am very glad I am to go to Yong Jung for awhile. I do not see how I could work here under the circumstances. If I could speak enough to do anything independently it would be different, but to assist with work like that!!"[33] Contributing to Murray's dismay over the quality of the work she was observing was the fear that, over time, it would become her way of practising too. Significantly, later that autumn she asked her mother to forward copies of the Canadian medical journal to which she subscribed "to help keep me from going to seed."[34]

Murray's temporary appointment to Yong Jung, Manchuria, to replace Dr. Stanley Martin, a young male colleague who was about to go on health leave, gave her a reprieve from conditions in Hamhung as well as an opportunity to work in a hospital that seemed better administered and equipped than the one in Hamhung, despite its remote location. But things went less smoothly in Yong Jung after Dr. Martin's departure, and soon her fear of falling behind in her profession returned to haunt her:

There is nothing like medicine for interest when you can dig right in ... and investigate your cases from both the clinical and laboratory side. One of the hard things out here is one is too busy to go into cases properly and has no one who can do lab work for one so one gets careless. I feel that after a year or two out here I shall be no good for anything else. It is impossible to spend enough time at the language to learn it properly and do a couple of operations every day and see thirty or forty out cases besides and attend the cases in the wards and superintend the dressings done by careless and ignorant dressers and still have enough time to do any of it as well as it ought to be done. And then you are disgusted with yourself for not doing things properly and you long for a blood count or a lab report or an x-ray plate and there is no one to do it and you haven't time yourself if you had the apparatus.[35]

Allotting increased hospital responsibilities to Korean medical personnel as a way to get more time for language study and her own work was not an option, in Murray's view, because while they were "very competent" in some things, they had yet to see what a "decent hospital" was like. "If they pattern their hospitals on the mission hospitals or the Japanese ones," she wrote, "they will fall a long way short of good scientific work."[36] Her criticism of Japanese hospitals probably referred to those in Korea, since she had not then seen any in metropolitan Japan, and she would later send staff members there to see "good" work and would sometimes go herself.

As for mission hospitals, the one that inspired her strongest disapproval in this period was the East Gate Hospital for Women in Seoul, an American Methodist institution run by a Dr. Stewart and Dr. Rosetta Sherwood Hall, the latter an 1889 graduate of the Woman's Medical College of Pennsylvania.[37] Murray voiced her criticism of East Gate and its doctors in the context of a trip that she made to Seoul in December 1922 as part of a mission committee to inspect medical facilities there and place orders for supplies prior to rebuilding the hospital at Hamhung, to which she was slated to return. The Hamhung hospital had closed some months earlier following the sudden death of Dr. McMillan and would not be allowed to reopen until renovations brought it up to standards acceptable to the colonial government.

In a long letter to her father, Murray expressed her disapproval of what she had seen of the work of the two women doctors at East Gate: with plenty of funds at their disposal, trained Western nurses, and two young Korean women doctors, they had only four in-patients in total. Yet because of their insistence on serving female patients exclusively, they had refused to affiliate with Severance Union Medical College and Hospital, an ecumenical mission institution in Seoul, despite the fact that it was "packed to the doors and short of funds." Their policy of treating women patients exclusively would be justifiable, Murray wrote, if they did their work well and in sufficient volume, but that was far from being the case. Rather, they had made the term "woman doctor" a byword for inferior standards, a situation she was determined to alter:

> After having seen these two and Dr. McMillan and their institutions I am not surprised that missionaries, medical and non-medical alike, ask me if I can do surgery ... These people have established the standard expected of women doctors. I understand now why Dr. Martin wasn't enthusiastic about turning his hospital over to me when he first heard I was coming to Korea ... my little job seems to be to transform Hamheung [sic] Hospital from what it was into one of the best and most flourishing mission institutions in Korea and incidentally demonstrate to the missionary community that women doctors are not necessarily cantankerous and inefficient.[38]

Murray faulted the two American doctors for their failure to keep abreast of new medical developments in the West as well as for persisting in a separate-spheres approach in the face of Severance's much greater needs. Named for Standard Oil magnate L.H. Severance, who had provided funds to establish the training hospital following an appeal from Dr. Oliver Avison (a British-born Canadian serving under an American Presbyterian board), the college had graduated its first class of doctors in 1908.[39] While only a scaled-down version of Avison's "ideal of medical education ... the University of Toronto,"[40] Severance was nevertheless the only mission facility in Korea staffed and equipped to provide training to Korean medical students at a level that brought government accreditation. As such, Murray believed, it ought to have first claim on the Western-trained missionary doctors and nurses and the ample resources she had seen at East Gate.

She was not, of course, unusual in favouring mergers and centralization. Such trends were a part of her era's "search for order" in religious as well as secular affairs. Indeed, L.H. Severance had chosen to make medical work in Korea the object of his largesse after hearing a speech by Avison on "Unity in Medical Missions."[41] In 1932 William Hocking's *Re-Thinking Missions: A Laymen's Inquiry after One Hundred Years* would recommend moves towards centralization and the creation of a few good, up-to-date medical institutions in the Asian mission fields whenever feasible as a way to help return medical missions to the pre-eminence they had enjoyed in the nineteenth century. Writing with particular reference to China, Hocking declared that "the trend toward union of women's hospitals with general hospitals is logical" and that limiting nurses only to women patients was "inefficient and unnecessary."[42] The Peking Union Medical College, funded, like the Laymen's Inquiry itself, by Rockefeller money, undoubtedly served as a model of what the modernizing laymen had in mind. It had acquired the reputation of a medical mecca, and it treated and trained both sexes.

But setting aside the question of efficiency, was there, in fact, a compelling need for separate, female-run medical services for Korean women in order to entice them to accept Western medical care? The answer seemed to depend on where within Korea such medical services were being offered, and to which social classes, and when. Traditional Confucian gender values in Korea called for female seclusion and strict segregation of the sexes and taught the inferiority of women.[43] In Seoul, where the most important *yangban* families (the hereditary elite) lived, early American women medical missionaries had emphasized respectable women's seclusion and, in an effort to win support among the elite, they accommodated rather than challenged seclusion practices. Dr. Hall, for instance, made house calls on the royal Min family and talked of starting a night clinic for respectable women, who could not appear in public in daylight hours. The missionaries stressed that such women were reluctant to be treated by male doctors, whether Korean or Western.[44] Nor was the preference for treatment by their own sex confined to elite women. Grant Lee's account of the tandem growth of Western medicine and Protestantism in Korea speaks of large numbers of Korean women coming for treatment to the pioneer Western women doctors who began providing their services specifically to women patients in the last two decades of the nineteenth century.[45]

But this preference was evidently weaker and also less feasible to maintain in northern Korea, where *yangban* families had traditionally been rare. There, the Koreans with whom the missionaries had readiest contact were the poor and uneducated, typically rural people.[46] Working in this northern setting, Murray seems not to have felt any strong local cultural imperative to restrict her medical practice to women.[47] Indeed, she obviously believed that, irrespective of their sex, the poor should have access to affordable Western medical care. Thus in 1925, when Dr. Hall of East Gate Hospital joined the McCully sisters, two elderly Canadian evangelistic missionaries, in urging Murray to restrict her practice to "women's work for women," she dismissed their suggestion in a joking fashion.[48]

Murray and the Koreans who became her interns or staff doctors – all but one of them male in the interwar era – *did* practise separate spheres medicine when it seemed necessary or feasible. It was the male doctors, for instance, who conducted medical examinations of applicants for the Hamhung mission's boys' high school.[49] But both Murray and her male colleagues treated patients of both sexes. And, significantly, they shared in teaching nursing students after the Hamhung hospital school of nursing was established in

1928.[50] When patients and hospital employees came from impoverished backgrounds, there was obviously less need for sensitivity to Confucian gender norms. The rural poor were a particularly important constituency, especially as Murray and the hospital's Korean Christian staff established and consolidated contacts with Christian communities and groups of enquirers outside Hamhung through evangelism and public health work.[51] While they often came to the mission hospital only as a last resort and not necessarily as an exclusive choice, patients from such backgrounds were willing to take a chance on Murray and her institution regardless of their sex.[52] Meanwhile, as modernization and Western influences took hold in Korea, there was some loosening of traditional gender norms even among the more affluent and respectable, a pattern that was accelerated by women's participation in the March First Movement.[53] Such changes made it more feasible to practise and teach medicine in a general hospital setting.

Murray's rejection of a separate-spheres approach to missionary medicine in Korea also reflected changes taking place in North American society in the interwar era relating to feminism and women's roles. I have referred to such changes in earlier chapters, but they merit further attention here as a means of contextualizing Murray's approach. Marriage, followed by family and full-time homemaking responsibilities, was, of course, still the norm even for highly educated women. But among the small proportion of such women who did not marry, or who continued working after marriage, there were some who were no longer satisfied to build professional careers exclusively around the needs of women and children. Nancy Cott has identified an unwillingness to be confined to a female-only sphere as one characteristic of the small band of "modern" feminists who emerged in the 1910s as a group with a more radical and broad-ranging agenda than that of mainstream social or maternal feminists. Cott's chapter on "Professionalism and Feminism" is particularly helpful for charting the ironic development whereby a feminist ambition to become a professional woman in the 1910s evolved in the interwar era into a professional identity so strong that it left conventional feminist concerns behind.[54] Similarly, Rosalind Rosenberg has written about a generation of social scientists who differed from their first-generation sisters in their unwillingness to be confined to a world of women. Those of Margaret Mead's era, she observes, "rejected the public side of feminism, with its ideology of female uniqueness and its organizational focus on female interests."[55] There are important ways in which Murray differed from the groups and patterns described by Cott and Rosenberg, particularly in her ongoing adherence to conventional religious and moral values and social norms and in her assumption that marriage necessarily terminated a woman's professional career. Yet in her unwillingness to be confined to a "women's sphere" in terms of her clients and colleagues, she shared common ground with them. And like the American women doctors who objected to the formation in 1915 of a national association of women doctors as a "divisive and retrogressive" step, she regarded integration rather than gender separation as the way forward, professionally.[56]

If a decline in rigid gender segregation in interwar Korea, especially among poor and Westernizing groups, made the avoidance of a separate-spheres approach seem feasible to Murray, it was this desire to be fully professional, to achieve the highest possible level of efficiency in scientific medicine within the context of an Asian medical mission, that made a women-only work world unattractive. The pages that follow deal with Murray's pursuit of scientific missionary medicine in the years prior to her repatriation to Canada in 1942.

Building a Medical Community

Returning to Hamhung in 1923 to reopen the mission hospital after her visits to East Gate and other sites in Seoul, Murray experienced a variety of setbacks rather than the rapid achievement of her goal to demonstrate what a good woman doctor could do. Early in 1924, a breakdown in health that seems to have been a combination of specific physical problems and emotional strain resulted in her being sent to the Peking Union Medical College.[57] When doctors there found no evidence of tuberculosis (the official diagnosis of missionary doctors in Seoul), she used the opportunity for professional development, taking a brief course in ophthalmology.[58] Once back in Hamhung, she returned to the challenge of building up the hospital's facilities, a task that involved a struggle for such conveniences as running water, electricity, and a bathtub, as well as for the most basic medical equipment.[59] What *had* changed – and this was a change that would become more pronounced in later years – was that Murray was learning to be less critical of Western and Korean co-workers and to make small compromises when local customs conflicted with her Western notions of good hospital administration.[60]

During her second and subsequent missionary terms, Murray worked for and publicized various technological and procedural advances, including the installation of x-ray equipment – still a rarity in South Hamkyung province in the early 1930s – and the development of systematic laboratory work.[61] Laboratory work emerged as a particular source of pride in a 1930 circular letter to supporters of her work: "Out of about twenty-five mission hospitals in Korea our hospital was one of four that had a laboratory report sufficiently complete to be of use to a research worker who was preparing a paper for the medical journals. The other three are much larger institutions than ours so it was gratifying to be able to come up to their standard."[62] As it became clear that tuberculosis was the biggest public health problem in the region, Murray established the first on-site facilities in the province for caring for tubercular patients and sometimes tried surgical techniques such

Map of Korea showing places where Dr. Florence Murray worked.

Florence Murray in 1919. When she graduated from the coeducational Faculty of Medicine, Dalhousie University, Murray already had a rich fund of practical experience, having worked with victims of the Halifax explosion in 1917 and, a year later, with victims of Spanish influenza in nearby Lockeport, where twenty-five people had died of the disease. Reproduced by permission of Heather Murray.

Dr. Murray and Dr. T.S. Lee with their arms full of babies (left) and with the entire team of doctors at the mission hospital, Hamhung (above). Dr. Hyo-Soon Kim, who began as a junior colleague and became a cherished friend, is on Murray's right. Dr. T.Y. Whang is at the far right. Both photos appeared in *The Korean Mission Field* in May 1941, a year before Murray was returned to Canada in an exchange of wartime internees. Reproduced courtesy UCA.

Dr. P.K. Koh replaced Murray as superintendent of the mission hospital, Hamhung, in 1941. In postcolonial South Korea he was briefly vice-minister of education before becoming a hospital and university administrator. Mandatory retirement cut short his term as president of Yonsei University. Reproduced from *The Korean Mission Field*, May 1941, courtesy UCA.

Dr. Helen Kim, president of Ewha Womans University, where Murray briefly served in the new medical department following her return to Korea in 1947. The first Korean woman to obtain a doctorate (Columbia University, 1931), Kim was a figure of enormous influence in postcolonial South Korea. She represented her country at international organizations such as the UN, UNESCO, and the Red Cross and was publisher of the *Korea Times* for three years. Photo courtesy Ewha Womans University.

Murray with Korean war orphan Soon-Kile. Injured during the war, Soon-Kile received an artificial leg at Severance Hospital. He was later adopted by a US army officer. Photo courtesy UCA and National Defence, Ottawa (UCA accession no. 76.001P/4133 N).

Murray and unidentified friends stand before the monument erected at "Murray Village" to recognize her multifaceted work with families affected by leprosy. Courtesy Maritime Conference Archives, United Church of Canada.

as those publicized in contemporary medical literature to treat diseased lungs. She developed her own pneumothorax apparatus for local compression of the lung and, on at least one occasion, performed the more formidable operation to collapse the chest wall over the infected area in her patient, using the latest books on tuberculosis for guidance.[63] In 1937 the hospital opened a new wing, and in August 1939, despite the tense international situation that was making many missions prepare for the departure of Western staff, Murray was authorized to draw up plans for a wholly renovated hospital facility.[64]

Paralleling these advances in the hospital's physical infrastructure were the steps taken to train staff and, to the extent possible, to develop specialities. A young man was hired to become the hospital's x-ray and laboratory technician as work in these areas grew.[65] A greater concern, of course, was with the training of nurses and interns. Murray's work with nurses will be briefly described before we turn to the relationships that most clearly took her beyond gender norms in the West and in Korea: those with male interns and colleagues.

In Canada, procedures for systematically training a staff of qualified, respectable women as hospital nurses had begun in the late 1800s and had taken shape in the early twentieth century as an essential part of the process of developing modern, scientific, hospital-based medicine.[66] It was not surprising, therefore, that Murray should have abandoned her predecessor's ad hoc approach to training assistants in favour of developing a full-fledged nurses' training school at the mission hospital. The new school's first class of three students graduated in 1932. To an even greater degree than in Canada, the establishment of a nurses' training program in colonial Korea had to overcome the early reluctance of respectable families to let their daughters enter such a program. Even male church leaders in Hamhung were at first surprised that nursing students could be *"nice* girls."[67] As in Canada, too, some young nursing students were unwilling to risk their reputation for respectability by caring for male patients, a problem that Murray resolved in the manner that Halifax's Victoria General Hospital had done, by training a few male nurses.[68] Beginning with girls who were elementary school graduates, Murray was gradually able to draw in some high-school students. Along with a public ceremony after six months to grant caps to probationers, and another after three years when black bands on these caps and the granting of pins signalled the young women's new status as graduate nurses, the higher education of some entrants helped to raise the status of hospital nursing.[69] The colonial government did not recognize the mission's nurses' training program as official despite the fact that it was a three-year course combining classroom instruction and practical experience, since most students were unable to pass qualifying examinations in the Japanese language. Nevertheless, Murray took great pride in her graduates, affirming that as a result of their skills and Christian character "nursing [in South Hamkyung province] rose in public esteem from a despised occupation fit only for those who would otherwise starve, to a respected vocation second only to that of teacher."[70]

Like most people in Korea and the West, Murray regarded nursing as normally women's work and the role of the physician as normally a man's vocation. No institution existed to train women as doctors when she arrived in Korea in 1921. During the preceding decade, the government medical college in Seoul had accepted a few female students under pressure from Dr. Hall, but it was unwilling to continue doing so. The Chosen Women's Medical Training Institute, established in 1928 by the indefatigable Dr. Hall and a Tokyo-trained Korean colleague, achieved college-level status a decade later, but there were significant constraints on the training it could offer.[71] As noted earlier, during her years as superintendent of the mission hospital at Hamhung, Murray had only one woman doctor on staff, Hyo-Soon Kim, who came as an intern in 1938 following training in Japan.[72] In a letter to her father in 1925, Murray explained why she was unwilling to follow Dr. Hall's example and work for the medical training of Korean women:

> I would like to see the girls get a chance for as much education as they want. But every girl in Korea gets married and looks after her husbands [sic] house and wardrobe and family and that takes the most of her time. I would rather put any money I have to spend that way into some man who will be likely to do something for his fellow country men and women than in training up a doctor who will just wait on her husband in the end after all. I think it is a waste of effort and I disappoint Dr. Hall terribly in not being enthusiastic over her pet scheme.[73]

Even in the West, Murray believed, marriage effectively meant the end of a woman's medical career.[74] If "every girl" in Korea did in fact get married, it seemed to follow that the loss to the profession there, where it could least be afforded, would be even greater.[75] Interestingly, Murray felt no such concern about the fact that most of her nurses married (some left the training program while still students to go into arranged marriages), since, as in the West, such training was regarded as a valuable asset in a woman's future family life.[76]

While the Korean men whom Murray took on as interns were not lost to the mission through marriage, they were often lost to it, ironically, by the very training that the Hamhung hospital was providing. As in other missions in East Asia, after a period of interning in a mission hospital, many doctors left for higher paying jobs elsewhere, or opened up their own private practice, while a small but significant number went abroad for specialized training.[77] Murray was quite distressed when doctors left for more lucrative work during her first term, especially if such men worked in direct competition with her hospital, and she was certainly disappointed in those who went abroad if they did not return to Korea.[78] Yet the departure of former interns or staff doctors for practice elsewhere in Korea was not seen as loss in the way that women doctors who married were seen as lost, for as she had told her father in the 1925 letter decrying Dr. Hall's "pet scheme," male doctors could be expected to go on contributing Western medical skills to the larger Korean community for the duration of their working lives.[79]

Since she regarded the training of such young men as an investment in Korea's future medical well-being, Murray took great pride in her own skills as a clinical instructor. Even when an intern came to her to do surgical work with no previous experience, she was confident that, with time, she could "make a surgeon of him."[80] If one of the most noteworthy aspects of her correspondence is the degree to which she wrote about details of her medical work (even in letters to recipients who were not in the same profession), what is even more striking is the degree to which, within such letters, she referred to her own mentoring function, despite the fact that she was not in charge of a medical school, and that the men who came to her as interns had their classroom years behind them.[81]

Murray's zeal for her tutorial role was potentially a recipe for tense cross-gender, cross-cultural relations, and during her first term that potential was often realized. Hers was not the only mission hospital in Korea where tensions developed when Western women doctors, imbued with a sense of their superiority as Western-trained *professionals*, tried to tutor young interns shaped by centuries of Confucian gender values and conscious of their own superiority *as men*.[82] But as Murray had acknowledged in an unusually frank self-assessment in 1924, she was a "hard taskmaster" in terms of her expectations of staff.[83] That tendency inevitably exacerbated already tense relationships with male interns and added to the difficulty of retaining them. Inevitably, too, interns who were not Christian would have been unable to contribute as fully to the life and outreach of the hospital as Murray would have wished. Accentuating these sources of tension was the significance that Murray attached to "race" when confronted with professional problems during the early years. If her tendency to "orientalize" individual interns' shortcomings as practitioners was made known to them in the way that it was conveyed in letters to her family, it was hardly surprising that such men found her a difficult mentor during that first term.[84]

By contrast, Murray's correspondence during her subsequent terms in northern Korea reflects a decided shift to more positive relationships with such men. Undoubtedly part of this change was due simply to the fact that as she came to feel more at home in Korea and more confident in her own role, she felt less need to demonstrate her authority and was thus less critical of others and more inclined to "positive" orientalism.[85] But there also appears to have been an increase in mutual professional respect between Murray and her Korean male colleagues in the years following her troubled first term, and a greater willingness on her part to facilitate their professional development.[86] In 1929 Murray was the first woman to be chosen president of the Medical Missionary Association of Korea.[87] In contrast to the situation in the Christian Medical Association of India, mission-employed doctors who were nationals were not a part of the association in Korea at this time. Still, the fact that Murray's mainly male Western colleagues had selected her for the role would perhaps have raised her status in the eyes of her Korean colleagues. It would have also served to boost her own confidence and provide a new outlet for her "taskmaster" tendencies. Meanwhile, in 1928 she had arranged for a promising young doctor who had served in her hospital during her furlough to obtain medical experience in a tuberculosis sanatorium in Canada.[88] Occasionally, other men would be sent to North America to gain Western medical experience. More commonly they went for shorter periods to Japan or China for specialized postgraduate study. This was the case in 1939, for instance, with a former intern who was to spend three months in Peking before taking over as "our Eye, ear, nose and throat man" from the hospital's former specialist in this field, who was entering private practice.[89]

Murray's ongoing efforts to upgrade her own skills were evident in her return to the Peking Union Medical College for a brief postgraduate course in 1929 and in her willingness to use holidays (as well as furloughs) partly for professional development.[90] When some Korean colleagues emerged as particularly valued and anxious to specialize, Murray tried to accommodate their professional interests within the hospital. Thus, in 1930 she spoke of surrendering much of the surgical work to Dr. P.K. Koh, who had joined her three years earlier, despite the fact that surgery was her "first love" and comprised "most of the interesting cases."[91] Arranging for the building of a three-storey brick house "like the other hospital buildings" for the Korean staff doctor was another way of signifying that professional status was to be recognized and rewarded.[92]

That Murray cared personally as well as professionally about her male associates' well-being, especially if they were young and promising and determined to overcome such obstacles as their own ill health,[93] undoubtedly contributed to improved relations with them. But perhaps what counted most was her growing willingness to learn from and with them. In 1937 she was the only woman and the only Westerner in a local scientific society that developed when meetings of the hospital staff expanded to accommodate other doctors who had "asked to come in with us on the scientific meetings." There was perhaps some condescension, but mainly pride, as she told her family about being part of this tiny scientific community with "nine Oriental gentlemen."[94]

Murray's zest for her role as hospital superintendent during the 1930s is evident in her correspondence. It is thus unlikely that initiatives for sharing responsibility for hospital management originated with her. Despite her increasingly cordial and mutually respectful relationships with Korean and Western colleagues, she retained what one relative remembered as "the habit of command," and was perhaps somewhat reluctant to relinquish her authority.[95] Yet as deteriorating relations between Japan and the United States and Britain made it seem likely that missionaries would have to resign from positions of responsibility in Christian institutions and perhaps withdraw altogether from Korea, it became expedient to make changes. By 1938 Murray was sharing internal hospital administration with newly created departmental committees.[96] As in other missions, a hospital board was also established, made up primarily of Korean Christians.[97] In March 1941, with most American missionaries already gone from Korea and war between the Allies and Japan increasingly likely, Murray prepared for the possibility of her own departure by acting on colleague William Scott's suggestion and asking a Korean to take over her role. Dr. Koh, her former surgeon and a man whose professional and personal qualities she greatly respected, was asked to come back to Hamhung from his post as professor of surgery at Severance Hospital to take over as hospital superintendent.[98]

Nor was this to be scaled-down work in the absence of Western staff. In 1940 Murray had gone to Japan to arrange for advanced training in a tuberculosis sanatorium for the nurse whom she proposed to put in charge of the hospital's enlarged tuberculosis building.[99] That building project went ahead, while housing left vacant by departing Westerners was turned into new hospital space, with a former YMCA residence becoming the new maternity annex under Dr. Hyo-Soon Kim.[100] Meanwhile, Murray urged Woman's Missionary Society officials and her sister Anna to continue sending x-ray film and other supplies regardless of the impending changes.[101]

When she had first seen the mission hospital in Hamhung in 1921, it had approximately ten beds and its medical staff consisted of Dr. McMillan and one Korean doctor. When she left twenty-one years later, it had one hundred beds and at least six Korean doctors.[102] Along with ordained colleagues E.J.O. Fraser and William Scott and nurse Beulah Bourns, she had delayed her departure as long as possible. While the two men had been interned and Fraser briefly jailed following the attack on Pearl Harbor in December 1941, Murray and Bourns had been permitted to continue working in the hospital until the day they left Hamhung, reportedly "the only persons so allowed in all Korea."[103] In June 1942, the four Canadians were repatriated as part of an exchange for Japanese internees in the United States and

Canada.[104] Despite the tense circumstances surrounding their departure and the difficulties that lay ahead for their Korean colleagues, Murray had good reason to believe that the type of medical practice she valued had taken root in Hamhung.

Postwar Patterns: Gender and Professionalism in a New Setting

Since the 1970s, serious questions have been raised about the appropriateness of the Western model of scientific medicine for non-Western settings. At the end of the Second World War, however, when Murray was preparing to return to Korea, no such challenges loomed. Thus, she could resume her career confident in the knowledge that Western medicine (if not always Western practitioners) was still welcome and that even those at home who no longer believed in evangelizing the world approved of the kind of work that medical missionaries did. Indeed, in the years ahead, newly emerging national governments as well as Western states, armies, philanthropic foundations, and aid organizations would eagerly support the cause of Western medicine in impoverished and wartorn postcolonial settings.

With the end of the war, Korea was free of Japanese colonial rule. While US troops moved into the south, Russian-assisted communists quickly assumed control in the north. Under these circumstances, United Church missionaries could not return to their former stations. Instead, they began work in South Korea, participating in immediate relief activities for refugees from the north[105] and undertaking "to serve, as called upon, in co-operative institutions" to meet needs defined by Korean Christian leaders. This approach was in keeping with recommendations of the Post-War Planning Committee of the Foreign Missions Conference of North America and with the views of the United Church's own deputation of mission board officials, who visited India and East Asia in 1947. The deputation instructed its mission staff "not to build up in South Korea a mission comparable to our former mission in the north."[106] Clearly, a new era had dawned. For Murray, it meant coming to terms with the loss of the physical plant and the public-health activities that she had built up over the years and over which, despite her increasingly collegial relations with senior Korean staff, she had largely exercised control. Living in Seoul from July 1947, she shared nostalgic memories with former hospital workers and others she had known in Hamhung and a sense of exile from the place that had been her home, as well as theirs, for some twenty years.[107] Given the professional gains and the personal growth she had experienced during those years, and the frustrations and difficulties attendant on beginning anew in the South – now in her fifties and no longer in charge – it would seem logical to think of the Hamhung period as her golden era and what followed as anticlimax. Yet as the following brief summary shows, she was to have a diverse and fulfilling second career, one that continued to be characterized by a commitment to "standards," albeit in conditions that often called for compromises and detours in the face of immediate human crises.

In 1946, the President of Ewha Womans University in Seoul, Helen Kim, had asked the Woman's Missionary Society of the United Church for three of its women missionaries to join her staff, with Murray identified as the priority appointment. A 1918 graduate of Ewha College, Kim had gone on to study in the US, achieving a PhD from Columbia University in 1931 and thus becoming the first Korean woman anywhere to obtain a doctoral degree.[108] Having persuaded government officials to upgrade Ewha from college to university status in the immediate postwar period, she was anxious to start a medical training program for women as part of the new university's offerings and wanted Murray's help in that task. Murray acceded to the request and, with her usual brisk efficiency, began making enquiries and arrangements for needed medical supplies. In one letter to the business agent of the New-York-based Ewha Co-operating Board, having fired off questions and a recommendation that he seek money or supplies from such bodies as the Red Cross, the Rockefeller Foundation, and federal war-surplus agencies, she realized that she might have been *too* ardent: "here am I giving advice to a business man. Excuse me. My zeal outruns my discretion."[109]

Yet she had grave misgivings about the new venture. Experienced and enthusiastic about instructing interns in a clinical setting, she was less confident about her ability to begin teaching in a classroom, and, not anticipating this new assignment, she had prepared for her return by gaining further expertise in the treatment of tuberculosis, both at a small sanatorium in Kentville, Nova Scotia, and at the famous Trudeau sanatorium at Lake Saranac in New York state.[110] Her greatest concern was about Kim's decision to start the new medical department immediately. Although the staff and physical facilities were sadly inadequate, even for a modest beginning, and no funding had yet been assured from North American supporters, Kim had already made a commitment to accept fifty-nine medical students. Once on the scene, Murray urged her either to make other arrangements for the students and postpone the opening of a medical training department at Ewha or to cooperate with Severance Union Medical College and Hospital in a joint coeducational program. Insisting on the necessity for separate higher education for Korean women and on the importance of an immediate beginning, Kim declined to consider either possibility.[111]

The Ewha Co-operating Board initially endorsed Murray's suggestion for a joint program with Severance. (Hers was just one of a number of voices urging a policy of consolidation and cooperation in the direction of a single, strong, multifaceted Christian university for Korea in preference to several small and struggling institutions.) But the board was ultimately persuaded by Kim's arguments to reverse its position and support the establishment of a medical department at Ewha.[112] As its deliberations on the matter revealed, the ECB was caught on the horns of a dilemma: it wanted to avoid supporting costly, inefficient and "old-fashioned" mission strategies, but it also wanted to avoid the decision-making style of an earlier era when home-base officials and missionaries had used their financial clout to impose Western solutions on indigenous Christian leaders. While the FMCNA's recommendation that postwar missionaries should take their cues from indigenous Christian leaders was an important aspect of "modernizing" missions, it was sometimes a difficult fit with more conventional and technical approaches to that task.

Murray began her short career at Ewha as associate dean of the medical department and assistant superintendent of the teaching hospital (the former East Gate Hospital). As various crises developed, she was asked to take on the senior position in both institutions. But these were not roles she was willing to retain, especially in the face of needs and opportunities in other institutions and her conviction that Ewha lacked an appreciation of the standards required to train properly qualified doctors as well as the resources to do so. She continued teaching there on a part-time basis until 1950, explaining in her 1949 annual report that she did not wish "to penalize the students for what is not their fault," but adding that "they deserve a better course than it is possible to give them." The United Church mission would retain close ties to Ewha, but Murray was clearly relieved to retire from its staff.[113]

After serving half-time on a committee to investigate internal difficulties at the new Seoul National University Hospital (difficulties which she attributed to communist agitators) and, later, as the government-appointed advisor to its beleaguered superintendent, she joined the staff at Severance, teaching in the medical school and becoming assistant superintendent of the hospital and temporary head of pediatrics.[114] Perhaps her most important contribution to Severance during this period was in serving as its official voice with the Cooperating Board for Christian Higher Education in Chosun. A North American board like the ECB and, like it, located in New York, it was more broadly ecumenical than its sister organization and thus more financially able to assist still-struggling institutions like Severance. In her letters to the board, Murray dispensed with formulaic pieties and social chat and instead presented detailed arguments for money and the types of Western specialists she thought Severance still needed. She also sought opportunities for Korean staff and students to go abroad for further training and experience.[115] Overseas experience was being promoted by the national government, which was sending Korean doctors to the US on scholarships, so that they could see medical work of a higher standard than that prevalent in the war-ravaged hospitals of Korea. Murray believed that missions should do the same: "Actual experience in a well equipped well run hospital will do more to raise the standards of hospitals in the east than any amount of talking by a few medical missionaries who are suspected of wishing to impose their own customs and culture on an independent people." To this end she asked her own church, as well as the Cooperating Board, to assist with overseas study scholarships, beginning with a request for assistance and placement for a former Hamhung colleague, Dr. T.Y. Whang.[116]

Like other missionaries, Murray was forced to leave Korea in June 1950 when civil war broke out. In October 1951 she returned, not to Seoul, which was twice captured by communist troops, but to Pusan on the southeast coast, to which South Korea's government and thousands of refugees had fled.[117] Missionaries like Murray who were allowed back by the military authorities did what they could on an ad hoc basis to help refugees and orphans. For a time, she also undertook translating and other non-medical duties among military and civilian patients on a Danish Red Cross hospital ship, work for which she was later decorated by the Danish government. By March 1952, she was back at Severance, which the US army was temporarily using as a treatment centre for Korean civilians in the service corps. She was, reportedly, the first Western civilian physician to return to Seoul. Severance's physical plant had been largely destroyed, and bombers heading north for the battle front could still be heard and seen overhead. Nonetheless, the hospital reopened under Severance Board auspices in April, and, under pressure from the government, the medical college began teaching in June, its students including women for the first time.[118] As well as joining the Korean staff in trying to rehabilitate the hospital and re-establish medical work,[119] Murray and veteran Canadian mission nurse Beulah Bourns also joined in wider relief work. As part of this work, they visited churches, nurseries, and other centres to distribute the supplies provided by overseas funds and by the UN's Civil Assistance Command for Korea (UNCACK), and other relief agencies. Murray's letters to her family from this period convey a remarkable sense of serenity, even *joie de vivre*, despite the harsh physical conditions in war-ravaged Seoul and the expectation that another attack on the city might be imminent. Far from wishing to be elsewhere, she seems to have thrived on the many roles that she was called upon to play. She rejoiced in Koreans' resilience in the face of extreme hardship and in the signs of international cooperation that were evident in the city, describing an ecumenical and interracial Easter Sunday service on a Seoul hillside as "a sort of foretaste of heaven."[120]

During the war period she had frequent, and usually friendly, contacts with Canadian and US military personnel as well as with UN relief and rehabilitation workers. Canadian soldiers' assistance to her hospital and relief work seems to have been provided mainly on an informal and individual basis (and may occasionally have involved military supplies "liberated" for her use).[121] UN agencies and US army units were in a position to do much more, of course, by way of helping to rebuild Severance and providing supplies, and here again Murray played an important role by acting as a liaison and describing specific needs. From time to time she was flown to military bases to address personnel on Korean medical matters or aspects of the country's history, welcoming such contacts as opportunities to promote "international and interracial understanding" as well as medical knowledge.[122] Similarly, when representatives of civilian relief agencies and the media began flocking to Severance, and to Seoul generally, in the last half of 1952, she welcomed opportunities to present Korea and its needs in an upbeat way, in spite of the many other demands on her time.[123] The contacts established during this period also enlarged Murray's social life. She disapproved of, but learned to tolerate, the drinking that prevailed at UN staff gatherings and other social events, while the drinking habits of Canadian soldiers received less attention in letters home than their many acts of kindness to civilian victims of the war, especially its child victims.[124]

Especially before the armistice in July 1953, Murray saw it as part of her role at Severance to exemplify and encourage a willingness to improvise and "make do" in the short run, while not losing sight of the long-term goals of high quality staff and facilities and Western medical standards.[125] It was these long-range goals that she presented to the New-York-based Co-operating Board in the immediate postwar years when she again took up her role as Severance's voice in its deliberations. She and fellow Canadian Ernest Struthers were the only foreign doctors on the staff in the spring of 1954, but she pressed the Board to locate and finance more Westerners, preferably with needed specialties, so that they could exert an upward influence on standards while there was still a place for foreign experts at the institution. She worried that Severance was hiring too many doctors with "indifferent training," while first-rate specialists like orthopedic surgeon Dr. P.K. Moon ("the best man on our staff") were leaving, frustrated by administrative problems, salary delays, etc. As the worst of the wartime conditions receded, she looked for faster progress in rehabilitating the hospital and the college and so was frustrated by, even testy about, delays in the arrival of funds from the Board and the inadequacy of the sums allotted. With the sudden departure of the superintendent, she temporarily took on his role as well as that of treasurer, along with her regular teaching and clinical work. Since some 35 percent of all doctors in South Korea at this time were said to be Severance graduates, she was conscious of the fact that the quality of the training they were receiving had widespread and lasting significance.[126] Also adding to the stress of this period were the protracted and delicate negotiations required to ensure that the US Eighth Army followed through on its commitment to build a memorial "chest hospital" on the new Severance campus to be located outside central Seoul.[127]

Following her furlough in the mid-1950s, Murray played a smaller role at Severance. She was now a comparatively elderly missionary and technically a generalist at a time when Korean specialists, including some who had trained abroad, were increasingly available, along with a few younger Westerners. After taking on several temporary assignments outside Seoul, she seemed resigned to "filling in" in various roles at Severance. It was in this spirit that she began the task of trying to organize medical records in the hospital in 1956. She also chaired the Medical College Library Committee, and continued as a correspondent with the Cooperating Board even after the administrative changes by which Severance became the College of Medicine of the newly formed Yonsei University in 1957, and the Cooperating Board became part of the United Board for Christian Higher Education in Asia (UBCHEA).[128]

Yet despite having celebrated her *whangnap* in 1954 (the birthday that marked the beginning of one's symbolically significant sixty-first year),[129] Murray had an opportunity to participate in the establishment of a new medical institution when in 1958 she was appointed "chairman" of the Wonju Union Christian Hospital Board and Building Committee. The new project was undertaken jointly by US Methodists and the United Church of Canada, with start-up help from the UN Korean Relief Agency (UNKRA), to serve a mountainous region southeast of Seoul that had limited medical facilities and had suffered greatly during the war. Murray was able to serve for one year as medical director of the new hospital before being required to retire from the United Church of Canada's mission staff. During this brief Wonju interval, she also operated a tuberculosis clinic and began multifaceted work with and for leprosy victims (she deplored the term "lepers"). Assisted by a church elder who located untreated leprosy sufferers in remote regions, she established a clinic for treatment. She took steps to establish small-scale agricultural projects for afflicted families and schooling for their children, and to educate local people, including Wonju Hospital staff, about the importance of accepting and integrating non-contagious members of afflicted families into the larger community. Subsequently, this project was taken over by the government, and, to Murray's great satisfaction, her assistant, himself a former leprosy patient, became part of its public health team.[130] A new village for former leprosy patients established under Murray's auspices was later named in her honour.[131]

Officially retired in 1961, Murray returned to Korea to fill in for two years in the "Mission to Lepers" clinic in Taegu in the absence of its British physician. Then, from 1964 to 1969, she was back at Severance at a task she had begun in the previous decade: attempting to organize a medical records system and set up a training program for medical records technicians. This was unglamorous work and by no means fully appreciated by some of Severance's senior administrators, despite the fact that she had been invited to undertake it. For obvious reasons, the keeping of full and systematic patient records could not have been a priority at the hospital during its many years of upheaval. At the same time, it was coming to be regarded as a necessary aspect of a fully modern hospital committed to teaching and research activities as well as patient treatment. In a letter to the Cooperating Board in 1953, Murray had identified a medical records librarian as one of the specialists that Severance needed in order to provide on-site training to a local person. No such person having been appointed, she had herself begun to organize records following her return from furlough in 1956. Now, at age seventy, she returned to this challenge, personally retrieving, cleaning, and sorting dusty records; pressing the administration for adequate space for their storage and use; even organizing conferences to which other hospitals were invited to send delegates in order to stimulate interest in, and raise the professional profile of, this aspect of medical work. While providing basic instructions in records keeping to a few young women, she sought United Church funding to sponsor a student for specialized professional training in this relatively new field. Her last newsletter from Korea reported that the church was providing a scholarship for Mrs. Suhn-Hei Kim to study at the Royal Columbian Hospital in British Columbia.[132]

Questions of Priorities

During the interwar years in the north and after the Second World War in South Korea, Murray thrived rather than merely endured in a work world where her professional colleagues and students were mainly men. Even outside work settings, she was often the only woman in a group of men, as, for instance, during the Korean War years, when she was flown to military bases to give talks or participate in medical gatherings, and in old age, when she was invited to a mess dinner by Canadian military officers in Seoul to meet visiting diplomatic officials.[133] Her status as a veteran missionary physician with a reputation for professionalism, initiative, and endurance brought her remarkable opportunities as an "honorary man" during those years. Because she obviously enjoyed that role, and because I have argued in this chapter that she put "standards" ahead of "sisterhood," readers might conclude that she was indifferent to the specific needs and concerns of women. Yet such a conclusion does not seem warranted.

Even in her student days at Prince of Wales College in Charlottetown, Prince Edward Island, Murray had been interested in political rights for women. A supporter of female suffrage, she had successfully pressed the principal to allow a debate on the subject, despite his strong objections. In later years she was particularly likely to comment on the more mundane burdens and inequalities that women experienced in marriage, especially in Korea, but also in the West.[134] Within her own work world, she deplored the ongoing tendency of Korean doctors to treat nurses like servants.[135] She realized that the leadership roles allotted to her at Severance in the early 1950s were unusual (and that her advice, coming from a woman *and* a foreigner, was not always welcome). She also knew that the treatment accorded to the first Korean women brought there to practise and study under wartime pressures was demeaning and inequitable.[136] In response to a question from the Cooperating Board about whether gender mattered in recruiting overseas doctors for Severance, she acidly commented that "women would be allowed to work as much as they like but would not likely be given the higher positions or put over men no matter what their qualifications or experience."[137] (Having spent most of her working life outside North America, she seemed not to realize that things were little different there for professional women.)

In her relationships with Korean women doctors, Murray was supportive in personal and practical ways. Chapter 1 referred to the evolution of her relationship with Hyo-Soon Kim, who began as a junior colleague and became a close friend. Each one assisted the other through difficult times over the years and also shared happier events, such as Murray's *whangnap*. Murray's friendship with another young doctor began unpromisingly in the late 1940s during her Ewha interval. Heung Joo Lee, a medical student at Ewha, initially regarded Murray as a stern and humourless teacher. Later, in other settings, Lee came to know her as a positive and practical kind of mentor and, even in old age, cherished her memory.[138] For many years, Murray met monthly with women doctors in Seoul for professional and personal fellowship and lent her own medical books and journals for their use. In the Korean war era, she also arranged for some of them to work and study in Canada and, after the war, helped out in the non-Christian Seoul Women's Medical College as it struggled to re-establish work in the wake of extensive damage.[139] Such things suggest that she was not without a "feminist consciousness" (though she would probably have deplored the term) or a personal sense of sisterhood. Nonetheless, when it came to rooting Western medicine in the soil of Korea, what mattered more to her than creating opportunities for women to become doctors was increasing the supply of well-trained practitioners, irrespective of their gender, practitioners imbued with a belief in the importance of professional standards as high as local circumstances permitted, and of keeping abreast of changes in the larger world of medicine.

Nor did Murray's commitment to Western-style medical professionalism preclude a concern for the cause of Christianity in Korea. Her response in retirement to questions about whether she had been a doctor or a missionary was to say that the two could not be disentangled and that "I hope I was both."[140] She was not being disingenuous. When *Re-Thinking Missions* was published in 1932, she had rejected what she interpreted as its message that medical missionaries should refrain from promoting their faith. Indeed, she seems to have been so irritated by this aspect of the Inquiry's report – and by the failure of the Laymen to include Korea on their itinerary – that she was not attentive to what she shared with them: a concern to make missionary medicine the best that it could be in any given set of circumstances.[141] As in other Christian hospitals, the work day at her hospital in Hamhung began with a morning worship service. Bible workers on its staff visited patients and former patients. As opportunities presented themselves, particularly when patients were receiving long-term treatment, Murray herself spoke to patients about the faith that had brought her to Korea. She also participated with her Korean co-workers in visits to rural areas, especially those from which patients had come or where nascent Christian communities existed, to do public health work and evangelism.[142] In Seoul after the Second World War and during and after the Korean War, she rejoiced in the zeal with which Christian refugees established – and then re-established – churches. She contributed willingly to this religious life, accepting invitations to visit and speak at the makeshift churches that sprang up in and around the city.[143] But again, one comes back to the fact that Murray was, first and foremost, a medical professional. Both as a newly arrived missionary physician in Hamhung, brashly determined to sweep away all the compromises with local constraints and evangelical priorities that her predecessors had made, and as a superannuated veteran at Severance Hospital in the 1960s, grumbling privately about the unduly long prayer service that delayed the start of the working day, she was a doctor first and an evangelist second.[144] Among many things that had changed in the intervening years, that had not.

Going Home

Murray had lived so long in Korea that the decision to retire permanently to Canada was not automatic. After some forty years in her adopted country, she had ceased to be an outsider in many ways. At a gathering of Christian medical workers near Seoul in 1967, she was proceeding to the stage to receive a small gift along with other foreign doctors when someone in the audience called out, "She's not a foreigner." She was obviously moved by this outburst. "Wasn't that a nice compliment?" she wrote in her next letter home.[145] There were Korean friends who wanted her to remain as part of their family. And there was a culture that she had long since tended to "orientalize" in generally positive rather than generally negative terms. Despite the damage that she thought had been inflicted on Koreans' morals and values by long years of US occupation, Korea still seemed more wholesome in many ways than the West. Writing to her siblings in 1967, she reflected sarcastically on the 1960s generation in Canada:

> I've had some copies of MACLEANS and one of SATURDAY NIGHT and find them somewhat disturbing as I do even the [United Church] Observer. Much of the language, if it is real language, is unfamiliar. Evidently do-gooders are

very wicked folk, though I have been under the impression all my life that it is better to do good than bad. And "square" is apparently a term of opprobrium though I'm not quite sure what it means. And "hippies" seem to be some kind of human or near human beings who prefer darkness and smoke to daylight and clean air, but how they got like that or if there is any hope of recovery I haven't been able to figure out. I think I fit in better here where people seem more civilized and can enjoy themselves without getting drunk or under the influence of narcotics or other drugs.[146]

But in the end, she decided that it was better to return to her siblings and her homeland than risk becoming a burden on Korean friends.[147] Living in Halifax from 1969, following her final retirement, a still-vigorous Murray maintained a variety of interests, Korea prominent among them. She kept in touch with the handful of Koreans who lived in Nova Scotia and welcomed immigrants en route further west.[148] As she had done prior to returning permanently to Canada, she spoke and wrote about the importance of opening up trade, immigration, and diplomatic links between Canada and Korea.[149] Like other retired missionaries in the years to come, she found another outlet for her international interests in volunteer work with Oxfam.[150] Although she had not given up on missions as a way to help needy countries, she had come to view secular organizations in this new era as an alternative route to the path that had opened in her own youth through foreign missionary service. As she had explained in the taped interview with church officials at the time of her official retirement, places like newly independent Nigeria, which she had then just visited, could use the services of able young Canadians with professional training. They need not go as missionaries, or on a permanent basis. But by undertaking even a short period of service they would be doing something that was worthwhile and interesting: participating in "an adventure in understanding and building world peace."[151] In a print interview in Halifax in 1969, she expressed a similar sentiment: "She cannot understand," her interviewer wrote, "why some young people are content to poke along at some dull job if they are capable of better things. 'The whole world is waiting.'"[152] With its note of slight impatience and still-youthful idealism, this was vintage Murray. A whole generation of secular idealists was about to take up her challenge.

Her own "adventure in understanding" came to an end after a short illness in 1975. She died just prior to Dutton's publication of the first volume of her memoirs and a decade before alumni of Yonsei University honoured her, and two Canadian male colleagues who had also served at Severance, by sending a memorial pagoda to Canada. It stands on the campus of Victoria University in the University of Toronto, the initials in lieu of first names on its surface concealing the fact that one of the three doctors honoured had been a woman in a medical world of men.[153]

4

Books for Africa: Margaret Wrong and the Gendering of African Literature, 1929-63

In 1949, a year after Margaret Wrong's sudden death in Gulu, Uganda, a group of fourteen men and women wrote a letter to the *Times* of London calling for the creation of a Margaret Wrong Memorial Fund "to encourage literary productions from Africa, either in English, French, or any other suitable language, and, if possible, to subsidize their production." The establishment of a literary prize, they suggested, would be a fitting tribute to a friend and colleague whose knowledge of Africa had been "unique in its depth, range, and sympathy." In addition to prominent members of the British missions bureaucracy, the group included the Nigerian churchman Seth I. Kale, Fabian Colonial Bureau Secretary Rita Hinden, Lord Hailey of *African Survey* fame, E.G. Hawkesworth, chief commissioner of Ashanti in the Gold Coast, W.E.F. Ward from the Colonial Office, and, from the scholarly community, the linguist Ida Ward and the anthropologist Margaret Read. In the years to follow, the Margaret Wrong Prize for African Literature would be awarded to African writers as different in style and subject matter as Rwanda's Abbé Alexis Kagamé and Nigeria's Chinua Achebe.[1]

The knowledge of Africa that Margaret Wrong's colleagues wished to commemorate had been acquired in the course of her career as secretary of the International Committee on Christian Literature for Africa (ICCLA). The London-based ICCLA had been established in 1929 with a mandate to foster "the preparation, publication, and distribution of literature for use in connection with missionary work in Africa."[2] Interpreting that mandate broadly and creatively, Wrong had played an important, though often behind-the-scenes, role in many activities affecting the development of education and literature in Africa. Her views on related but larger issues in colonial affairs had been sought and given a respectful hearing not only in Britain and its African colonies but also in North America. In its settings and professional concerns, Wrong's career was markedly different from that of either of the two medical missionaries featured in the preceding chapters. Nevertheless, like Choné Oliver and Florence Murray, Wrong had personal and professional interests that converged with shifts in missions and colonial politics to take her beyond the traditional world of women's work for women.

This chapter focuses on one aspect of Wrong's expansive role as secretary of the ICCLA: her concern to promote the development of written literature *by* Africans. As I explore this aspect of her work, Wrong herself may at times seem to fade into the background. This is only because the nature and limits of what she attempted cannot be understood in isolation from the larger context, since the strategies implemented by the ICCLA to encourage the development of indigenous literary activity were part of an interrelated network of liberal missionary and colonial social-reform initiatives. The practical effect of those initiatives was to make literary production a masculine activity. Quite simply, the work of the ICCLA had the effect of augmenting the head start that African men already had in the realm of Western-style cultural production as a result not only of their greater literacy but also of their greater exposure to teaching and mentoring in secular and missionary institutions.[3]

Such a pattern emerged despite the fact that, like Oliver and Murray, Wrong was sympathetically attuned to contemporary issues of women's rights. In the case of African women, she expressed concern about the lack of provision for educational opportunities from the time of her first visit to the subcontinent, in 1926, and also about the hard physical conditions and gender-based inequities in their daily lives.[4] Her long-time companion, Margaret Read, was something of a pioneer in her scholarly attention to the roles of women and children in African societies; Read's anthropological research undoubtedly added to Wrong's insights and interest.[5] One might, then, have expected to find her working to subvert the gender norms of the era's colonial culture: practising resistance rather than complicity, to use Chaudhuri's and Strobel's terms.[6] Certainly as early as that first visit, she did pay more than lip service to meeting what she perceived to be African women's educational needs; her commitment would increase following the outbreak of the Second World War.[7] Yet in addition to being constrained by indigenous and colonial values that favoured and facilitated the modernization of African men, Wrong had concerns and priorities of her own that ultimately had a similar effect. She was intensely interested in the "big" economic and political questions animating interwar Africa, and was concerned with issues of racial injustice that, in practice, impinged mainly on male elites.[8] Moreover, as a kind of cultural gatekeeper, Wrong wanted to shield African societies from what she deemed to be destructive or inappropriate Western influences, including those that seemed to her likely to bring about a premature disruption of existing gender systems.[9]

What also needs to be taken into account is the symbiotic relationship that developed between modernizing African men and the ICCLA as it sought to promote the development of literature by Africans for Africans. Like other instruments of liberal missionary reformism, the ICCLA both needed and could assist upwardly mobile young men. In its goal of promoting the development of "suitable" reading matter for Africans, the ICCLA came to recognize the importance, indeed the necessity, of seeking out and supporting African talent. The mission-educated young men who were the most likely sources of such talent[10] would, in many cases, reject their mission ties in later years as they grew to resent even the humane and serviceable aspects of missionary paternalism and turned in new literary and political directions. Peter Abrahams, a "Cape Coloured" South African writer who achieved prominence in the 1940s and 1950s, and whose links with the ICCLA are discussed below, is a case in point.[11] Still, the ICCLA, and the cluster of initiatives for promoting literature and literacy with which it was linked, were a part of the literary heritage of many such writers. This chapter describes such initiatives and explains why their absence from women's experience remains significant for gendered patterns of literary production in Africa.[12]

As a final word of introduction, it may be useful to explain the frequently invoked phrase "encouragement of indigenous literature." The word "literature" is used as it was by the ICCLA itself to refer to a variety of forms of religious and secular literary production: books, booklets, tracts, periodicals, and even posters. As opportunities arose, the ICCLA encouraged original imaginative work in some of these media as part of what it called "general literature," but its stock in trade was inspirational and didactic reading matter.[13] That being the case, there was sometimes *de facto* censorship, rather than "encouragement," of literary offerings – a pattern akin to the informal censorship that took place in missionary publishing generally.[14] Nevertheless, involvement in the production of such matter, however indirectly, and in translating European classics and transcribing local legends, could serve as a point of creative departure both for the production of the inexpensive "market literature" that became especially popular in colonial Nigeria and for more sophisticated literary work.[15] Especially for the son of a Christian teacher or pastor, there was, at a minimum, an awareness of such material as a cultural artifact that Africans as well as Europeans could produce, and a point of contact with mentors and facilitators of new opportunities.[16] But if such contacts led to the production of "indigenous" literature, it is nonetheless important to be clear about what that category involved. A good deal of what African writers wrote in British colonial Africa would in fact be in English rather than a vernacular despite the efforts of agencies like the ICCLA and its more secular counterpart, the International Institute of African Languages and Cultures, and of prominent linguists like Ida Ward to encourage writing in African languages.[17] The choice of English as a medium of expression was not open to more than a handful of African women writers, and yet it was a choice that would have profound significance in giving African authors access to pan-African and Western audiences.

An Intertwined Personal and Professional Background

Margaret Wrong had the benefit of a privileged background and more than a decade of experience in Christian social service and recruitment work when, in 1929, she was asked to take on responsibility for the International Missionary Council's (IMC) new committee, the ICCLA. Born in Toronto in 1887, she was the oldest of five children in a close and prominent family. Her maternal grandfather, Edward Blake, had served successively as premier of Ontario, federal Liberal leader, and member of parliament in the British House of Commons. George Wrong, her father, ordained as a low-Church Anglican clergyman, bypassed parish work for an academic career during which he effectively established the history department at the University of Toronto and sought to make Canadian history something more than the province of amateurs. A Canadian nationalist, he was also an Anglophile and imperial enthusiast whose trans-Atlantic connections opened many doors for his children.[18]

In 1911, after studying and then teaching part-time at Havergal Girls' School, Margaret (Marga to family and friends) left Toronto for Oxford University, along with her brother Murray, who would stay on as a history don at Magdalen College, and family friend Vincent Massey, a future Canadian Governor General. After three years of history studies at Somerville College, Marga returned to Canada and a six-year association with the University of Toronto, first as a YWCA secretary, then as an MA student and part-time instructor and an organizer of residential and social facilities for women students.[19] From 1921 to 1925, she worked from Geneva as travelling secretary for the World Student Christian Federation (WSCF), and from 1926 to 1929, from London as a missions secretary for the British Student Christian Movement (SCM). Her role as catalyst for the SCM's "Africa Group" reflected the fact that the continent had become an abiding interest following a six-month tour of sub-Saharan Africa in 1926 with Mabel Carney of Teachers College, Columbia University.[20] On the 1926 tour, as in her earlier work with the WSCF, Wrong demonstrated adaptability and enthusiasm, and liberal tendencies on race questions. Along with her Canadian identity, these qualities made her a congenial figure for the reform-minded mission bureaucrats within the IMC who were engaged during the 1920s in efforts to restructure missions' educational work in Africa.[21]

J.H. Oldham, the leading figure in this restructuring project, was also the person responsible for recruiting Wrong (though the first choice for the new position had been the missionary-anthropologist Edwin Smith).[22] Wrong had no missionary background, in Africa or elsewhere, but her previous work experience and her interest in Africa had already led to the offer of a job as headmistress at the Gold Coast's Achimota College.[23] Writing to her parents in the fall of 1928 about alternatives to the Achimota position and then, early in 1929, about Oldham's offer, she made no reference to a sense of religious calling but instead spoke of her interest in "interracial work" and of the challenges and responsibilities of the larger Africa job, which would draw on her previous experience in "co-operative" and "pioneering" work.[24]

The absence of traditional religious discourse to express her sense of calling was characteristic of Wrong, as it was of a generation of young men and women who came to Christian social service through the early SCM. Recalling his friendship with Wrong at the University of Toronto, where they had both been leaders in establishing the SCM and he a controversial professor under siege at Victoria College, Samuel Henry Hooke wrote that Wrong had "never had much use ... [for] conventional piety."[25] Nor did she feel it necessary to adopt the type of retiring and modest behaviour once considered appropriate, if not absolutely *de rigueur,* for evangelical Protestant women. It was not that she shunned a missionary identity – she cheerfully told a Jewish fellow-traveller during a 1930 shipboard encounter that she was "to all intents and purposes a missionary."[26] But neither did she fit the stereotype of the sexless and ascetic spinster missionary. Hooke maintained that he had at first found her beauty "a little intimidating," while Mabel Carney recalled that, during the 1926 tour, a drunken Scottish administrator on the Gold Coast, carried away by her good looks and outgoing manner, had tried "to make love to her one dark night during the return drive from a native dance."[27] Missionary bureaucrats like Oldham would not have been deterred by the fact that Wrong did not fit the conventional image of a "lady missionary." Probably quite the contrary, especially since, like Carney, they could see that she both charmed *and* was taken seriously by people in authority and that her interest in social issues was linked to an intense if generally unverbalized Christian faith.

As for her interest in interracial and cooperative activities, it had already been demonstrated in her home life as well as in her work with the WSCF and the British SCM by the time she accepted Oldham's offer. From the fall of 1926, when she and Margaret Read had established a home together in the London suburb of Golders Green, their house had been a place where overseas visitors, and particularly students from Asia and Africa, could come for a visit, a meal, or an extended stay.[28] Her home life intersected with her work in another way in that, following Murray's death in Oxford in 1928, Wrong was the primary caregiver for a number of years for three of his six children. Like her colleagues and friends, they, too, would remember the Golders Green house as a kind of way station for overseas visitors. They also remembered that as teenagers they were expected to help out with tasks related to literature production. At intervals, then, Wrong had to structure her work, and especially her international travels, around her domestic responsibilities. But far from allowing these duties to diminish her involvement with the ICCLA, she remained at its centre and expanded its reach. ("The ICCLA *was* Margaret Wrong," one colleague commented following her death.[29]) She coped by moving briskly through long work days, increasingly giving short shrift to such "trivialities" as matters of dress, and by working in a rare personal and professional partnership with Margaret Read. Like Wrong, Read was for some years a surrogate parent to her expatriate brother's two children.[30] Together, the "two Margarets" combined the private and public spheres of their lives in productive and satisfying ways.[31]

At Edinburgh House

Wrong's official work for the ICCLA had three distinct aspects. Her base of operations was Edinburgh House, London, the converted Belgravia dwelling where the committee shared space with the Conference of British Missionary Societies (CBMS), the IMC, and other ecumenical groups.[32] Tours of sub-Saharan Africa took place approximately every third year and were generally of some six months' duration. Often these were followed up by trips to North America to obtain money and support for the cause.[33] In the four years preceding her first major tour of Africa for the committee, Wrong publicized existing literature resources in vernacular and colonial languages, identified what appeared to be missions' most pressing literature needs, and proposed strategies to meet them. To further these goals, she established consultative and cooperative relationships with missionary societies and their workers in the fields, and with publishers, colonial officials, and scholars whose Africa interests overlapped with her own. Although it was to function primarily as a clearing house for information about literature resources and publishing opportunities rather than as a publisher itself, the ICCLA did publish two periodicals, *Books for Africa* and *Listen: News from Near and Far*.

Even at the end of Wrong's lifetime, the content of these two periodicals came overwhelmingly from Westerners. Nonetheless, in their very different ways, each provided some encouragement for African voices. *Listen,* launched in January 1932, seemed to hold special opportunities for women writers. Intended to serve as a simple reader for Africans new to literacy and the Christian faith, it particularly targeted villagers, women, and children. For this audience it employed a simplified form of English, a practice which, inevitably, contributed to its condescending tone. It was designed so that individual sections could be translated into African languages, or French or Portuguese, and reissued in other formats. A significant portion of *Listen*'s content was devoted to "women's issues." As such, it dealt with indigenous domestic matters and subsistence farming as well as with African Christian family life and adaptations of the latest Western teachings on nutrition,

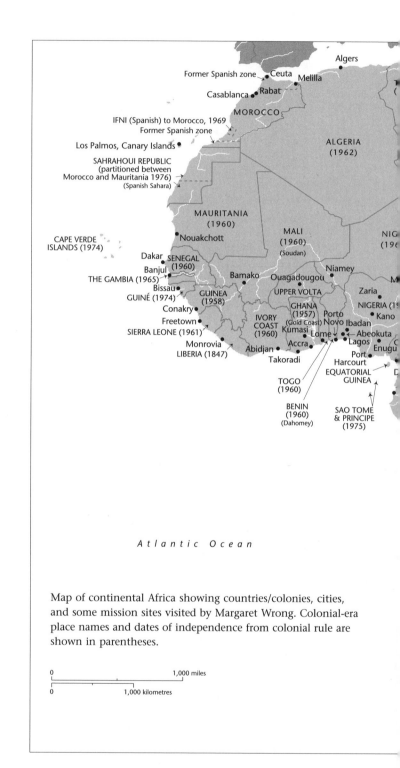

Map of continental Africa showing countries/colonies, cities, and some mission sites visited by Margaret Wrong. Colonial-era place names and dates of independence from colonial rule are shown in parentheses.

Mediterranean Sea

CYRENAICA   Cairo •Suez
LIBYA   •   •
1951)
                   EGYPT
       FEZZAN   (1922)

                              Red Sea

CHAD   Khartoum
(1960)   •   Former frontier
                                    ← of Eritrea
'Djamena   SUDAN
er   (1956)   DJIBOUTI
ers   (1977)   Former frontier
ish   Addis Abbaba ←   between British
roons   •   and Italian
CENTRAL AFRICAN   ETHIOPIA   Somaliland
UBLIC (1960) (Ubanghi-Shari) Yambio Juba
angui•   •   •
        •Gulu
        (1962)   KENYA
RWANDA   •Kampala (1963)   •Mogadishu
DEMOCRATIC (1962)
REPUBLIC   Kigali • •
OF CONGO   BURUNDI Nairobi   Indian Ocean
azzaville (1960) (1962)•
        (formerly Zaire) Bujumbura
ashasa (Belgian Congo)   •Mombasa
eopoldville)   TANZANIA   Zanzibar
a   (1961)   •
              (Tanganyika) Dar es Salaam
              MALAWI (1964)
              (Nyasaland)
                              COROMOS
ANGOLA   •Ekwendeni   (1975)
(1975)   Lilongwe   •Diégo-Suarez
       ZAMBIA (1964)
       (Northern Rhodesia) •Blantyre
       Lusaka Harare   Tananarive
AMIBIA •   (Salisbury)   • (Antananarivo)
/ AFRICA) ZIMBABWE (1980)
       (Southern Rhodesia) •Beira
       BOTSWANA Bulawayo MALAGASY REPUBLIC (1960)
ndhoek (Bechuanaland)   (MADAGASCAR)
     Gaborone•
  Mafeking•   •Pretoria •Maputo
   Johannesburg• •Mbabane
  Bloemfontein SWAZILAND (1968)
     •   •Maseru
SOUTH AFRICA •Durban
(1910) Fort Hare ← LESOTHO (1966) (Basutoland)
     Lovedale• •Umtata
Town   Transkei Territories

Margaret Wrong (Marga) with her father near Murray Bay, Quebec, 1906. George Wrong's trans-Atlantic connections opened many doors for his daughter, which she readily acknowledged. In old age he took great pride in her international work and came to accept the fact that he could not lure her back to a job in Toronto. Family photo courtesy Jo LaPierre.

Marga, probably as a teenager, at the Wrongs' country home near Whitby, Ontario (right), and in the 1930s (below). Professor Samuel Henry Hooke, who first met Wrong between these two intervals when both were at the University of Toronto, later recalled her beauty as "a little intimidating." Family photos courtesy Chris Armstrong and Jo LaPierre.

Wrong, left, and Margaret Read, right, in front of a village hut, possibly the one in which they lived in 1936 during their three-week stay in a Nyasaland (Malawi) village. Elsie Gordon, centre, a Canadian friend of Wrong's, had travelled with "the two Margarets" on the voyage to South Africa but seems not to have stayed with them during their interval in the village. Photo courtesy Institute of Education, University of London, Margaret Read collection.

Wrong displaying pictures and books at a makeshift stall in a village market, Nyasaland, 1936. "I had the proud distinction of drawing as large a crowd as the local butcher." Photo courtesy the Library, School of Oriental and African Studies, University of London.

The Dick-Whittaker Dairy Parlour, Mason County, Alabama, 1947. Wrong is on the left beside Christopher Cox, Educational Adviser to the Secretary of State for the Colonies. To his right are Mr. and Mrs. Dick and their daughter, Mrs. Whittaker, who, like her husband, was a graduate of Tuskegee, she in home economics and he in agriculture. Wrong, Cox, and others like Jackson Davis of the Rockefeller Foundation's General Education Board were anxious to publicize the achievements of modernizing African Americans like the Whittakers and, where possible, have their expertise adapted to particular African contexts. Photo courtesy Institute of Education, University of London, Margaret Read collection.

Dr. Christian G. Baëta was an impressive young delegate from Ghana to the IMC conference at Tambaram in 1938. As a delegate to the IMC conference at Whitby, Ontario, in 1947 he was, with other delegates, a guest at the nearby Wrong home. Later, as vice-chairman of the IMC, he helped orchestrate its merger with the World Council of Churches (WCC). Photo courtesy Oikoumene, WCC, Geneva.

Joseph H. Oldham some four decades after he had become the first general secretary of the International Missionary Council in 1921. A distant but oft-quoted guru for Choné Oliver, he was simply "Joe" to Wrong, whom he had recruited for the ICCLA, and to other colleagues at Edinburgh House. A powerful influence at the Colonial Office as well as in the international missions bureaucracy, Oldham had a particular interest in African affairs. Photo courtesy Oikoumene, WCC, Geneva.

sanitation, and childcare. Occasionally such material was written by African women, a development that Wrong was anxious to promote, especially in later years when *Listen* contained a specially designated Women's Page.[34] But in practice, few African women were in a position to become contributors even when the subject matter was within their "sphere." They were even less well positioned to benefit from the existence of the ICCLA's senior periodical, *Books for Africa*.

Established as a quarterly in 1931, *Books for Africa* served as an important professional journal for mission educators, including senior African personnel. As such, it described experiments in education that could be adapted from outside Africa or from one part of the continent to another, and it publicized Colonial Office and local government initiatives related to the development of literacy. It promoted the vernacular literary competition for African authors conducted by the International African Institute (IAI) and drew readers' attention to the IAI's journal, *Africa*, as an important source of information about literature related to the continent. Publicizing such literature was, of course, its own chief raison d'être. In addition to topical articles, there were brief "notices" about new, adapted, or translated works in English, French, and Portuguese, and a list of new vernacular publications arranged alphabetically by language group as regular features of the journal.

The first issue signalled the kinds of literary activity that the ICCLA would be encouraging, as well as the type of work already in existence that it wished to bring to the notice of educators. The latter included brief descriptions of newly available health posters and Bible pictures with accompanying vernacular texts and an overview of the Bible societies' recent annual reports. The popularity of Georgina A. Gollock's *Lives of Eminent Africans* and Edwin W. Smith's *Aggrey of Africa* was cited as evidence that "Africans welcome lives of their own people" and a call was issued for "willing scribes, both African and European ... to take down the material stored in the minds of old men and women which will otherwise be lost at their death."[35] Among nine brief notices about other biographies, was one about Booker T. Washington's *Up from Slavery* and three on works about Africans. One of these books, *Life of Titus Mtembu: An African Priest and Pastor,* was written by his son. Significantly, however, the notice that followed, about a Malagasy Christian woman martyr, was written by a European author rather than a female relative.[36]

Future issues of *Books for Africa* would continue to publicize writing by, as well as about, Africans, some of it less ephemeral and didactic than James Mtembu's brief biography of his father. Thomas Mofolo's eponymous *Chaka*, a fictionalized account of the exploits of a renowned Zulu warrior published by the IAI in 1931 (some twenty-one years after it had first been shown to missionaries) and often cited by scholars as the first African novel, was "noticed" in 1932.[37] Along with the IAI's *Africa*, then, and the IMC's *International Review of Missions (IRM), Books for Africa* would become a key vehicle for spreading the word internationally that Africans were writers as well as readers.

On Tour

Wrong's first major tour of Africa for the ICCLA took place in 1933.[38] It served as a get-acquainted exercise with her various constituencies in the continent. A number of broad themes emerged on the tour that Wrong would reiterate on later journeys and in speeches, periodicals, and books. There was, for instance, the controversial question of which African languages to privilege in publishing new vernacular materials and translating European works, and, in regard to content, an emphasis on the importance of creating literature that reflected indigenous conditions and spoke to African needs.[39] She stressed the urgency of achieving a much greater degree of inter-mission and mission-government cooperation, along with the need for cooperation with scientific researchers in such tasks as recording music and legends, and identifying the reading interests of such key groups as migrant workers. The need to seek out and assist African writers was mentioned, but not featured, in reports written during the 1933 tour and in Wrong's *Africa and the Making of Books*, published a year later.[40]

By contrast, discussing literature needs with Africans and seeking out writers who could meet those needs seems to have been a priority on Wrong's 1936 tour of southern and southeastern Africa (a journey of some eight thousand miles, financed by the Carnegie Corporation). The most important such contact came through the Rev. R.H.W. Shepherd, a member of the publications bureau of Lovedale Mission in Cape Province and editor of its monthly, *The South African Outlook*. Shepherd had invited Wrong to be present for what was subsequently described as the first conference of black South African writers.[41] Held at the Transvaal home of Rheinallt Jones, the Director of the South African Institute of Race Relations, the conference was arranged "to encourage and assist African writers, and to consult with them regarding the steps which can be taken for the development of the literature of the Bantu languages of Southern Africa."[42] Here Wrong met a number of writers whose names and works she would later publicize, among them the Zulu poet and playwright H.I.E. Dhlomo and the Xhosa educator and politician D.D.T. Jabavu. Others who were invited but unable to attend included Thomas Mofolo and poet J.J.R. Jolobe.[43] In late twentieth-century studies of African literature, these writers are identified primarily for their pioneer work and their cultural links with white liberal sympathizers, or for their civil rights aspirations, rather than as creators of lasting literature. But in the interwar era, they were black South African authors of importance, and significant as role models for aspiring young writers like Peter Abrahams, who, like them, would find support for his literary aspirations among white Christian liberals so long as he eschewed politically sensitive issues.[44]

Prior to the Transvaal writers' conference, Wrong had also met with the African Reading Circle at the University of Witwatersrand, chaired by Zulu poet and professor Benedict Vilakazi. Elsewhere, still in her role as talent scout, she also endeavoured to meet promising musicians and visual artists (the artists, ideally, would illustrate books).[45] Wrong's 1936 tour exemplified patterns that would be ongoing in her efforts to recruit Africans for the work of the ICCLA: in addition to meeting black South African intellectuals, she had focused on such practical matters as how to finance and arrange for the publication of their work and for further training where necessary; how to improve on the meagre library resources available to non-Europeans, and how to encourage the retrieval and recording of traditional songs.

In 1936 and afterward, Wrong's role on the ground was that of a catalyst. As a result of her travels, she was conscious of the dearth of print literature and the waste involved in isolated effort. She was, therefore, a strong advocate of cooperation among missions, and between missions and colonial officials. Before leaving South Africa, she participated in the first meeting of the literature subcommittee of the newly formed Christian Council of South Africa. Chaired by Shepherd and made up of Europeans and Africans, the subcommittee was to arrange for local literature committees to be set up in each of the language areas in which the Council had work. For Wrong, it marked "a great step forward."[46]

By comparison with other parts of sub-Saharan Africa, South Africa was well served by indigenous authors and publishing opportunities, a fact made more evident to Wrong as she travelled north, staying first in Nyasaland (Malawi) and then the Rhodesias (Zimbabwe and Zambia). In Nyasaland, she linked up with Margaret Read, who was doing fieldwork among the Ngoni and thus able to help her with grassroots connections. Living for three weeks in a grass hut in the centre of a village, beside the chief's house – "a public and very interesting life" – Wrong attempted to establish a range of contacts and to discern and cultivate literature interests.

> I had opportunity of talking over books needed with various African people, ranging from clerks in government or commercial service who knew English well to old men who knew only the vernacular. I attended two weekly markets held at the village of the paramount chief and sat there showing pictures and books to all and sundry. There I had the proud distinction of drawing as large a crowd as the local butcher; many, indeed, came from him to me and held their gory, unwrapped purchases perilously near my wares in the excitement of the moment. One old chief came and asked for a book explaining British administration.[47]

From grass huts and village markets she went on to more elite contacts and accommodation: talks with the Acting Director of Education in Lusaka, for instance, and, in Salisbury, a stay with the Chief Justice while attending various meetings. The first of these officials invited her to "submit concrete proposals for the increase of literature for Africans."[48] The discussions Wrong initiated during this portion of her tour led a year later to the creation of the Northern Rhodesia Literature Committee, sponsored by government but involving missionaries and Africans. Later, as the Northern Rhodesia and Nyasaland Joint Publications Bureau, it would become one of the first publishing houses in south-central Africa.[49]

By 1939, when Wrong was on her fourth major sub-Saharan tour, financed, like the previous one, by the Carnegie Corporation, her knowledge of Africa and African elites had grown considerably.[50] The elites included many expatriates, especially students, for whom, as noted, Wrong and Margaret Read kept a kind of open house. In addition to traditional leaders, local notables whom Wrong met on her travels included pastors, teachers, and journalists. It was on members of these groups, she believed, that adequate provision for Africa's literature needs would increasingly depend, since, the more she saw of Africa, the more she realized that outsiders like herself could accomplish little while working on their own. She was especially eloquent on this point following a meeting in Kaimosi, Kenya, with an area literature committee that included local African teaching staff as well as representatives of missions and educational officers:

> Meetings such as this are very helpful. Too often in such a rapid tour there is no time for them and I feel increasingly with every journey in Africa which I make that life is going on of which I only catch fugitive glimpses, and of which I lack understanding almost as completely as I lack understanding of the marine life seen through the glass-bottomed boat at Port Sudan. I am more than ever convinced that the need of literature can only be met through the closest cooperation with Africans both in defining the need and in writing to meet it.[51]

Wartime and Postwar Initiatives
Given this perspective, Wrong was understandably anxious to involve Africans in the new opportunities for literacy and literature work that came with the Second World War. The desire for literacy, which had become stronger in some parts of Africa even before 1939, developed markedly under wartime conditions.[52] At the same time, with the coming of the war, the British government was under increased pressure to improve social services within Africa and to enlarge educational opportunities, this last with a view to "preparing" Africans for eventual self-government. Such pressures came from within Africa and from the anti-colonial critiques of the Roosevelt

administration. But they also came from within Britain itself. Groups such as the Fabian Colonial Bureau, of which Wrong was a member, operated both as a left-wing pressure group *and* in cooperative relationships with liberal imperialists in the Colonial Office in order to facilitate what historian J.D. Hargreaves has termed "progressive social engineering."[53] Such circumstances produced a new level of state support for the kind of work in which Wrong and the ICCLA had been engaged.[54]

The British Council, for instance, offered to distribute free copies of *Listen*, on request, to African schools. Encouraged by this and other instances of practical state aid for the periodical, Wrong sought articles from prominent African Christians such as the Nigerian churchman (later Bishop) Seth I. Kale.[55] She also had access to new institutions, among them the BBC, where, from 1941, she worked half-time, on loan from the ICCLA, as a section officer for the African Division of the London Transcription Service. Working with Africans, she was to develop scripts for broadcast in Africa.[56]

In terms of significance for the ICCLA's mandate, perhaps the most important wartime initiative to come out of the Colonial Office was the new emphasis on adult literacy movements. These movements potentially had special importance for women, since women so seldom had access to regular schooling. As a member of the subcommittee that prepared the Colonial Office's important *Mass Education in African Society,* Wrong contributed a list of suggested reading materials for adult literacy campaigns. The titles on the list, printed originally in *Books for Africa*, dealt with a wide range of subjects and were written in simple English and as such were considered suitable for translation into vernaculars.[57] Wrong's 1944-45 tour of West Africa and the Belgian Congo brought her into contact with Africans who could do such translations as well as produce original literature. Following the tour, which had been undertaken partly in response to invitations from the Nigerian and Gold Coast governments, she prepared her "Report on Literacy and Adult Education in the Gold Coast." The report provided strong arguments for adult literacy programs, an effort, clearly, to woo local colonial officials, some of whom remained decidedly skeptical about their value. It outlined in detail the steps that needed to be taken to bring about the production of literature in both local vernaculars and English for use in such programs.[58] Subsequently, she acted as a liaison between Gold Coast education officials and authors, and publishers in England, to arrange for the publication of short vernacular manuscripts.[59]

During and after the war, working with like-minded colleagues, Wrong took additional steps to encourage the development of indigenous literature. Her friend Ida Ward, as head of the department of African languages and cultures at the School of Oriental and African Studies (SOAS), was a key figure in assisting West Africans with the scientific study of their own languages. Like Wrong, Ward was anxious to convince Western-educated

Africans that writing instructional literature in their own language was a task worthy of their talents.[60] Wrong's 1942 paper on "The Importance of Literature in African Languages," prepared for the Royal Anthropological Society, endorsed Ward's call for scholarships to enable African students to undertake language study at SOAS and called for the establishment in London of a central collection of African publications and texts as a useful resource for such students.[61] Africans, especially South Africans, were doing impressive translations of Western classics, including Shakespeare, she told her audience, but their creativity in their own languages must also be assisted, for "without the encouragement of African authorship, there can be no literature in the true sense of the term, in African languages."[62]

This was also a time when Wrong's American connections were strengthening in ways significant for African intellectuals, and perhaps especially for those with links to the IAI. Along with government and mission grants, Rockefeller money had helped the IAI expand its activities in the 1930s. With the outbreak of war, its work was interrupted and its journal, *Africa*, temporarily suspended. Wrong was part of the interim committee that helped the IAI through its wartime difficulties, thereby enabling it to resume publication of its journal and re-establish its vernacular literary competition, which had proven to be an important stimulus for African writers in the 1930s.[63] Wrong's links to the Rockefeller-funded General Education Board (GEB) were particularly important in helping the Institute find a new level of advocacy and support in the mid-1940s in the US. The GEB's primary focus was, and remained, the American South. But especially after its associate director, Jackson Davis, and African American agricultural specialist Thomas Campbell had joined Wrong for part of the 1944-45 tour of West Africa and the Belgian Congo, Davis demonstrated a keen interest in promoting knowledge of, and links with, Africa in the US. Unlike Melville Herskovits, an emerging African studies scholar, who regarded the IAI as too "colonial," Davis promoted it as an ideal vehicle for making the US more Africa-minded. His support undoubtedly reflected the close personal relationship he had developed with Wrong, but it also attested to the interest he shared with her and the Institute in supporting the agendas of liberal colonial officials and "responsible Africans" in order to "lay the basis for collaboration and constructive tasks of education, self-government, and economic development."[64]

Finally, convinced that not only authorship but also the mechanisms for identifying and assisting authors and publishing their work must increasingly be located *in* Africa, Wrong renewed her call for the establishment of literature bureaus with full-time staff in all the British colonies in Africa, and for cooperative efforts by missions and colonial officials to bring these about. The East African Literature Bureau, one of the most important regional publishers in late twentieth-century Africa, reflected these efforts, coming into existence within months of her death in 1948.[65]

Unequal Opportunities and Matters of Representation

The opportunities for authorship promoted and publicized through the ICCLA mainly served male writers. The most fundamental reason was women's lack of literacy. Even at the primary level, girls' schooling lagged significantly behind boys', and the gap widened at more advanced levels. As late as the war years, secondary schooling for girls was still confined mainly to South and West Africa. Almost all of the Africans who went to Britain to study were men.[66] Thus, women were generally not able to benefit from the contacts and resources available to would-be writers in either Africa or the imperial metropolis. Similarly, they were seldom among the educated Africans who travelled to the US for study and work experience when groups within missions and philanthropic agencies such as the GEB cooperated with each other and with British colonial officials to increase such contacts in the 1940s.[67]

The push for adult literacy that began in wartime would seem to have provided an opportunity to recruit at least some women to become writers, given the emphasis that was then being placed on simple materials in vernaculars. And, in her "Report on Literacy and Adult Education in the Gold Coast," Wrong had pointed out the particular importance of making such literature available for women, since they so infrequently had exposure to spoken or written English. The people she was seeking to create this literature, however, would ideally be well schooled in English as well as their own tongue and "at home in the modern conditions of the world" (to use Ida Ward's phrase).[68] Wrong came to know several South African women whose familiarity and ease with Western ways accorded with Ward's description. They were, however, fully engaged in social service and other work that missions valued. I have found no evidence that Margaret Wrong sought to recruit them for vernacular literature work or that she actively sought out such women elsewhere.[69] Almost invariably, therefore, such writers were men.

Especially outside South Africa, reading material in vernaculars remained scarce despite the increased interest in fostering its development during the war years. There were other practical constraints that particularly affected women. African women lived primarily in rural areas, where heavy work loads, as well as their physical environment, militated against personal reading even if they did manage to acquire basic literacy. Night came early in African villages and was unbroken by the electric light that allowed literate male workers in urban and industrial work sites to use their precious leisure hours for reading.[70] In the libraries for non-Europeans that gradually began to be established in urban centres, there were English as well as vernacular books to serve intellectually ambitious young men. In his autobiographical *Tell Freedom*, Peter Abrahams recalled the sense of elation that had come to him when, in the 1930s, he had first discovered "American Negro literature" in the Carnegie Non-European Library of the Bantu Men's Social Centre in Johannesburg: "In the months that followed I spent nearly all my spare time in the library ... I read every one of the books on the shelf marked: American Negro Literature. I became a nationalist, a colour nationalist through the writings of men and women who lived a world away from me."[71]

Not only did literate women seldom have access to such mind-stirring resources as those discovered by Abrahams; the book and pamphlet literature created specifically for them, like the domestic content in *Listen,* typically emphasized home- and family-linked matters. In *Africa and the Making of Books*, Wrong cited the request of an "elderly pastor" for just such reading matter for young women: "It is good to have a book such as the Bible ... But now I would ask for still more books which speak specially to certain people. I would ask first of all for a little book for the women, which will teach them all they should know about the care of children and the care of the house and the growing of food. This is one of the books we need most today."[72] This "elderly pastor" became a kind of stock figure in Wrong's reports, but it seems clear that the message she attributed to him was one that she heard regularly. Occasionally she cited African women as sources of such requests.[73] However, usually her informants on "appropriate" reading matter for African women were missionaries, African male teachers, and "elderly pastors" or traditional leaders.

Books such as Georgina A. Gollock's *Daughters of Africa*, published in 1932 and recommended in *Listen's* "Books to Read" column at the end of that year, *did* include women in non-domestic roles, but they were typically historic, distant figures. A few of her 1930s "daughters" were training to become midwives, nurses, or teachers, but most were homemakers – albeit able, modern, Christian, homemakers. Writing at a time when nationalist activism was increasing among Western-educated men, Gollock concluded *Daughters of Africa* by calling upon women to trust in "the slow, sure justice of God" and the love of "white folk" as a way of persuading the men in their lives to forgo agitation.[74]

When Wrong herself spoke out on African women's roles, she avoided the condescending language used by Gollock and attributed to the "elderly pastor." She also expressed confidence that the number of women obtaining higher education and undertaking professional roles would increase. And yet, for the rank and file, she did not anticipate a future markedly different from that envisioned by other "authorities." Her contribution in 1935 to a series of articles in *West Africa* collectively titled "West Africa ...

The Next Fifty Years?" is illuminating in this regard. "To emphasise a woman's place in the family," she wrote, "is not to deny to her spheres of activity outside the family, nor is it to throw doubt on higher education for women. African women in the next 50 years will probably qualify for professional life in increasing numbers." Nonetheless, she went on to sound a cautionary note:

> It is to be hoped that the spread of education among women ... will result in increased sensitiveness to the needs of the community and in the bringing of trained intelligence to bear on the meeting of those needs. A small, educated aristocracy of women cut off from the majority of the people but in a position to exploit their ignorance by reason of superior knowledge would be a menace, whereas educated women, animated by a spirit of public service, would be a blessing.

In responding to her own question – "What has education to contribute to the life of the rank and file of African women whose sphere is, and will continue to be, children, house and the growing and preparation of food?" – she showed a keen awareness of the need to be attentive to specific contexts and existing knowledge and skills: "The teaching of domestic science needs to be planned against a local background, so that it will emphasise and pass on knowledge already possessed by women in the community, and supplement that knowledge where it is deficient." Clearly, however, "the needs of the community" or, more precisely, of specific communities, rather than individual women's own interests, were being identified as the central focus of women's educational and literary activities.[75]

African women, in short, were being encouraged to see themselves primarily in homemaking, nurturing, supportive roles. The same had been true in nineteenth-century England when novelists like George Eliot and Jane Austen had used domestic themes to produce outstanding imaginative work. And it would still be true in late twentieth-century Africa, when a few women writers would be able to draw on familiar themes of home and family life to produce such powerful novels as Buchi Emecheta's *The Joys of Motherhood* (1979) and Mariama Bâ's *So Long a Letter* (1980).[76] Nonetheless, certain preconditions had to exist before even the most gifted women could transfuse their experiences in women's worlds into effective fiction: access to adequate light and leisure and writing materials, exposure to stimulating, empowering literature, and, of course, literacy.[77] Even in the late twentieth century, few African women had access to all these things.

A final factor has to be mentioned here. If it was not a prerequisite, the active encouragement of female creativity was at least a desirable ingredient. In *So Long a Letter*, Miriama Bâ's Senegalese letter-writer and her friend Aissatou received such encouragement as schoolgirls from "the white woman who was the first to desire for us an 'uncommon destiny.'"[78] But a more common experience was probably that described by Nigeria's Buchi Emecheta in her autobiographical *Head above Water:* confessing to one of her teachers at the Methodist Girls' High School her desire to become a writer, she is warned reproachfully that "Pride goeth before a fall."[79] When such "guidance" from Western mentors was coupled with the general reluctance of African parents to invest in their daughters' education or allow them unsupervised contact with foreign environments (whether in Africa or the West),[80] the opportunities for women to learn from the world of letters, much less add to its stock, were negligible.

African men of literary talent were far more likely than their female counterparts to have direct contact with the language and the institutions of the colonial power. These factors proved instrumental in their ability to demonstrate their creative gifts and, in the last half of the twentieth century, to achieve eminence as authors on the world's stage as well as within their own region. And these men typically wrote in English or French, unless a strong commitment to a shared Christian faith or to the related notion of using their talents for the "uplift of their people" prompted them to act on the pleas of reformers like Wrong and Ward and write in their own language. Their schooling had been primarily in the colonial language, and through that medium, they realized, lay opportunities for an audience far wider than that of their own language group.[81]

For subject matter, the first generation of writers to achieve international recognition turned to the encounter between colonial and missionary institutions and the institutions of their own people. In doing so, they created a powerful imaginative literature, offering African narratives of colonial contact to challenge those in such classic texts as Conrad's *Heart of Darkness* or Carey's *Mr. Johnson*. The prototype of this genre (labelled "clash of cultures" novels by one scholar) is *Things Fall Apart*, Chinua Achebe's moving account of the disintegration of a proud man and his West African community in the face of missionary and colonial incursions.[82] The novel's female characters are "shadowy figures" as critic Florence Stratton has observed, but given its theme, their marginality seems appropriate: like African women historically, they experience colonial contact, in both its cultural and political forms, as a delayed, often second-hand, and less vivid, phenomenon.[83]

The Margaret Wrong Prize

In 1954, twenty-five years after the founding of the ICCLA, Claude de Mestral, who was to preside over the tranfer of the ICCLA's work to Africa,[84] invoked his predecessor's legacy in an effort to shame the churches into giving more (and more collegial) support to African writers who could serve their faith through literature:

Thanks mainly to the initiative of Margaret Wrong, the British Territories now have publication Bureaus, which are responsible for the publication of school books and of health and community welfare literature, and which devote much attention to the needs of the reading public in the vernaculars. This has greatly helped in securing a larger measure of agreement as to orthography and grammar. It has also launched many African authors upon their careers.[85]

Much of what de Mestral was citing, and what I have been describing in this chapter, was not what is commonly understood as "literature." Nevertheless, such material, and the agencies behind it, fostered writing skills and creative opportunities and thus contributed to the establishment of a talent pool from which skilled imaginative writers could emerge. Moreover, fiction writing, while not a priority, had been encouraged from the outset by the ICCLA and associated literature committees as part of a desirable body of "general literature."[86] What had not been deliberately fostered, of course, was the sharp critique of missions and colonialism that was to emerge in a lot of African fiction – although even that would eventually be sanctioned in the Margaret Wrong Prize for African Literature.

The prize was the most tangible link between Wrong's legacy and African creative writing – and the most dramatic indication of its gendered outcome. During the years before 1963 (the period for which information is most accessible), the Margaret Wrong Prize was sometimes awarded for writing in African languages, as well as for work in French and Portuguese. Most commonly, however, it was given for literature in English. Among the recipients were a number of African writers who would later become internationally recognized, including the two most celebrated, Chinua Achebe and Wole Soyinka. Their fellow Nigerian Amos Tutola did not succeed in winning the prize, but he reportedly wrote his controversial *The Palm-Wine Drinkard* in three days after hearing about its existence.[87]

Nor did Peter Abrahams ever win the prize, despite his considerable output in fiction and autobiography. Nonetheless, Abrahams was the most prominent African author to be closely associated with the ICCLA. He had moved from South Africa to England in 1941, where he became active in the pan-Africanist liberation movement, serving as publicity secretary for the Pan-African Congress in Manchester in 1945.[88] He was a featured speaker at a dinner in Wrong's memory in 1954 and, with Joyce Cary, a judge of manuscripts submitted for the award.[89] Names of nominees were put forward by senior educators or civil servants in Africa, by spokesmen for publishers, the British Council, and the IAI, and by others similarly positioned to identify African writers of promise or achievement. Claude de Mestral put one name forward in 1958, and at least one writer nominated himself.[90]

No woman writer appears even to have been nominated for an award, much less to have been a recipient, in the years before 1963.

Given the obstacles facing African women who sought advanced education and non-domestic roles, and the fact that it was not until 1966 that the first recognized novel by a black African woman was published in English,[91] their absence from the nominee list is scarcely surprising. And yet it is not inconceivable that it could have been otherwise, especially since the war had produced some new opportunities for advanced schooling for women.[92] Moreover, almost from the beginning, the terms and conditions of the award had been contested subjects among those administering the Margaret Wrong Fund (among whom were Margaret Read and several other women). Faced with the small capital endowment for the award, the many countries to be considered, and the necessity for taking nationalist sentiments into account in deciding on which languages to recognize in a given year, a few trustees in fact became quite inventive about invoking Wrong's "real" vision for African literature to conform with their own perception of how the fund should be used.[93] Yet this inventiveness did not extend to an awareness of gender questions. With the late twentieth-century women's movement still beyond the horizon, there was no external stimulus to suggest that the absence of women writers from lists of nominees was a problem, much less a problem justifying interventionist action analogous to that initiated some thirty years earlier when Margaret Wrong and the ICCLA had recognized that Africans could be assisted to become writers as well as readers.

"The Interdependence of Cultural Terrains"
Modern imperialism, Edward Said has observed, was characterized not by separate worlds of colonizer and colonized, or of imperialism and culture as discrete realms, but rather by "the overlapping experience of Westerners and Orientals, the interdependence of cultural terrains."[94] In this chapter, I have suggested that the cultural projects of Margaret Wrong and the ICCLA and of modernizing African men were not merely overlapping, but symbiotic. As such, they were largely free of overt conflict. Whether because they shared the Christian faith and values of Wrong and her committee – and many clearly did – or because they recognized that ICCLA resources could advance their personal and nationalist ambitions, members of this generation of male intellectuals participated actively in a variety of ICCLA-initiated literary and ancillary endeavours.

To locate Wrong's collaborators in two distinct camps in this fashion is of course somewhat misleading, since many African Christians were also strong nationalists; not a few became national leaders.[95] At a certain stage in their transition from mission-educated prodigies to nation builders, Wrong could serve as a resource even for men whose interests were not primarily literary. Thus, after six years of graduate studies in the US, Kwame Nkrumah could turn up at Edinburgh House in 1945 with a letter of introduction from Thomas Jesse Jones, enquiring about job possibilities at Achimota College and seeking advice about necessary qualifications. In the same year he would help organize the Pan-African Congress; twelve years later he would head the new nation of Ghana, and in 1961 *Books for Africa* would advertise an affordable, abridged edition of his autobiography.[96] Nor was Nkrumah an isolated case. Especially following their joint tour of West Africa and the Belgian Congo, the GEB's Jackson Davis directed Africans as well as Africa-minded black and white Americans towards Wrong for advice and expertise.[97]

The cooperative response of male elites to ICCLA initiatives was also facilitated by Wrong's gradualist and selective approach to cultural change, particularly regarding matters of gender. As we have seen, when the ICCLA turned its attention explicitly to women, its primary concern was to promote changes in specific domestic practices rather than alterations in fundamental roles, with the literature for this purpose almost always written *for* women rather than by them. *Listen,* for example, gave particular attention to women and to "women's issues," and by the 1940s it was more actively seeking women contributors. But whether its vastly increased "volume of correspondence, enquiries, answers to competitions and contributions from readers" (130 letters in the mail from West Africa during one week in early 1947) included many publishable contributions from women is doubtful. Literary materials written in Basic English, as *Listen* was, were decidedly unattractive as reading matter to West Africa's educated elite, so it is unlikely that the few women among this elite with the skills to become authors would have wanted to devote their talents to writing on domestic subject matter for a publication like *Listen.*[98]

The predominant emphasis on domestic matters in the ICCLA's literature for women was a congenial emphasis for modernizing men seeking up-to-date wives, and perhaps also for most women, since marriage and child-rearing were near-universal norms. The emphasis on domesticity was, furthermore, part of a much larger pattern in women's education that continued into the postcolonial era.[99] But it was not an approach that served creative women well. Only in the late twentieth century would African women writers come into their own and begin to find an enthusiastic audience at home and abroad. By then, the Margaret Wrong prize, like the person for whom it was named, was a largely forgotten fragment of Africa's literary history.[100]

5
Women in a Transitional Era: Links and Legacies

Some three weeks after Margaret Wrong's death, Canon Rowling, the elderly cleric who had worked part-time in the 1920s on the cause of literature for Africa, wrote to the family to suggest that Marga's body be disinterred from the Church Missionary Society cemetery in Gulu and transported to the cathedral at Kampala for reinternment. She would rest there beside Alex Mackay, "the pioneer," Bishop Hannington, "the martyr bishop," George Pilkington, "the most gifted translator," and other stars in the church's firmament of Uganda missionary heroes. Hume Wrong's veto of this suggestion was polite but clear: Marga's body was to remain in the spot where it had been buried on the day of her death.[1] While Hume Wrong did not elaborate on the reasons for his and his sister Agnes's decision to decline this intended honour, it seems to have been motivated by several considerations. Agnes Wrong Armstrong recalled their objections to the purely physical aspects of the transfer of Marga's remains.[2] There may also have been a reluctance to emphasize her ties to a movement that Hume, at least, had continued to regard with a certain condescension despite his respect for her own work and, perhaps most importantly, an awareness that Marga would not have wanted to be the object of such a dramatic exercise in old-style missionary sentimentality.[3]

The proposed reburial and the response it evoked highlighted the liminality of the interwar missionary enterprise as well as the ambiguous nature of Margaret Wrong's position during the years between 1929, when she had been appointed secretary of the ICCLA, and 1948, when she died of heart failure shortly after beginning her fifth major African tour for the committee. Unlike Choné Oliver and Florence Murray, Wrong had not been a missionary. Yet like Oliver and Murray, she had been engaged in work that marked a transitional stage between the conversion-focused Christian social service that had been practised by mainstream Protestant missions in Asia and Africa prior to the First World War and the largely secular social welfare activities that would be undertaken under the rubric of "development work" on these continents after the Second World War. The careers of the three women reflected new patterns and trajectories in the foreign missionary movement in the interwar era as it responded, on the one hand, to increasingly secular tendencies in the West and, on the other, to the goals of modernizing and nationalizing elites in colonized and missionized societies. These were tendencies and goals that significantly challenged the conduct and content of "mission." Moderates and liberals in the movement responded to the challenges by broadening the range and upgrading the quality of the practical services offered by missions while de-emphasizing proselytization. Their work was also characterized by a decline in ethnocentrism, a greater openness on "race" issues, and a new willingness to assist Asian and African Christians (and non-Christians) in their personal and professional development. With regard to educated indigenous co-workers, the goal was, as Oliver said in reference to Indian Christian doctors, to facilitate their becoming "colleagues and eventually successors."[4] Inevitably however, old ways and attitudes coexisted with the new, and there was still plenty of scope for missionary paternalism.

At a more personal level, the careers of Oliver, Murray, and Wrong reflected a new stage in Western feminism. The three were part of a cohort of well-educated career women who felt no need to justify their participation in the public sphere in terms of women's work for women and children, the rationale used by an earlier generation of social or maternal feminists to explain their extra-domestic involvements. Certainly, they were more conventional in their ideas about married women's roles than such high-profile interwar figures as Pearl Buck and Vera Brittain, who determinedly combined writing and activism with their family lives. Nonetheless, they shared common ground with such women in advocating broader rights and opportunities for their sex while not choosing personally to make "women's interests" their exclusive constituency.[5] Nor do they seem to have been under pressure to do so from supporters at home. North American women who had traditionally supported women's work in missions on the basis of familiar stereotypes of downtrodden heathen sisters had some difficulty in reconceptualizing their overseas interests in the broader framework of Christian internationalism. Yet by the 1940s, influenced by that concept and by practical financial considerations, they were ready to support such new departures as coeducation at Christian Medical College, Vellore. In Canada, the United Church Woman's Missionary Society was a proud supporter of Murray's work in general medicine and the leading Canadian organization supporting Wrong's activities. Likewise, British women, not all of them Christian, were a supportive constituency for Wrong.[6] In an interwar climate that emphasized international "brotherhood," the broader focus seemed logical.

The three women's work worlds were spacious in ways that went beyond gender. They engaged in a good deal of cooperative work with groups with whom they had shared or overlapping interests, groups whose concerns in later years would often be distinct from, or even hostile to, those of the world of missions: colonial and local government officials, for instance, nationalists and future national leaders, anthropologists, foundation officials, and academics. Of the three women, Oliver probably had fewest links beyond the world of missions and indigenous Christians. But even in her case, work for the CMAI and especially the medical college project necessitated meetings with local political and academic figures, while a shared interest in moral and medical issues affecting women led to contacts with non-Christian women like Dr. Muthulakshmi Reddi, the first Indian woman legislator.[7] During her years in Hamhung, Murray might have grumbled privately about Japanese colonial officials (whose reputation for efficiency was, she thought, undeserved), but as the superintendent of a hospital over which they had ultimate control she had no choice but to deal with them on a wide variety of matters. After the Second World War and especially during the Korean War era, there were more, and usually more congenial, dealings with officialdom in the form of Korean and American civilian and military men. While these dealings were undertaken for professional purposes, they also enlarged her life. As well, she had the satisfaction of seeing former protegés and colleagues like Dr. P.K. Koh become prominent figures in independent South Korea (in Koh's case, vice-minister of education in 1951-52 and later president of Kyongpook and Yonsei universities).[8]

Wrong's circle of contacts was widest of the three, and here, too, although pragmatism initially motivated such contacts, it did not preclude collegial relationships and even the development of friendships. During her early Africa years, Wrong was sometimes taken aback by the ignorance and sheer ineptness on race issues of some British colonial agents in East and West Africa. And in 1929 when South Africa's General Smuts was at Oxford to give the Rhodes lectures, she expressed disappointment about favourable media coverage of his "premises about the necessary benefits [to Africans] from white civilization," especially since they were "unmodified by information on the actual situation which Western industry creates."[9] But neither these concerns nor, later, her Fabian connections prevented her from working in collaborative relationships with the Colonial Office and men on the ground.[10] With some officials, such as the Canadian-born governor of the Gold Coast, Gordon Guggisberg, the most powerful member of what Nkrumah called the "great triumvirate" behind Achimota College, she developed a close friendship, commencing with her first visit to Africa.[11] Similarly, anthropologist Bronislaw Malinowski, Margaret Read's mentor at the London School of Economics, became a friend despite his militant agnosticism and penchant for ribald humour.[12] A letter from Wrong to her parents, written in 1928 when she was still with the SCM (Student Christian Movement), shows the diversity, even then, of her networks as well as her sense of the bizarre in some of her involvements, in this case a conference on "sex hygiene & how to teach it to primitive peoples":

> Sir Gordon Guggisberg is in the chair & often quite lost when it becomes too psychological – very much on the spot [? illeg.] at other times. If he can manage it he treats me to a large wink or a broad grin at crucial points. Prof. Malinowsky [sic], one of his assistants in anthropology from the London School of Economics, – several biologists & a psychologist or two and assorted missionaries & me representing the S.C.M. & Lady Williams as a free lance make up the 20 to 30 odd – I forgot some gov't educational officers. Prof. Malinowsky prepared a somewhat provocative memorandum on native customs & we are going through [? illeg.] it – all day it's been monogamy vs polygamy and the pros and cons of birth control – he's delighted that so free a discussion is possible in a group of nearly 30 people including both sexes & married & unmarried. But as I say father's hair would have risen.[13]

Missing from this conclave on their sex lives were any Africans themselves (though it is possible that some were invited).[14] A decade later, Jomo Kenyatta, mission educated and a student of Malinowski's, would defend customs like female circumcision against missionary intervention as part of a larger and pioneering assertion of cultural pride in his *Facing Mount Kenya* (introduced by Malinowski).[15] But other educated Africans, and African Americans, would continue to seek assistance from and collaborate with missionaries and like-minded reformers during these transitional decades in the project of selectively remaking African community and family life. During the war years, even Haille Selassie's London-based daughter came to see Wrong about obtaining books in appropriate vernaculars on health and welfare for use in Ethiopia.[16] African American Max Yergen, in South Africa for many years with the local equivalent of the YMCA, and later, back in the US, the founder of the International Committee on African Affairs and an adherent of the Communist Party, emerged as the most significant of Wrong's long-term contacts among black Americans concerned with Africa's "uplift," but he was by no means a unique figure.[17]

For Oliver and Murray, and especially for Wrong, the world of interwar missions was, then, a multifaceted world. Their particular skills and interests intersected with opportunities and crises in the larger societies around them and with the ambitions and agendas of Western and non-Western modernizers to give the three women expansive roles.

All three women were tangibly honoured within their work worlds at the time of their retirement or death: through the Oliver Fund, the Margaret Wrong prize, and, in Murray's case, the naming of "Murray Village" and much more. Wrong's sudden death brought tributes from well beyond the world of missions. Past, present, and future Canadian prime ministers wrote to her family, as did Britain's Colonial Secretary, Arthur Creech Jones, whom she had known through Colonial Office committees and the Fabian Colonial Bureau. Tuskegee's Thomas M. Campbell, the African American agricultural specialist who (along with Jackson Davis) had joined Wrong on the West Africa tour of 1944-45, shared his memories of her, as did many other public figures.[18] Some of the tributes were undoubtedly linked to the prominence of her father and her brother Hume, by then Canada's ambassador to the US. But her broad-ranging work had become known on its own merits through such vehicles as the US foundations, the Institute of Pacific Relations, and her wartime Circular Letters, the mailing list for which included such varied figures as Professor Karl Polanyi and Dr. Marion Hilliard in Toronto, and African American Ralph Bunche at the United Nations as well as more predictable mission-linked constituencies.[19] Nor did those who wrote obituaries in such papers as *West Africa* and the *Manchester Guardian,* or the African students who reportedly comprised about half of those in attendance at the memorial service for Wrong in London in May 1948 ("coming in singly and in twos and threes, not in an institutional crocodile") have significant links to her family.[20] In her twenty-nine years with the ICCLA she had earned an international reputation of her own, both as an authority on, and a "friend of Africa."[21]

Murray would work for many more years than Oliver and Wrong and live long enough to enjoy two honorary degrees from Dalhousie University as well as decorations from the governments of Denmark and South Korea. (The Danish award was presented in 1952 in the name of the King of Denmark for her wartime work on the Red Cross ship *Jutlandia.* South Korea's Order of Civil Merit was given by the President in 1969 to recognize Murray's long years of service in Korea.) Unlike Anglo-Saxon missionaries who had worked in British colonial settings, former Korea missionaries like Murray were not vulnerable to charges of having been agents of the colonial power and thus, even in the postcolonial era, they received tributes from institutions and individuals who felt no need to distance themselves from this aspect of their colonial past.[22] Indeed, even in the 1990s there were elderly Korean doctors who could still recall Murray's contribution to the development of Western-style medicine in Korea and, in one case, her personal mentorship, without experiencing the conflicting concerns and emotions of men and women in British colonial Asia and Africa who had collaborated with Anglo-Saxon missionaries, the colonialists' cultural kin.[23]

Within a few years of their deaths, Oliver's and Wrong's careers were largely lost to public memory. Murray's name lingered longest among Canadians because she was the youngest of the three and lived longest, but by the time I began research for this project in 1990 even Murray was largely unknown except among a few United Church people, mainly in Atlantic Canada, and among some Koreans and expatriate Koreans. Even before she died, the missionary era was effectively over as an activity of mainstream women and men and of mainstream Protestant churches.[24] As I point out in the introduction to this book, missionaries, particularly American missionaries, were going to the "Third World" in record numbers at the end of the twentieth century, but they were part of a new wave of evangelicals, most notably Pentecostalists.[25] The legacies of Oliver, Wrong, and Murray, and of other like-minded men and women from the transitional era, were reflected not in these new evangelical missions but in the projects of NGOs and in state-aided development work.[26]

Development work. The term was evidently new to Murray when she responded to an Oxfam questionnaire on the subject in the early 1970s by asserting that if it meant "copying the conditions in western countries" and such things as "high rise apartments and huge factories, I am not interested."[27] But in fact "development work" had already been in use for some decades as an umbrella label to identify a wide range of privately and publicly funded projects concerned with promoting the social and economic advance of poor, typically postcolonial, societies.[28] Indeed, by the time that Murray answered the Oxfam questionnaire, a wide range of development-type interventions in the South had passed the stage of being regarded as unproblematically altruistic and were starting to come under critical scrutiny: from Marxists, feminists, and others in (or from) the West, from non-Westerners concerned about adverse outcomes and neocolonial agendas, and from frustrated volunteers and aid administrators themselves.[29] Two types of intervention that have come under particular fire and that are germane to the subject matter of this book are Western-style medicine and forms of development work that targeted – or failed to target – women.

With regard to Western medicine, some 1970s critics focused on its putative role as a velvet glove in the service of capitalism and imperialism in Asia and Africa, first via missions and later in more sophisticated and efficient forms such as those funded by Western foundations and governments. Others also offered a "cultural critique," which they applied to health care in the world's richest as well as its poorest nations. The cultural critique challenged the assertion that Western-style medical care is "effective, humane, and desirable," portraying it instead as a form of "social control." In the 1960s a Rockefeller study indicted its own past foundation practices for funding an elitist approach to medicine rather than training local auxiliaries, providing community health centres, etc.[30] By the 1990s, scholars like David Arnold were producing more theoretically sophisticated and more factually grounded analyses of the links between Western medicine and imperialism than those offered in earlier works.[31] And as the West itself grew more attracted to "traditional" (especially "Chinese") healing techniques and to holistic and community health approaches to health and well-being, it was the positive emphases on these kinds of alternatives in the "cultural critique" of Western medicine in non-Western societies, rather than charges of its inhumanity, that seemed most apt.

Not surprisingly, mission-founded medical institutions did not escape the criticism. The state government of Tamil Nadu threatened to close Christian Medical College, Vellore, in the 1970s, charging that it was an agent of Western interests. For some years Vellore was isolated and financially punished by the Christian Medical Commission of the World Council of Churches on the grounds that its involvement in high-tech medicine for the rich resulted in the "total irrelevance" of its work for the majority of Indians. The Indian medical personnel who were largely responsible for Vellore as it faced these crises responded to the first charge by showing that ownership of the college was constitutionally vested in Indian churches rather than overseas missions, and, to the second, by defying the Christian Medical Commission's paternalism and persisting in its "both/and" approach (high-tech, high-cost medicine for the rich *and* community service and affordable medical care for the poor), insisting that such an approach was both necessary and functional.[32]

In taking a "both/and" approach, Vellore was reflecting practices that dated back to the era of Dr. Ida S. Scudder and Dr. Choné Oliver. Indeed, Scudder had instituted mobile roadside clinics in the early days of Vellore. In Oliver's case, as Chapter 2 has shown, the establishment of a fully professional Christian medical college with up-to-date staff and infrastructure was the project that most absorbed her during her years as CMAI secretary. Yet she and her colleagues were by no means indifferent to community and family health measures and preventive work, as even a casual perusal of the CMAI *Journal* for this era makes abundantly clear. A resolution passed at the CMAI's third biennial conference called for closer involvement with existing movements "for promoting public health and rural uplift" and for "one-third of the annual contributions from mission hospitals and dispensaries [to] be devoted to this branch of our work."[33] A major obstacle to following through on such resolutions in India and elsewhere was the fact that, for many practitioners, and especially for those who financed their work, public health activities lacked the *cachet* of the sophisticated medicine undertaken in big urban hospitals.[34] A public health emphasis was, meanwhile, a good fit with Oliver's belief in body, mind, and spirit links in health and healing, which, as noted earlier, was something of a hobby horse with her. It was also an important reason for her attraction to Gandhi, despite his periodic criticisms of Western medicine generally and medical missions in particular. When she met him in 1935, latrine building and his book on self-restraint versus self-indulgence proved to be congenial topics of conversation.[35]

During her years as CMAI secretary, Oliver seems to have had relatively little to say regarding India's classic Ayurvedic and Unani systems of medicine, perhaps because she herself was not actually practising medicine and because nationalists with an interest in medicine were, unlike Gandhi, often eager modernizers. In Korea, meanwhile, Murray remained a strong critic of indigenous medicine (though it seemed to be less of an issue for her in the post-Second World War years when she was working in South Korea). From a present-day perspective, her strong and exclusive commitment to Western practices and standards may appear at best naïve, at worst culturally arrogant and counterproductive. Yet it is important to keep in mind that the practices and assumptions of scientific medicine that began in the West and that missionaries sought to transfer are ones that medical professionals in Korea, India, and other Asian countries have made their own, notwithstanding the continuing importance of indigenous medicine to large segments of Asian societies.[36] Furthermore, practices like acupuncture that have recently won a measure of acceptance in the West were ones that doctors like Murray often came to know through circumstances where lack of sanitation or poor techniques had exacerbated existing medical problems. Their lack of openness to indigenous medicine was obviously influenced by their confidence in the superiority of the Western product, but other factors were also at play. Finally, as Chapter 3 of this book suggests, while Murray held fast to Western medical standards as long-term goals for Korea, she learned a good deal over the years about the need to make short-term compromises in response to immediate circumstances.

Concerns about what development has done to, or failed to do for, women in the underdeveloped world have received a great deal of attention since the 1970s. The concerns emerged as feminist activists and academics succeeded in highlighting problems that appeared to have received little attention from early development workers and their colonial-era predecessors. Esther Boserup's 1970 book, *Women's Role in Economic Development,* was a pioneering work in this field. It argued that policies first implemented by settlers, colonial administrators, and technical advisors had fatally ignored African women's importance in subsistence farming and that missionaries had focused too narrowly on women's domestic education.[37] In the years since Boserup's book appeared, there has been a wealth of literature emphasizing the negative social consequences of neglecting women in development planning – or of approaching them in the wrong way[38] – and, conversely, the value of the "right" kinds of development for women, not just for their own advancement but for the well-being of their communities. In the 1990s, the message about the widespread benefits to be derived from effective WID (Women in Development) projects was being presented even by Lawrence Summers, the Chief Economist of the World Bank, an organization whose debt policies have been widely regarded as exacerbating the problems of Third-World women and the societies in which they live. In his Foreword to *Women's Education in Developing Countries,* Summers claims that "investment in the education of girls may well be the highest-return investment available in the developing world."[39]

It could be argued that Oliver, Murray, and Wrong, by not making women the main targets of their work, contributed to the "neglect of women" pattern "discovered" in the last third of the twentieth century. In this book I have shown that their personal interests and professional priorities intersected with indigenous and colonial gender values and contexts to shape their careers, careers that, while ostensibly gender-neutral in the groups they sought to assist, most often gave them male colleagues and clients. It seems undeniable that their career paths did give them access to more capacious and interesting work worlds than would have been possible if they had adhered to the "women's work for women" paradigm of the previous era in missions. The elderly George Wrong knew this: much as he wanted his unmarried daughter back in Canada, trying at times to interest her in such things as a forthcoming job at the University of Toronto's St. Hilda's College in the mid-1930s, he recognized the breadth and challenge of her ICCLA work. And in the late 1930s when she declined an offer to become head of a proposed women's college in Uganda, he congratulated her on a recent success in New York (probably in obtaining a foundation grant) before adding, "I do not wonder that you do not choose to give up this work to become the head of a College for Women. No one else could, I think, have done what you have done."[40] Their personal interests and satisfactions aside, all three women presumably believed that their respective professional goals and approaches would yield long-term benefits for communities of men *and* women.

Critiques of the impact on women of colonial- and missionary-era development work have, as noted, focused on sins of commission as well as omission, especially regarding the single-minded emphasis on domesticity. Here, a brief return to the role of Wrong and the ICCLA in the sphere of domestic education is in order. As Chapter 4 shows, in the literature it produced and promoted specifically for women, the ICCLA took essentially the same approach as most missionaries did towards African women's education: it focused mainly on altering particulars within an existing world of family, community, and subsistence farming rather than facilitating the broadening of women's "career" horizons.[41] Undertaking the former approach, it seemed clear, would win support from many male modernizers and even some traditional leaders. Undertaking the "broader horizons" approach would alienate even most modernizers. It would also deflect women from the role being assigned them as the continent's "stabilizing element" and have the effect of getting them "all dressed up with no place to go."[42] In an important 1940 article on "The Education of African Women in a Changing World," Wrong also justified the domesticity approach on the grounds that "for a long time to come" it would be congruent with "the interests of the majority of African women ... [in] marriage and child-bearing." But she warned that no amount of training for homemaking would improve the quality of family life unless there was accompanying improvement in "the provision for social services, wage rates and standards of life in country and town." She also warned that "home-making must offer adequate scope for women's powers" and that "diversity of function of men and women must not imply servility of status for women."[43] Overall, the article showed both conventional thinking (and naïveté) *and* a keen awareness of structural and ideological obstacles that inhibited advances for African women. Scholars of underdevelopment in colonial societies have drawn attention to missionaries' "blind spots" on gender,[44] but they have not often credited them with a countervailing recognition of barriers facing women. When one turns from Wrong's 1940 article to recent literature on problems in the realm of women and development in the late twentieth century, one experiences a sense of déjà vu and an awareness of the limited success of most outside interventions, however varied and well intentioned.

The fact is that despite much soul searching and critical analyses from within and outside development circles, and experiments with such strategies as providing easy credit for women's income-generation projects, the most popular approach remains "to bring women into development as better mothers."[45] Advocates of these and other approaches to assisting and "empowering" poor women (and, through them, their families) all recognize the centrality of education for girls and hence the need to overcome barriers like physical distance from schools, parents' assumptions about the unprofitability of educating daughters, and mothers' need for their labour in preparing meals and obtaining fuel and water.[46] But, again, none of these insights is new. Many women missionaries of Wrong's acquaintance recognized that educating girls had positive, long-term ramifications for family and community life. Prominent African educators and activists of her era like James Aggrey and the Reverend I.O. Ransome-Kuti also acknowledged this fact.[47] On the basis of her fieldwork in Nyasaland (Malawi), Margaret Read wrote with conviction about the importance of such seemingly mundane things as a nearby water supply in increasing women's willingness to send their daughters to school.[48] Then, as now, there was an awareness of the value of promoting education and development for women in underdeveloped societies – and of the barriers to doing so. In recent years, investment in studying and overcoming the barriers has greatly increased, and the would-be problem-solvers are no longer mainly outsiders, but the gaps between women and men in literacy and related skills, and in consequent opportunities for economic and social advance, remain formidable.[49]

If Oliver, Murray, and Wrong and other professional women in the missionary enterprise in the interwar era had devoted their skills and resources more exclusively to women in an updated version of the "women's work for women" paradigm, would it have made a difference? The example of Ewha Womans University in Seoul, where Murray briefly served, provides an interesting case study. Under Helen Kim's strong leadership as a high-profile and well-connected Christian feminist, Ewha went on to become the largest women's university in the world. In the 1960s it was still responsible for educating more than half of South Korea's university women. It thus seems to illustrate the gains to be reaped by a single-minded focus on creating opportunities for women. Yet Ewha was slow to win recognition in such fields as medical education, and there were those in the late twentieth century, even among its graduates, who spoke of it as still being handicapped by a finishing-school image.[50] And of course Ewha's growth and accomplishments took place within a country whose success in the last few decades of the century marked it out as an "economic miracle."

Very different conditions prevailed in India and sub-Saharan Africa. Had Oliver and Wrong been able and willing to use the resources of their respective organizations more assertively on behalf of women's interests, it is at least conceivable that a few more Indian women might have become doctors and a few more African women well-educated professionals, perhaps even professional writers. Yet among the criticisms directed at Christian Medical College, Vellore, in its later years, the neglect of women's interests seems not to have been a major issue (though there was a very long gap in the years between its first and second female head). And in sub-Saharan Africa, as the preceding brief review of development efforts has suggested, even though concerns about the neglect of women's interests have become more focused in recent decades, the gender gap has not narrowed significantly in many countries.

A later generation of feminists may regret that women as talented as Oliver, Murray, and Wrong did not devote their careers more single-mindedly to those of their own sex, especially in countries where the needs were particularly great. Yet I want to resist the contention that they simply "sold out" to male professional and missionary/colonial agendas in the face of viable, "feminist" alternatives. It remains to be shown that there *were* realistic alternatives to the paths they took. It is surely significant that Dr. Ida S. Scudder ultimately saw no choice but to accept a coeducational successor to the all-women's institution she had founded at Vellore and to which she and other strong women had devoted so much energy for so many years. I would argue that within the framework of the choices they made, and were free to make – and with due recognition of the limits of *any* outside interventions in dealing with formidable social and economic problems – the things that Oliver, Murray, and Wrong accomplished were significant. Their contemporaries, non-Western as well as Western, women as well as men, saw much to admire in their efforts and achievements. Small, incremental gains, often carved out of compromises with local and colonial agendas, seemed to the three women and their contemporaries – as they seem to me now – eminently worthwhile.

That they pursued their careers within the framework of colonialism is clear; that they were mere "pawns in the imperialist game" is not.[51] However paradoxical it may seem, Wrong, who was unquestionably the closest of the three to Britain's "imperial project," was also the most active in anti-racist work and, in a low-key, Fabian way, in furthering moves towards decolonization. Paradoxically, too, Murray, working until 1942 in Japan's empire and undeniably affected by constraints, nonetheless, by dint of adapting pragmatically to the status quo, experienced opportunities for popular acceptance and service that were unavailable to her fellow missionaries in the British Empire. Sharing the broad goals and strategies of those "imperial" missionaries, she was, at the same time, free of their problematic relationship to empire.

Finally, Oliver, Murray, and Wrong were women of faith, their humanitarianism and international vision sustained and energized by a belief in the social relevance of Christianity. One does not, I trust, need to share their faith to find human interest as well as scholarly significance in their lives. After almost ten years of encountering their vivid personalities in their own and others' words, I continue to marvel at their perseverance, their empathy, and their capacity for personal growth. They bowed to circumstances when necessary and they rose to many occasions.

Appendices

Appendix 1

List of people interviewed. Interviews were conducted in person unless otherwise indicated (w: written communication; t: telephone).

Belle Choné Oliver and the Christian Medical Association of India
Dr. Fred Anderson, Toronto
Dr. V. (Dassen) Benjamin, Bangalore, India
Sonu Canara, RN, Ratlam, India (w)
Dr. Jacob Chandy, Kottayam, India
Mrs. Ancilla D'Costa and Miss Najoo Dungore, Nagpur, India
Mrs. Glenna Jamieson, Vancouver (w, t)
Rev. Hilda Johnson, Toronto
Dr. Lawrence Barnabas Maduram Joseph, Vellore, India
Dr. Cherian Thomas, New Delhi
Mrs. Choné Williams, Mississauga, ON

Florence Jessie Murray
Rev. Fred Bayliss and Olive Bayliss, Toronto
Marion Current, MPH, Toronto
Rev. Elda Daniels Struthers Davy, Toronto
Dr. George Dewar, O'Leary, PEI
Mrs. Shirley Ellis, O'Leary, PEI
Dr. Bong Hak Hyun, Suwon, Korea, and Edison, NJ (w, t)
Rev. Yu-Rak Kim, Hamilton, ON
Olive Murray Kayama, Toronto
Dr. Heung Joo Lee, Seoul (w)
Rev. Sang-Chul Lee, Newmarket, ON (w)
Dr. Helen Mackenzie, Balwyn, Australia (w)
Heather Murray, Montreal
Dr. Anna Murray Dike Musgrave, Clarkesburg, ON
Marion Pope, RN, Toronto
Dr. Ian Robb, Halifax
Dr. Hugh Rose and Marilyn Rose, Clarkesburg, ON

Dr. Margaret Storey, Seoul
Dr. Horace G. Underwood, Seoul
Rev. Reid Vipond, London, ON
Dr. Tai-Yun Whang, Toronto
Dr. Kilchai K. Yim, Flushing, NY (w, t)

Margaret Christian Wrong and the International Committee on Christian Literature for Africa
Venerable B. Adelaja, Lagos, Nigeria
Mrs. Agnes Ayodele Taylor Adesegibin, Lagos, Nigeria (w)
Archdeacon E.O. Alayande, Ibadan, Nigeria
Mrs. Agnes Wrong Armstrong, Toronto
Prof. C.G. Baëta, Accra, Ghana
Dr. Jill Wrong Cant, Oxford (w)
Prof. Jo LaPierre, Montreal
Newlove Mamattah, Accra, Ghana
Prof. Rosalind Wrong Mitchison, Ormiston, Scotland (w)
E.M.K. Mulira and Rebecca Mulira, Kampala, Uganda
Modupe Oduyoye, Ibadan, Nigeria
Prof. Kenneth E. Robinson, Chipping Norton, UK (w)
Dr. June Wrong Rogers, Ottawa
Rev. Canon John H.B. Rye, Toronto
Mabel Segun, Ibadan, Nigeria
Charles Wrong, Vancouver (w, t)
Dr. Oliver Wrong, London, UK (w)

Appendix 2

Colonies/countries visited by Margaret Wrong during her tours of sub-Saharan Africa. First reference to colonial name is followed by postcolonial name(s), in parentheses, where applicable.

March-August 1926
Tour with Mabel Carney, Teachers College, Columbia University
  Gold Coast (Ghana), arriving in Accra, 2 March
  Liberia
  Sierra Leone
  South Africa
  Southern Rhodesia (Zimbabwe)
  "Portuguese East Africa" (Mozambique)
  Tanganyika (Tanzania)
  Kenya
  Departure for England from Suez, 5 [?] August

April 1930
  Egypt

March-September 1933
First major tour as ICCLA secretary, accompanied by B.D. (Betty) Gibson
  Gold Coast, probably arriving in Accra first week of March
  Nigeria
  Sierra Leone
  British Cameroon (Cameroon)
  French Cameroun (Cameroon)
  Belgian Congo (Zaire; now Democratic Republic of Congo)
  "French Congo"
  Southern Sudan (Sudan)
  Uganda
  Kenya
  Tanganyika
  Northern Rhodesia (Zambia)
  Belgian Congo
  Angola
  Departure for England from Lobito Bay, Angola, 27 August

April-October 1936
Second major tour as ICCLA secretary
  South Africa, arriving in Cape Town, 27 April
  Northern Rhodesia
  Southern Rhodesia
  Nyasaland (Malawi)
  Tanganyika
  "Portuguese East Africa"
  Departure for England from Cape Town, 30 October

January-May 1939
Third major tour as ICCLA secretary
   Kenya, arriving in Mombasa, 6 January
   Uganda
   Sudan
   Nigeria
   Gold Coast
   Departure for England from Takoradi, Gold Coast, 28 May

September 1944-February 1945
Fourth major tour as ICCLA secretary, first studying literature needs for the
Education Department of the Gold Coast government and then accompany-
ing Thomas Campbell and Jackson Davis on their tour of West Africa and the
Belgian Congo
   Gold Coast, arriving in Takoradi, 22 September
   Belgian Congo
   French Equatorial Africa (Chad, Central African Republic, Congo, Gabon)
   French Cameroun
   Nigeria
   Sierra Leone
   Departure for England by plane from Freetown, 26 February

March-August 1948
Itinerary as planned for fifth major tour
   Egypt, for arrival in Cairo and departure for Sudan
   Sudan
   Kenya
   Tanganyika
   Nyasaland
   Northern Rhodesia
Actual itinerary: arrived Cairo; by plane to Khartoum; by plane to Juba;
merchant's truck to Yambio, Southern Sudan, and thence on to Gulu, Uganda,
10 April; died at Gulu, 11 April.

Notes

Abbreviations Used in Notes

AICs	African independent churches
Armstrong Collection	Uncatalogued collection of Mrs. Agnes Wrong Armstrong (deceased)
BFA	*Books for Africa: The Quarterly Bulletin of the International Committee on Christian Literature for Africa*
CBMS	Conference of British Missionary Societies
CMAI	Christian Medical Association of India
CMC	Christian Medical College, Vellore, India
CMS	Church Missionary Society
CO	Colonial Office
DUA	Dalhousie University Archives
EWUL	Ewha Womans University Library
FMCNA	Foreign Missions Conference of North America
GEB	General Education Board (of the Rockefeller Foundation)
IAI	International African Institute
ICCLA	International Committee on Christian Literature for Africa
IMC	International Missionary Council
IRM	*International Review of Missions*
ISR	*Indian Social Reformer*
KMF	*Korea Mission Field*
LFMI	Laymen's Foreign Missions Inquiry
NCC	National Christian Council of India
NCL	New College Library, Edinburgh
PANS	Public Archives of Nova Scotia
PUMC	Peking Union Medical College
PRO	Public Record Office
RAC	Rockefeller Archive Center
SCM	Student Christian Movement
SOAS	School of Oriental and African Studies, University of London
UBCHEA	United Board for Christian Higher Education in Asia
UCA	United Church/Victoria University Archives
UCC	United Church of Canada
WMS	Woman's Missionary Society of the United Church of Canada
WSCF	World Student Christian Federation
YDL	Yale Divinity School Library

Introduction

1   Like their famous mission-linked contemporary Pearl Buck, they may have disliked feminism as a label, given some of its connotations, but it was certainly in use in their era and,
like Buck, they supported goals for which it serves as an appropriate signifier (Peter Conn,
Pearl S. Buck: A Cultural Biography [Cambridge: Cambridge University Press, 1996], 235).

2   Nancy F. Cott, *The Grounding of Modern Feminism* (New Haven: Yale University Press, 1987),
especially chap. 7. Cf. Pat Thane, "The Women of the British Labour Party and Feminism,
1906-1945," in *British Feminism in the Twentieth Century,* ed. Harold Smith (Aldershot: Edward
Elgar, 1990), 125-43.

3   In considering my subjects' relationship to cultural facets of interwar modernity, I have
taken Ann Douglas's *Terrible Honesty: Mongrel Manhattan in the 1920s* (New York: Farrar,
Straus, Giroux, 1995) as a useful basis for comparisons, since she focuses on the city that
epitomized modernity in the decade when their careers began. Douglas features men and
women who were aggressively and self-consciously modern in their disavowal of conven-
tions in such matters as race and gender relations as well as religion, and in their disdain
for the idealized and "self-infatuated" mother figure of the Victorian era with her claims to
special virtues and moral responsibilities (220). On religion and modernization see Steve
Bruce, ed., *Religion and Modernization* (Oxford: Clarendon Press, 1992), especially introduction and chap. 2.

4   The reference to dinner and wine in Germany is in the Margaret Wrong segment of
uncatalogued family papers in the collection held (at the time of this research) by Agnes
Wrong Armstrong, Toronto, now deceased (hereafter Armstrong Collection); Margaret Wrong
to Mother, 23 May 1930.

5   Murray's judgmental attitudes as a young woman are discussed in Ruth Compton Brouwer,
"Home Lessons, Foreign Tests: The Background and First Missionary Term of Florence Murray,
Maritime Doctor in Korea," *Journal of the Canadian Historical Association*, n.s., 6 (1996):
103-28.

6   Dane Kennedy, "Imperial History and Post-Colonial Theory," *Journal of Imperial and Commonwealth History (JICH)* 24, no. 3 (1996): 345-63, quotation at 346.

7   For instance, Dana L. Robert, *American Women in Mission: A Social History of Their Thought
and Practice* (Macon: Mercer University Press, 1996), especially part 2. A reverse kind of
essentialism also took place, as in the case of negative stereotyping of American women by
nationalist-minded Indian men who were angered by Katherine Mayo's incendiary *Mother
India* (1927); see Kumari Jayawardena, *The White Woman's Other Burden: Western Women
and South Asia during British Rule* (New York: Routledge, 1995), 95-100.

8   Andrew Porter, "'Cultural Imperialism' and Protestant Missionary Enterprise, 1780-1914,"
JICH 25, no. 3 (1997): 367-91; Brian Stanley, *The Bible and the Flag: Protestant Missions and
British Imperialism in the Nineteenth and Twentieth Centuries* (Leicester: Apollo, 1990); and
Mary Taylor Huber and Nancy C. Lutkehaus, eds., *Gendered Missions: Women and Men in
Missionary Discourse and Practice* (Ann Arbor: University of Michigan Press, 1999).

9   On this point see Geoffrey A. Oddie, "'Orientalism' and British Protestant Missionary Constructions of India in the Nineteenth Century," *South Asia* 17, no. 2 (1994): 27-42; Andrew
Porter, "Cultural Imperialism," 368; and Huber and Lutkehaus, eds., *Gendered Missions*, 5-6.

10   For instance, Jane Haggis, "White Women and Colonialism: Towards a Non-Recuperative
History," in *Gender and Imperialism*, ed. Clare Midgley (Manchester: Manchester University
Press, 1998), 45-79, and also her "'Good Wives and Mothers' or 'Dedicated Workers': Con-
tradictions of Domesticity in the 'Mission of Sisterhood,' Travancore, South India," in
Maternities and Modernities: Colonial and Postcolonial Experiences in Asia and the Pacific, ed.
Kalpana Ram and Margaret Jolly (Cambridge: Cambridge University Press, 1998), 81-113.
For the quotation see Susan Thorne, *Congregational Missions and the Making of an Imperial
Culture in Nineteenth-Century England* (Stanford: Stanford University Press, 1999), 25.

11   Jean Comaroff and John Comaroff, *Of Revelation and Revolution: Christianity, Colonialism,
and Consciousness in South Africa* (Chicago: University of Chicago Press, 1991) and *Ethnography and the Historical Imagination* (Boulder: Westview Press, 1992). The Comaroffs' sophisticated work allows for subtlety, variety, and change in the interaction between missionaries
and indigenous people and a degree of compassion not often matched by colonial agents

and white settlers, but the religious element in the "long conversation" is given short shrift in their ultimate emphasis on missions as "the ideological arm of empire" (*Revelation*, 314) and missionaries as "footsoldiers of colonialism, the humble agents of a global movement" (*Ethnography*, 33). On the conflating of mission Christianity and colonialism, see also Antoinette Burton's fascinating *At the Heart of the Empire: Indians and the Colonial Encounter in Late-Victorian Britain* (Berkeley: University of California Press, 1998). Chapter 2 provides a portrayal of Pandita Ramabai, a Christian social reformer and convert from Hinduism, that presents her differences with her would-be spiritual mentors as essentially an expression of resistance to colonialism rather than an act of theological defiance or a disagreement over alternative courses of action. "Pandita Ramabai recognized," Burton asserts, "that, in the struggle for [social] reform in India, evangelical orthodoxy was a metaphor for imperial authority" (105).

12 Louise White, "'They Could Make Their Victims Dull': Genders and Genres, Fantasies and Cures in Colonial Southern Uganda," *American Historical Review* 100, no. 5 (1995): 1379-1402. For accounts of missionary doctors changing in response to indigenous medicine and/or their own lack of success see Lian Xi, *The Conversion of Missionaries: Liberalism in American Protestant Missions in China, 1907-1932* (University Park: Pennsylvania State University Press, 1997), chap. 1, and Terence O. Ranger, "Godly Medicine: The Ambiguities of Medical Mission in Southeastern Tanzania, 1900-1945," in *The Social Basis of Health and Healing in Africa*, ed. Steven Feierman and John M. Janzen (Berkeley: University of California Press, 1992), 256-82.

13 As, for instance, in Nicholas Thomas's *Colonialism's Culture: Anthropology, Travel and Government* (Cambridge: Polity Press, 1994), which ranges widely over south Pacific settings, and Gauri Viswanathan's, "'Coping with (Civil) Death': The Christian Convert's Rights of Passage in Colonial India," in *After Colonialism: Imperial Histories and Postcolonial Displacements*, ed. Gyan Prakash (Princeton: Princeton University Press, 1995), 183-210. Viswanathan's close analysis of a legal controversy in nineteenth-century India presents the agendas of converts, missionaries, and colonial officials as distinct from one another. While Susan Thorne's *Congregational Missions and the Making of an Imperial Culture* acknowledges complexity and change in relations between missions and imperial politics, it gives almost no attention to Christian converts and indigenous evangelists as dynamic influences on the missions/colonial nexus at home and abroad.

14 Ranger's "The Invention of Tradition in Colonial Africa," in *The Invention of Tradition*, ed. Eric Hobsbawm and Terence Ranger (Cambridge: Cambridge University Press, 1983), 211-62, has been helpful in my work at a broad level, while his *Are We Not Also Men? The Samkange Family and African Politics in Zimbabwe, 1920-64* (Harare: Baobab, 1995) has been useful as a case study for Chapter 1.

15 Stanley, *Bible*, 67; William R. Hutchison, *Errand to the World: American Protestant Thought and Foreign Missions* (Chicago: University of Chicago Press, 1987), 111.

16 Porter, "Cultural Imperialism," 371. The term, he observes, involves the conjoining of two "notoriously slippery" concepts (372).

17 T.O. Beidelman, "Social Theory and the Study of Christian Missions in Africa," *Africa* 44, no. 3 (1974): 235-49.

18 James G. Greenlee and Charles M. Johnston, *Good Citizens: British Missionaries and Imperial States, 1870-1918* (Montreal and Kingston: McGill-Queen's University Press, 1999).

19 See also A. Hamish Ion, *The Cross in the Dark Valley: The Canadian Protestant Missionary Movement in the Japanese Empire, 1931-1945* (Waterloo: Wilfrid Laurier University Press, 1999).

20 See Patricia R. Hill, *The World Their Household: The American Woman's Foreign Mission Movement and Cultural Transformation, 1870-1920* (Ann Arbor: University of Michigan Press, 1985), 168, and Robert, *American Women in Missions*, especially 273, 304-305, 313. By the 1920s, Hill writes, the national administrators of women's foreign missionary societies in the United States had renounced "a special and limited mission to women." Robert observes the same postwar phenomenon in the discourse of home-base women. It was not within the scope of either work to explore the overseas implications of shifts in domestic missionary discourse or of organizational changes that merged women's boards with men's.

21 Margaret Prang, *A Heart at Leisure from Itself: Caroline Macdonald of Japan* (Vancouver: UBC Press, 1995).

22 William Richey Hogg, *Ecumenical Foundations: A History of the International Missionary Council and Its Nineteenth-Century Background* (New York: Harper and Brothers, 1952).

23 On Perham see Barbara Bush, "'Britain's Conscience on Africa': White Women, Race and Imperial Politics in Inter-war Britain," in *Gender and Imperialism*, ed. Clare Midgley (Manchester: Manchester University Press, 1998), 200-23, and John W. Cell, "Colonial Rule," in *The Oxford History of the British Empire*, vol. 4, *The Twentieth Century*, ed. Judith M. Brown and Wm. Roger Louis (Oxford: Oxford University Press, 1999), especially 241, 247. See also Marion Shaw, *The Clear Stream: A Life of Winifred Holtby* (London: Virago Press, 1999), 172ff, for Holtby's involvement with the black labour movement in South Africa.

24 In *A World Mission: Canadian Protestantism and the Quest for a New International Order, 1918-1939* (Montreal and Kingston: McGill-Queen's University Press, 1991), Robert Wright argues that the "Christian internationalism" of the mainstream Protestant missions community left it largely uninterested in "secular international organizations" like the League of Nations (4). There is much evidence to refute this claim. Following the formation of the United Church of Canada in 1925, the Dominion Board of the Woman's Missionary Society opted to become a corporate member of the Canadian Society of the League of Nations and went on record as "whole-heartedly endorsing the League of Nations as the world's greatest instrument of peace" (*First Annual Report of the Woman's Missionary Society of the United Church of Canada*, 1925 and 1926, 19). Margaret Wrong's early support for the League of Nations fit seamlessly with her work with needy and often mutually hostile student groups during her Geneva-based WSCF years and also with her later work for African literature. The same continuity seems to have existed for two prominent Canadian political figures who were strong supporters both of overseas missions and of the League: former Ontario Liberal leader N.W. Rowell and Cairine Wilson, Canada's first woman senator. See N.W. Rowell, "The League of Nations and the Assembly at Geneva," *International Review of Missions* 10, no 3 (1921): 402-15; and Franca Iacovetta, "'A Respectable Feminist': The Political Career of Senator Cairine Wilson, 1921-1962," in *Beyond the Vote: Canadian Women and Politics*, ed. Linda Kealey and Joan Sangster (Toronto: University of Toronto Press, 1989), 63-85.

25 Dana L. Robert, "Shifting Southward: Global Christianity since 1945," *International Bulletin of Missionary Research* 24, no. 2 (2000): 50-58 (quoted phrase at 53).

26 Ralph D. Winter and Bruce A. Koch, "Finishing the Task: The Unreached People's Challenge," *Mission Frontiers* 22, no. 3 (2000): 22-26, 31-33.

27 Rebekah Chevalier, "Where Have All the Missionaries Gone?" in *Fire and Grace: Stories of History and Vision*, ed. Jim Taylor (Toronto: United Church Publishing, 1999), 37-42; Pamphlet entitled "Where in the World? The United Church of Canada participates in Development," Division of World Outreach/United Church of Canada, n.d. [1999].

Chapter 1: Challenge and Change in Interwar Missions

1 J. Paul S.R. Gibson, "Ideals of the Missionary Enterprise," *Indian Social Reformer* (hereafter *ISR*), 18 August 1934, 807-808; also "The Message of Christianity," *ISR*, 25 August 1934.

2 On the gap that could exist between the policy and the practice of women's work for women, even in the Victorian era, see Ruth Compton Brouwer, "Canadian Presbyterians and India Missions, 1876-1914: The Policy and Politics of 'Women's Work for Women,'" forthcoming in *North American Foreign Missions, 1810-1914: Theology, Theory, and Policy*, ed. Wilbert Shenk (Grand Rapids: William B. Eerdmans, 2002).

3 Andrew F. Walls, "The American Dimension in the History of the Missionary Movement," in *Earthen Vessels: American Evangelicals and Foreign Missions, 1880-1980*, ed. Joel A. Carpenter and Wilbert R. Shenk (Grand Rapids: William B. Eerdmans, 1990), 1-25. The US already had more than half the Protestant mission force in China by 1914. Even in India some 44 percent of Protestant missionaries were from the US by the early 1930s (missionaries were by far the largest American presence there); see Lian Xi, *The Conversion of Missionaries: Liberalism in American Protestant Missions in China, 1907-1932* (University Park: Pennsylvania State University Press, 1997), 6; and Laymen's Foreign Missions Inquiry (LFMI),

Fact-Finders' Reports, vol. 4, *India-Burma,* ed. Orville A. Petty, suppl. ser. (New York: Harper and Brothers, 1933), 24.

4 William Richey Hogg, *Ecumenical Foundations: A History of the International Missionary Council and Its Nineteenth-Century Background* (New York: Harper and Brothers, 1952), chaps. 4 and 5; Ruth Rouse and Stephen Charles Neill, eds., *A History of the Ecumenical Movement, 1517-1948* (London: SPCK, 1954), 366-73; and Keith Clements, *Faith on the Frontier: A Life of J.H. Oldham* (Edinburgh: T and T Clark, 1999), especially part 2 and 254-60.

5 Brian Clarke, "English-Speaking Canada from 1854," in *A Concise History of Christianity in Canada,* ed. Terrence Murphy and Roberto Perin (Toronto: Oxford University Press, 1996), 341-43; and Jessie H. Arnup, *A New Church Faces a New World* (Toronto: United Church of Canada, 1937), 240-42.

6 Hogg, *Ecumenical Foundations,* 202-10; William R. Hutchison, *Errand to the World: American Protestant Thought and Foreign Missions* (Chicago: University of Chicago Press, 1987), chaps. 5 and 6; George M. Marsden, *Fundamentalism and American Culture: The Shaping of Twentieth-Century Evangelicalism* (New York: Oxford University Press, 1980), 164ff, 221-22; and Robert Wright, *A World Mission: Canadian Protestants and the Quest for a New International Order* (Montreal and Kingston: McGill-Queen's University Press, 1991), 110-11.

7 Hogg, *Ecumenical Foundations,* chap. 6 and 286-304; Clements, *Oldham,* 78; Hans-Rudi Weber, *Asia and the Ecumenical Movement, 1895-1961* (London: SCM Press, 1966), 155; and Terence Ranger, *Are We Not Also Men? The Samkange Family and African Politics in Zimbabwe, 1920-64* (Harare: Baobab, 1995), 65.

8 Hogg, *Ecumenical Foundations,* 334-53.

9 Rouse and Neill, *Ecumenical Movement,* 368.

10 Hogg, *Ecumenical Foundations,* 211-14, 267, 333; K. Baago, *A History of the National Christian Council of India, 1914-1964* (Nagpur: National Christian Council, n.d. [1965]). In response to criticism from his New York counterpart about the amount of time he was giving to affairs in British Africa in the 1920s, Oldham pointed out that there was no mission organization in Africa equivalent to the national Christian councils in India, China, and Japan, where "the centre of gravity is in the field itself"; see New College Library, Edinburgh (NCL), Special Collections, J.H. Oldham Papers, box 4, ref. no. 4.8, Oldham to A.L. Warnshuis, 20 November 1928. Regarding divisions in Korea's Christian council see Yale Divinity School Library and Archives (YDL), microfiche of IMC Archives, Staff and Officers' Correspondence, mf box 26.11. 49, mf no. 14, William Paton papers, Travel Diary, Paton to Dear Friend, 7 December 1935.

11 Brian Stanley, *The Bible and the Flag: Protestant Missions and British Imperialism in the Nineteenth and Twentieth Centuries* (Leicester: Apollo, 1990), 155.

12 R.F. Jones, "Secular Civilization and the Christian Task," in *The Christian Life and Message in Relation to Non-Christian Systems: Report of the Jerusalem Meeting of the International Missionary Council, March 24th-April 8th, 1928,* vol. 1 (London: International Missionary Council, 1928), 338; and Clements, *Oldham,* 261.

13 Clifton J. Phillips, "Changing Attitudes in the Student Volunteer Movement of Great Britain and North America, 1886-1928," in *Missionary Ideologies in the Imperialist Era: 1880-1920,* ed. Torben Christensen and William R. Hutchison (Aarhuis, Denmark: Farlaget Aros, 1982), 131-45; William Ernest Hocking, *Re-Thinking Missions: A Laymen's Inquiry after One Hundred Years* (New York: Harper and Brothers, 1932), 289-90; and Wright, *World Mission,* 143.

14 Public Archives of Nova Scotia, Halifax (PANS), MMKC, vol. 2257, no. 85, Louise McCully to Edith McRae, 15 June 1923.

15 R. Laurence Moore, "Secularization: Religion and the Social Sciences," in *Between the Times: The Travail of the Protestant Establishment in America, 1900-1960,* ed. William R. Hutchison (Cambridge: Cambridge University Press, 1989), 233-52, quotation at 236.

16 For these tendencies in Oldham's life see Kathleen Bliss, "J.H. Oldham/1874-1969: From 'Edinburgh 1910' to the World Council of Churches," in *Mission Legacies: Biographical Studies of Leaders of the Missionary Movement,* ed. Gerald H. Anderson, Robert T. Coote, Norman A. Horner, and James M. Phillips (Maryknoll: Orbis Books, 1994), 577-78, and Clements, *Oldham.* Oldham's willingness to engage with the secular, scientific world, welcoming its benefits for humanity but challenging its indifference to spiritual concerns and the

centrality of human relationships is an ongoing theme in Clements's book, the first part of which incorporates some of Bliss's draft biography.

17 Grant Wacker, "Second Thoughts on the Great Commission: Liberal Protestants and Foreign Missions, 1890-1940," in *Earthen Vessels,* ed. Carpenter and Shenk, 292-94; "Mr Gandhi and Missions," *National Christian Council Review* 52, no. 1 (1932): 25-32; and NCL, Oldham Papers, Oldham to Sir A.F. Whyte, from Poona, 19 January 1922. By the late 1930s, attitudes to Gandhi had become more complex and fissured in reaction to his strong stand against mass movement evangelism; see Susan Billington Harper, *In the Shadow of the Mahatma: Bishop V.S. Azariah and the Travails of Christianity in British India* (Grand Rapids: William B. Eerdmans, 2000), chap. 9

18 Wright, *World Mission,* chap. 6.

19 For brief reference to these movements in Canada, see Clarke, "English-Speaking Canada," 343-48; also David B. Marshall, *Secularizing the Faith: Canadian Protestant Clergy and the Crisis of Belief, 1850-1940* (Toronto: University of Toronto Press, 1992), 201-204, and chap. 8; and Nancy Christie and Michael Gauvreau, *A Full-Orbed Christianity: The Protestant Churches and Social Welfare in Canada, 1900-1940* (Montreal and Kingston: McGill-Queen's University Press, 1996), 227-35. On the Oxford Group impact in Britain, see D.W. Bebbington, *Evangelicalism in Modern Britain: A History from the 1730s to the 1980s* (London: Unwin Hyman, 1989), 235-42.

20 Christie and Gauvreau, *Full-Orbed Christianity,* 227-34 and conclusion. A concern with strengthening social Christianity was also an important factor in the initial willingness of leading Canadian universities to bring sociology and social service within their purview, but a (putatively) disinterested approach to the "science" of social redemption eventually triumphed over religion and idealism; Marlene Shore, *The Science of Social Redemption: McGill, the Chicago School, and the Origins of Social Research in Canada* (Toronto: University of Toronto Press, 1987), and Sara Z. Burke, *Seeking the Highest Good: Social Service and Gender at the University of Toronto, 1888-1937* (Toronto: University of Toronto Press, 1996).

21 Clements, *Oldham,* chap. 17; Peter Ackroyd, *T.S. Eliot* (London: Hamish Hamilton, 1984), 243, 257.

22 Clements, *Oldham,* 255.

23 United Church Archives, Toronto (UCA), Glenna Jamieson Fonds, 3330, accession 88-002, box/file 003, Oliver, Notebooks and Diaries, diary for 1934, for example, entries for 22 February, 7 April, 15 December (hereafter Oliver diary/diaries with specific entries).

24 Hutchison, *Errand,* 138-45, quotation from Augustus Strong at 143.

25 For example, Richard Elphick, "The Benevolent Empire and the Social Gospel: Missionaries and South African Christians in the Age of Segregation," in *Christianity in South Africa: A Political, Social, and Cultural History,* ed. Richard Elphick and Rodney Davenport (Berkeley: University of California Press, 1997), 347-69.

26 UCA, Jamieson Fonds, Oliver diary, entry for 22 March 1937.

27 R. Fletcher Moorshead, *The Way of the Doctor: A Study in Medical Missions* (London: Carey Press, n.d. [1926]), chap. 8, quotation at 102-103.

28 Hocking, *Re-Thinking Missions,* 202.

29 Wright, *World Mission,* 135, 137-38. Wright maintains that Gollock's views on missionary preparation influenced the curriculum of the Canadian School of Missions, established in 1921.

30 Xi, *Conversion of Missionaries,* chap. 4.

31 James Dale Van Buskirk, *Korea: Land of the Dawn* (Toronto: Missionary Education Movement of the United States and Canada, 1931), chap. 5; UCA, William Scott, "Canadians in Korea: Brief Historical Sketch of Canadian Mission Work in Korea," typescript, 1975, 93-95. See also Bruce Cumings, *Korea's Place in the Sun: A Modern History* (New York: W.W. Norton, 1997), 57.

32 M.K. Gandhi, *Christian Missions: Their Place in India* (Ahmedabad: Navajivan, 1941), 44. This book brought together writings published periodically over the preceding decades, some of them based on talks to missionaries.

33 "The Reformer and Christian Missions," *ISR,* 18 November 1933, 187-88.

34 Judith M. Brown, *Modern India: The Origins of an Asian Democracy* (Delhi: Oxford University Press, 1985), 198; Baago, *National Christian Council,* 29-30; J.H. Oldham, "The Question of

a Conscience Clause in India," *IRM* 6 (1917): 126-41; Irene Mason Harper, "Tendencies in the Religious Education of India," *IRM* 17 (1928): 515-27, especially 520-21; Eleanor McDougall, "The Place of Religion in Indian Education," *IRM* 18 (1929): 358-69; and Hocking, *Re-Thinking Missions*, 127-28.

35 Lesslie Newbigin, *Unfinished Agenda: An Autobiography* (London: SPCK, 1985). Regarding Hilda Johnson, I am drawing on several conversations from the late 1980s as well as evidence in mission records, for instance, *Twenty-First Annual Report of the Woman's Missionary Society of the United Church of Canada, 1945-46*, 209-10, and *Twenty-Eighth Annual Report, 1952-53*, 174. By the latter date, Johnson, who now had a graduate degree in theology, was teaching at Union Theological Seminary in Indore. She also worked with the students' wives and did some evangelistic work with other women in the city, since, as she reported, "There has been no W.M.S. evangelistic worker in Indore for many years."

36 Lammin Sanneh, *Translating the Message: The Missionary Impact on Culture* (Maryknoll: Orbis Books, 1989); Richard Gray, *Black Christians and White Missionaries* (New Haven: Yale University Press, 1990); and Adrian Hastings, *The Church in Africa, 1450-1950* (Oxford: Clarendon Press, 1994). Hastings's study begins with the Ethiopian Church on the eve of Portuguese missionary activity. See also David Maxwell, "New Perspectives on the History of African Christianity," *Journal of Southern African Studies* 23, no. 1 (March 1997): 141-48.

37 Examining the work of the Church Missionary Society in Africa, T.O. Beidelman contended that in order to sustain interest at the home base, missionary propaganda deliberately misrepresented the realities of missionaries' roles: "Long after C.M.S missionaries became almost totally absorbed with administrative and technical duties, missionary training and literature ... continued to picture missionaries as directly encountering natives, speaking the languages of savages, and saving souls, even when missionaries rarely encountered untutored and illiterate Africans outside the fixed routine of a work or service situation in which prolonged proselytization was between Africans;" "Social theory and the Study of Christian Missions in Africa" (*Africa* 44, no. 3 [1974]: 235-49, quotation at 243). This is something of an overstatement for the contexts with which my research is most concerned, but it rightly emphasizes the existence of a gap between the literature and the reality.

38 A. Hamish Ion, *The Cross in the Dark Valley: The Canadian Protestant Missionary Movement in the Japanese Empire, 1931-1945* (Waterloo: Wilfrid Laurier University Press, 1999), chap. 2.

39 Ion, *Cross*, especially chaps. 9 and 10; Van Buskirk, *Korea*, chap. 2, quotation at 48.

40 Ranger, *Samkange*. Regarding the less well-known phenomenon of independent Protestant churches in China, see Daniel H. Bays, "The Growth of Independent Christianity in China, 1900-1937," in *Christianity in China from the Eighteenth Century to the Present*, ed. Daniel H. Bays (Stanford: Stanford University Press, 1996), 307-16.

41 Lamin Sanneh, *West African Christianity: The Religious Impact* (Maryknoll: Orbis Books, 1995), 169-73; and Harper, *Azariah*, chaps. 4 and 5 (quotation at 9). Despite Azariah's successes, however, no other Indian was made a bishop during his lifetime, not only because of the opposition of white Churchmen, Harper observes, but also because divisions among Indian Christians led them to regard a European bishop as less likely than an Indian one to favour his own subgroup.

42 Weber, *Ecumenical Movement*, 161.

43 M.K. Kuriakose, comp., *History of Christianity in India: Source Materials* (Madras: Christian Literature Society, 1982), 303-308, for Azariah's Edinburgh address; Carol Graham, "V.S. Azariah, 1874-1945: Exponent of Indigenous Mission and Christian Unity," in *Mission Legacies: Biographical Studies of Leaders of the Missionary Movement*, ed. Gerald Anderson, Robert T. Coote, Norman A. Horner, and James M. Phillips (Maryknoll: Orbis Books, 1994), 324-29, for changing percentages of conference delegates; and Hogg, *Ecumenical Foundations*, 293, for the quotation.

44 Ranger, *Samkange*, especially chap. 3, "Tambaram: A Re-making." On Baëta, see J.S. Pobee, ed., *Religion in a Pluralistic Society: Essays Presented to Professor C.G. Baëta* (Leiden: Brill, 1976), preface and chapter 10 by M.A.C. Warren. Baëta, who spoke four languages, went on to become vice-chairman of the IMC.

45 V.S. Azariah, for example; see Harper, *Azariah*, chap. 2, for his early years in YMCA work.

46 Xi, *Conversion*, 49, 163ff.

47 In using "race" as I do in this sentence, I am not seeking to vivify a discredited concept. It is, however, the word that would have been used in my subjects' era for differences now typically identified as national or ethnic differences.

48 UCA, Jamieson Fonds, Oliver diary, entry for 22 November 1940.

49 Ibid. Oliver's diaries reveal increases in the number and variety of her contacts with educated Indians and, especially with the new pressures created by the Second World War, greater self-consciousness among missionaries about their relationships with Indians. For examples, see entries for 21 and 31 January 1936; 10 March, 22 and 29 November, and 7 December 1940.

50 P.V. Benjamin, "Presidential Address," *Journal of the Christian Medical Association of India, Burma and Ceylon* 18, no. 3 (May 1943): 153; and interview with Dr. V. (Dassen) Benjamin, Bangalore, India, 10 November 1999. Although the missionary mentor in this case was Danish, Benjamin remembered him as having "a streak of British imperialism."

51 Newbigin, *Unfinished Agenda*, 41. The automobile has, of course, remained both a medium and a metaphor for social distance in postcolonial India, although "race" is no longer what separates the privileged insiders from those on the outside; see Pankaj Mishra's "The Other India," *New York Review of Books*, 16 December 1999, 98, 100, for a vivid example in the context of electioneering. I am grateful to Ramsay Cook for drawing this article to my attention.

52 Kuriakose, *Source Materials*, 303-308 for Azariah's address; and Ranger, *Samkange*, chap. 3, quotation at 70.

53 Elazar Barkan, *The Retreat of Scientific Racism* (Cambridge: Cambridge University Press, 1992). As Barkan points out, the new ideas that undermined scientific racism did not reach down to a mass public, but through such figures as anthropologist Bronislaw Malinowski they would have been familiar to missionary statesmen like Oldham, who in 1924 published *Christianity and the Race Problem* (London: SCM Press, 1924).

54 UCA, Jamieson Fonds, Oliver diaries, entries for 25 June 1935, 19 October 1936, and 14 February 1940.

55 The evolution of Murray's relations with Korean Christians emerges chiefly in the extensive correspondence with her family on which I draw for Chapter 3, where some of the friendships are discussed more fully.

56 Ranger, *Samkange*, chap. 5.

57 Because they typified my three subjects' experiences and that of missionaries generally, I have chosen in this section to focus on work-related and social relationships rather than on the shared homemaking arrangements and close same-sex friendships that sometimes developed between Western and indigenous Christian women, or occasional cross-race marriages such as that between Choné Oliver's Nagpur friend Irene Mott Bose (daughter of John R. Mott), and her Indian husband, Vivian Bose, a High Court judge. (For the Boses see Mary Ann Lind, *The Compassionate Memsahibs: Welfare Activities of British Women in India, 1900-1947* [New York: Greenwood Press, 1988]). For the same reason I have not dealt with missionary friendships with non-Christian nationals, although some of these evidently became quite close. See, for example, John Munro, comp., *Beyond the Moon Gate: A China Odyssey, 1938-1950. Adapted from the Diaries of Margaret Outerbridge* (Vancouver: Douglas and McIntyre, 1990).

58 Edward W. Said, *Out of Place: A Memoir* (New York: Knopf, 1999), 15.

59 T.J. Jones, *Education in Africa: A Study of West, South and Equatorial Africa* (New York: Phelps-Stokes Fund, 1922), and *Education in East Africa* (London: Edinburgh House Press, 1925); Clements, *Oldham*, 220-24 (quotation at 220); Richard Gray, "Christianity," in *The Colonial Moment in Africa: Essays on the Movement of Minds and Materials, 1900-1940,* ed. A.D. Roberts (Cambridge: Cambridge University Press, 1986), chap. 3, especially 182-90.

60 J.H. Oldham and B.D. Gibson, *The Remaking of Man in Africa* (London: Oxford University Press, 1931) is essentially a textbook for this gatekeeping approach to educating Africans. Interestingly, however, the word "remaking" in the title, which now seems to epitomize missionary imperialism, was borrowed from W.E. Hocking's *Human Nature and Its Remaking,*

a book about the philosophical basis for Christian education generally, which Oldham, who reviewed it, greatly admired; see Clements, *Oldham*, 213-14, 249-50.

61 For example, Edward H. Berman, "Educational Colonialism in Africa: The Role of American Foundations, 1910-1945," in *Philanthropy and Cultural Imperialism: The Foundations at Home and Abroad*, ed. Robert F. Arnove (Boston: G.K. Hall, 1980), 179-201, and, in a similar vein, Kenneth James King, *Pan-Africanism and Education: A Study of Race Philanthropy and Education in the Southern States of America and East Africa* (Oxford: Clarendon Press, 1971). Cf. John W. Cell, ed., *By Kenya Possessed: The Correspondence of Norman Leys and J.H. Oldham, 1918-1926* (Chicago: University of Chicago Press, 1976), introduction, especially 67-71. Cell recognizes the pragmatism that led Oldham to ally himself with various groups and individuals in pursuit of his causes and suggests that his approach made him "arguably the single most influential individual in the shaping of British official thinking and colonial policy toward Africa between the wars" (83). However, some of Oldham's fellow humanitarians, among them Leys and Victor Murray, believed that his pragmatism sometimes led him to betray his own causes. Thus, Leys, a physician and Christian socialist who briefly collaborated with Oldham in a struggle against the introduction of forced labour in Kenya, read his 1924 *Christianity and the Race Problem* with "great admiration and nearly complete agreement" but deplored his willingness to work cooperatively within the existing colonial framework (Clements, *Oldham*, 208, 246). Victor Murray, a British educator of missionaries, strongly criticized Jones and the Phelps-Stokes approach in *The School in the Bush* and thought that Oldham should do likewise. Oldham's response, characteristically, was that while the two Phelps-Stokes reports on Africa had "their limitations," Jones's involvement had the effect within the US of creating unprecedented interest in Africa and stimulating the work of mission boards; see NCL, Oldham Papers, box 5, ref. no. 5.4, Murray to Oldham, 8 January 1930, and Oldham to Murray, 18 January 1930. While collaboration such as that in which Oldham engaged may seem at first glance to confirm an impression that the "missionary project" was part of the larger "imperial project," close-grained analyses of his career (such as those provided by Cell and Clements) suggest a much more complex pattern.

62 Gray, "Christianity," 189. For a qualified illustration of Gray's point see Nnamdi Azikiwe, *My Odyssey: An Autobiography* (London: C. Hurst and Co., 1970), especially 37, 272-73.

63 A.D. Lindsay, *Report of the Commission on Christian Higher Education in India: An Enquiry into the Place of the Christian College in Modern India* (London: Oxford University Press, 1931), 3-5 (hereafter Lindsay Commission, *Report*). On Lindsay as a liberal Christian imperialist see Gerald Studdert-Kennedy, "Christian Imperialists of the Raj: Left, Right and Centre," in *Making Imperial Mentalities: Socialisation and British Imperialism*, ed. J.A. Mangan (Manchester: Manchester University Press, 1990), 127-43.

64 Lindsay Commission, *Report*, 349-50, 353.

65 Arthur Mayhew, "The Commission on Christian Higher Education in India," *IRM* 20 (1931): 512-24; Baago, *National Christian Council*, 50-52; Eleanor M. Jackson, *Red Tape and the Gospel: A Study of the Significance of the Ecumenical Missionary Struggle of William Paton (1886-1943)* (Birmingham: Phlogiston Press and Selly Oak Colleges, 1980), 112-21; and Hogg, *Ecumenical Foundations*, 274-75.

66 See *ISR*, 24 February and 10 and 17 March 1934 for articles and correspondence on the Christian colleges issue in the wake of the *Report*, and, for a useful overview, Mayhew, "Christian Higher Education." Despite its ostensible ongoing interest in making converts, the *Report* acknowledged the colleges' lack of success in this matter: "It is not probable that the total number of baptisms from all these colleges in the last ten years would be more than, if as many as, a dozen" (108).

67 See Hocking, *Re-Thinking Missions*, foreword and chap. 1, and Hutchison, *Errand*, chap. 6 for background; and Hocking, introduction to *Regional Reports*, vol. 1, for the concern with responding to criticism.

68 Hocking, *Re-Thinking Missions*, 15, 16.

69 Ibid., chap. 2 and summary at 326-27.

70 Hutchison, *Errand*, chap. 6; Xi, *Conversion*, 191-99; and Peter Conn, *Pearl S. Buck: A Cultural Biography* (Cambridge: Cambridge University Press, 1996), 148-51.

71 Jackson, *Red Tape*, 113-21 (quotation at 121); and Clements, *Oldham*, 269-71.

72 Hutchison, *Errand*, 175; Oliver, "On Re-Thinking Missions," *The New Outlook*, 18 January 1933, 58; and Hocking, *Re-Thinking Missions*, xiv. Wright's *World Mission*, 172, seems to me to overstate the negative reaction in the Canadian missions community. As he acknowledges, it was put forward as a mission study book by various groups.

73 Hogg, *Ecumenical Foundations*, 221-26, 263-65, 277-79, 322-25; and Baago, *National Christian Council of India*, 46, 87.

74 UCA, Jamieson Fonds, Oliver diary, quotation in entry for 15 November 1936.

75 Hogg, *Ecumenical Foundations*, 224; NCL, Oldham Papers, box 2, ref. no. 2.6, Gibson to "Dear Family," from India, December 1921; and box 4, ref. no. 4.9, Oldham to Dr. Lerrigo, 1 January 1929, and box 6, ref. no. 6.3, E.W. Thompson to Oldham, 2 October 1931, and Max Yergan to Gibson, 13 October 1931.

76 Jackson, *Red Tape*, 177; see also introduction, 14, regarding his unease with some women colleagues.

77 Hocking, *Re-Thinking Missions*, 169; "Secretarial Notes," *The Journal of the Christian Medical Association of India* 14, no. 1 (January 1939): 143; Report of All-India Women's Conference, *ISR*, 25 August 1934, 821; and Lindsay Commission, *Report*, 250-57 (quotation at 255). Debates about coeducation also took place among missionaries and colonial educators concerned with British Africa in the interwar era, but they had more to do with "moral" issues than with issues of quality, efficiency, and economy in higher-level educational institutions. In reality, so few upper-level schools existed in this era, especially outside South and West Africa, that coeducation was largely a non-issue as far as the employment of Western women was concerned. While some prominent senior educators in West Africa, including Aggrey and Principal Alex Fraser at Achimota, and the Rev. I.O. Ransom-Kuti at Abeokuta Grammar School in Nigeria, favoured coeducation as the best way to provide for and signal the importance of educating girls, there were others, both men and women, who saw segregated education as necessary to ensure that girls received access and attention. Interestingly, when higher education for women was being discussed in Uganda in the late 1930s, a separate women's college was envisioned; however, a decade later, Makerere College had been made coeducational and included at least one prominent woman faculty member. Oldham and Gibson, *Remaking*, chap. 9; Edwin W. Smith, *Aggrey of Africa: A Study in Black and White* (New York: Friendship Press for Phelps-Stokes Fund, 1929), 247-48; W.E.F. Ward, *Fraser of Trinity and Achimota* (Accra: Ghana University Press, 1965); Cheryl Johnson-Odim and Nina Emma Mba, *For Women and the Nation: Funmilayo Ransome-Kuti of Nigeria* (Chicago: University of Chicago Press, 1997), 43; and Sylvia Leith-Ross, *African Women: A Study of the Ibo of Nigeria* (1939; reprint, New York: Praeger, 1965). The Uganda situation is discussed in Chapter 5 in connection with Margaret Wrong's career.

78 Jessie Gregory Lutz, *China and the Christian Colleges, 1850-1950* (Ithaca: Cornell University Press, 1971), 157-58.

79 Hocking, *Re-Thinking Missions*, 266-68. See also YDL, microfiche of Joint IMC/CBMS Archives: India, NCC and CMAI records, mf box 398, mf no. 77, Choné Oliver to William Paton, 13 December 1929, 3, regarding several provinces that had introduced this requirement in legislation on nursing regulations.

80 Geraldine Forbes, *Women in Modern India*, The New Cambridge History of India, IV, 2 (Cambridge: Cambridge University Press, 1996), 72-83; and "Our Greatest Enemy is Purdah," *ISR*, 4 November 1933, 153.

81 On the slowness of devolution in women missionaries' work see Hocking, *Re-Thinking Missions*, 279-83.

Chapter 2: "Colleagues and Eventually Successors"

1 *Journal of the Christian Medical Association of India, Burma and Ceylon* (hereafter *Journal*) 18, no. 2 (March 1943): 102-103; quotation from C.S. Lewis, *The Screwtape Letters* (London: Geoffrey Bles, 1942), 21.

2 K.K. Pilley, *History of Higher Education in South India*, vol. 2, *University of Madras, 1857-1957, Affiliated Institutions* (Madras: Associated Printers, 1957), 234-38; and Gillian Paterson, *Whose Ministry? A Ministry of Health Care for the Year 2000* (Geneva: WCC Publications, 1993), vii, 2-3.

3 Edith Blumhofer, *Aimee Semple McPherson, Everybody's Sister* (Grand Rapids: William B. Eerdmans, 1993); and Janice Dickin, "Pentecostalism and Professionalism: The Experience and Legacy of Aimee Semple McPherson," in *Challenging Professions: Historical and Contemporary Perspectives on Women's Professional Work*, ed. Elizabeth Smyth, Sandra Acker, Paula Bourne, and Alison Prentice (Toronto: University of Toronto Press, 1999), 25-43. McPherson began her career in religion as a missionary wife in China.

4 G.N. Emery, "Oliver, Adam," *Dictionary of Canadian Biography*, vol. 11 (Toronto: University of Toronto Press, 1982), 651-53. Adam Oliver's political troubles were by no means uncommon in his era, and the charges against him arose in a context of sharp political party rivalries. Still, such controversies were not typical in Canadian missionaries' backgrounds.

5 This account of Choné Oliver's family background draws on Glenna Jamieson and Choné Williams, "Dr. Belle Choné Oliver, Woman Doctor: Healing the Whole Person, Body, Mind and Spirit," manuscript, chap. 1. I am grateful to Ms. Jamieson for providing me with duplicate copy of this and other materials on Choné Oliver, which she subsequently donated to the United Church/Victoria University Archives (UCA). See UCA, Glenna Jamieson Fonds, 3330, Accession 88.002, box/file 001-2, and Accession 88.029C, box/file 001-02, for Oliver's autobiographical "B.C. Oliver: Early Years and Story of School and College Life," written for her friend Margaret Coltart.

6 Kate Campbell Hurd-Mead, *Medical Women of America: A Short History of the Pioneer Medical Women of America and of a Few of Their Colleagues in England* (New York: Froben Press, 1933), 69-72; and Steven J. Peitzman, *A New and Untried Course: Woman's Medical College and Medical College of Pennsylvania* (New Brunswick, NJ: Rutgers University Press, 2000), 24-26, 65-67, 129.

7 Reasons for this development are discussed in Chapter 3.

8 Veronica Strong-Boag, "Canada's Women Doctors: Feminism Constrained," in *A Not Unreasonable Claim: Women and Reform in Canada, 1880s-1920s*, ed. Linda Kealey (Toronto: Women's Press, 1979), 109-29.

9 UCA, Jamieson Fonds, Oliver, "Early Years." Much of what the British called Central India is now part of Madhya Pradesh.

10 For women's role in the mission see my *New Women for God: Canadian Presbyterian Women and India Missions, 1876-1914* (Toronto: University of Toronto Press, 1990). For illustrations of Oliver's spiritual concerns in this period, see UCA, Jamieson Fonds, 88.002, box/file 003, Notebooks and Diaries, diary for 1903-1905 (includes some 1906 entries), entries for 22 January, 25 April, 24 May, 1903; 5 February and 5 November 1905; 14 and 27 January, 20 and 30 March, and 7 April 1906.

11 That the Oxford Group movement for a time attracted a good deal of attention in India as well as Europe and North America is evident from a series of articles and letters in the non-Christian and nationalistic *Indian Social Reformer* (*ISR*) in July and August 1934. Manilal Parekh wrote in the 11 August issue that in spite of its "bourgeois mentality," the movement served a useful purpose by ignoring doctrine and ritual and focusing on "the ethical and spiritual life."

12 On Jones's interest in ashrams, see Richard W. Taylor, "E. Stanley Jones, 1884-1973: Following the Christ of the Indian Road," in *Mission Legacies: Biographical Studies of Leaders in the Modern Missionary Movement*, ed. Gerald H. Anderson, Robert T. Coote, Norman A. Horner, and James M. Phillips (Maryknoll: Orbis Books, 1994), 339-47. Oliver, "Mr Gandhi and Missions," *Journal* 6, no. 3 (July 1931): 217-18; also ibid., 193, for Dr. Frimodt-Möller's article on the same subject; UCA, Jamieson Fonds, Notebooks and Diaries, diary entry for 18 March 1935.

13 UCA, Jamieson Fonds, box/file 001-02, "Dr. B.C. Oliver," autobiographical sketch.

14 Oliver worked, for instance to improve opportunities for Indian and Western nurses, called for more places for women in national and international mission councils, and strongly favoured the ordination of women in the United Church of Canada. See Yale Divinity School Library and Archives (YDL), microfiche of Joint International Missionary Council/Conference of British Missionary Societies Archives, India, National Christian Council and CMAI records (hereafter NCC-CMAI records), mf box 398, mf no. 77, Oliver to William

Paton, 13 December 1929 and mf no. 80, Oliver to Paton, 28 May 1936; UCA, Jamieson Fonds, Oliver diaries, entries for 13 April 1935, 22 and 30 March 1937, and 2 and 5 August 1940.

15 Discussed in Brouwer, *New Women*, chap. 5, especially 159.

16 "In Loving Memory of Dr. B. Choné Oliver," *Journal* 22, nos. 4-5 (July-September 1947): 187.

17 Ibid., 188; UCA Jamieson Fonds, "Dr. B.C. Oliver" (contains quotation). The *Survey of Medical Missions in India* was discussed under "Editorial Comment" in *Journal* 4, no. 4 (September 1929): 155-56, and in 6, no. 1 (March 1931): 41ff.

18 "Constitution and By-laws," *Journal* 1, no. 3 (July 1926): 108.

19 R. Fletcher Moorshead, *The Way of the Doctor: A Study in Medical Missions* (London: Carey Press, n.d. [1926]), chap. 8, especially 101-103.

20 Oliver, "Medical Missions at the Jerusalem Council," *Journal* 3, 3 (July 1928): 102-104.

21 Frimodt-Möller, "Medical Work and the Church," *Journal* 3, 4 (September 1928): 143-46.

22 Christian Medical Association of India (CMAI), *The Ministry of Healing in India: Handbook of the Christian Medical Association of India* (Mysore: Wesleyan Mission Press, 1932); and *Journal* 19, no. 4 (July 1944): 164.

23 CMAI, *Ministry of Healing*, 1, 2, 6.

24 For instance, Rev. William McE. Miller, "The Relation of Evangelism to Medical Missions," *Journal* 5, no. 3 (July 1930): 113-20, and, for Frimodt-Möller's and Oliver's replies, ibid. (September 1930): 229-30, and (November 1930): 286-88.

25 Quoted by Oliver in "The Why of Medical Missions," *Central India Torch* 6, no. 7 (December 1927): 1. Cf. Mary-Ellen Kelm, *Colonizing Bodies: Aboriginal Health and Healing in British Columbia, 1900-1950* (Vancouver: UBC Press, 1998), 146. Kelm perceives no such change among medical missionaries in BC in roughly the same period: "Proselytizing and assimilation were on the medical missionary agenda, and field workers were reminded that they worked for God first and science second. However elaborate the medical infrastructure they created, the reformation of Aboriginal bodies was only meant to carry out the task of winning souls."

26 She would later refer on several occasions to having begun the journey to a more satisfying understanding of the purpose of medical missions as a result of reading Dugald Christie's *Thirty Years in Moukden, 1883-1913* in 1915; see "Some Furlough Experiences," *Journal* 4, no. 6 (January 1930): 254, and "The Moukden Medical College," *Journal* 9, no. 6 (November 1934): 397.

27 The *Survey* had received favourable attention from such secular medical publications as the *India Medical Gazette* and the *British Medical Journal* as well as from Western mission organizations; National Council of Churches Library, Nagpur, *Proceedings of the Fourth Meeting of the National Christian Council* (hereafter NCC *Proceedings*, with date, or Executive Committee Meeting, with date), 17-20 December 1930, 21.

28 "Dr. B.C. Oliver," *Journal* 19, no. 4 (July 1944): 163.

29 David Arnold, *Colonizing the Body: State Medicine and Epidemic Disease in Nineteenth-Century India* (Berkeley: University of California Press, 1993), especially 13 and chap. 6. This was a general colonial pattern; Roy Porter, *The Greatest Benefit to Mankind: A Medical History of Humanity* (New York: W.W. Norton, 1997), 466, 478-79.

30 On the Dufferin Fund, see Maneesha Lal, "The Politics of Gender and Medicine in Colonial India: The Countess of Dufferin's Fund, 1885-1888," *Bulletin of the History of Medicine* 68 (1994): 29-66. For this pattern of imperial recognition in Oliver's own mission see Brouwer, *New Women*, chap. 6.

31 NCC *Proceedings*, 6-11 November 1926, 20; "Editorial Comment" on the *Survey, Journal* 4, no. 4 (September 1929): 156.

32 CMAI, *Ministry of Healing*, 44; Laymen's Foreign Missions Inquiry, *Regional Reports of the Commission of Appraisal*, vol. 1, *India-Burma*, ed. Orville Petty (New York: Harper and Brothers, 1933), 190.

33 Mary Pauline Jeffery, *Dr. Ida: The Life Story of Dr. Ida S. Scudder* (New York: Fleming H. Revell, 1938). The photograph is also reproduced in Kumari Jayawardena, *The White Woman's Other Burden: Western Women and South Asia during British Rule* (New York: Routledge, 1995), 79.

34 C.E. Vail, "Wanless, Sir William," *Journal* 8, no. 3 (May 1933): 193; Christopher H. Grundmann, "Wanless, William J[ames]," in *Biographical Dictionary of Christian Missions*, ed. Gerald H. Anderson (New York: Simon and Schuster and Prentice Hall, 1998), 717. For Gandhi's occasional use of Western medical treatments despite his aversion to interference with natural healing processes, see Roger Jeffery, "Doctors and Congress: The Role of Medical Men and Medical Politics in Indian Nationalism," in *The Indian National Congress and the Political Economy of India, 1885-1985*, ed. Mike Shepperdson and Colin Simmons (Aldershot: Avebury, 1988), 166-67.

35 LFMI, *Commission of Appraisal*, chap. 6, and *Fact-Finders' Reports*, vol. 4 *India-Burma*, suppl. ser., pt. 2 (New York: Harper and Brothers, 1933), 415-59, and William Ernest Hocking, *Re-Thinking Missions: A Laymen's Inquiry after One Hundred Years* (New York: Harper and Brothers, 1932), chap. 9; "The Survey," *Journal* 4, no. 4 (September 1929): 156.

36 CMAI, *Ministry of Healing*, chap. 7; LFMI, *India-Burma*, vol. 1, 192. The "examinations for licensure" at the medical schools led to degrees with varying designations, that at Vellore being a Licensed Medical Practitioner (LMP). The schools accepted some non-Christian students.

37 Indian Christians, Eurasians, and Parsis were very much over-represented in medical colleges before the First World War; Roger Jeffery, *The Politics of Health Care in India* (Berkeley: University of California Press, 1988), 84.

38 Jeffery, *Politics*, 74, 86; Arnold, *Colonizing the Body*, conclusion. After the First World War, as Jeffery notes, even the elite Indian Medical Service (IMS) began yielding more places to Indians. Arnold takes his account just up to 1914 but maintains that, already by that date, India's emerging elites with "their own political programs and professional agendas to pursue ... were beginning to see a more active, a more public-oriented, role for [Western-style] state medicine than colonialism had ever thought politically expedient or financially desirable" (294).

39 Judith M. Brown, *Modern India: The Origins of an Asian Democracy* (Delhi: Oxford University Press, 1985), 198. Admittedly, standards of medical training remained a "reserved subject" for the Government of India, and within the provincial governments there were those who worried the central government with their seeming willingness to advance indigenous systems of medicine and to relax Western standards in the institutions under their control, but as Jeffery points out, many nationalist politicians were really at one with the central government in favouring the exclusive advancement and the upgrading of Western medicine in India; see Roger Jeffery, "Recognizing India's Doctors: The Institutionalization of Medical Dependency, 1918-1939," *Modern Asian Studies* 13, no. 2 (1979): 301-26, especially 314, 323. See also his "Doctors and Congress."

40 Jeffery, "Recognizing India's Doctors," 306-8, 315-19.

41 The assumption that most Indian Christians were indifferent or opposed to nationalism was widespread and not ill-founded. Those Christians who were vocal nationalists and anxious to convert their fellow Christians to the cause tried to show that the two ideologies were not antithetical; see, for example, Cyril Modak, "To Christian Indians," *ISR*, 2 September 1933. This was the first in a series of such articles.

42 The Indian Christian community was very much a minority community. While more numerous than the Sikhs, Christians were less concentrated geographically, and, as noted, their religion, unlike that of the Sikhs, was deemed foreign. As Judith Brown has observed, the 1920s "saw increasing minority fears of the local use to which majority communities could put the resources of the new provincial power structures"; *Modern India*, 230. See also her "Who Is an Indian? Dilemmas of National Identity at the End of the British Raj in India" (paper presented at "Missions, Nationalism, and the End of Empire" conference, University of Cambridge, 6-9 September 2000).

43 Hocking, *Re-Thinking Missions*, 198.

44 YDL, NCC-CMAI records, mf no. 78, William Paton to Oliver, 9 March [1931], and mf no. 77, T.J. Joseph to Dr. Firor, 19 March 1931. The second of these concerns tended to be discussed in a low-key way rather than highlighted in publicity materials because, as Paton put it, there was a risk of their being perceived as "racial point[s]."

45 Ibid., letter of Joseph, and "Findings of the Committee on a Christian Medical College for Men for India," 5 and 6 September 1930; Douglas Forman, "Some Phases of Co-operation with Nationals in Christian Medical Work," *Journal* 11, no. 5 (September 1936): 377.

46 Oliver would have agreed with Gandhi that "morals are closely linked to health" although not with his statement that a "perfectly moral person alone can achieve perfect health"; see Joseph S. Alter, "Gandhi's Body, Gandhi's Truth: Nonviolence and the Biomoral Imperative of Public Health," *Journal of Asian Studies* 55, no. 2 (1996): 301-22 (quotation on 301). Likewise, while she sympathized with some of the teachings of Christian Science, she rejected its unwillingness to accept the role that scientific medicine could contribute to healing; see "Christianity and the Cure of Disease," *Journal* 8, no. 1 (January 1933): 1-13. The degree to which mind-body links in medical matters were in the air at this period and the pragmatic ways in which such ideas could be deployed is well illustrated in an editorial in the *Indian Social Reformer*. Arguing against admitting Jewish refugee doctors to practise in India, the editor maintained that such doctors would be ignorant of Indians' religious and cultural customs, and "the psychology of the patient ... is becoming recognized as the essential part of medicine"; see "Influx of Foreign Doctors," 3 March 1934, 420.

47 *Journal* 4, no. 1 (March 1929): 45; 4, no. 2 (May 1929): 91; and 4, no. 5 (November 1929): 238; YDL, NCC-CMAI correspondence, mf no. 77, Oliver to Paton, 13 December 1929.

48 YDL, NCC-CMAI records, mf no. 38, minutes of meeting of College Committee, 6 and 7 April 1931, and "Concerning the Proposed Union Christian Medical College for Men" (quotation at 3).

49 CMAI, *Ministry of Healing*, 45-46, 68; and Hilda Lazarus, "The Sphere of Indian Women in Medical Work in India," in *Women in Modern India*, ed. Evelyn C. Gedge and Mithan Chowski (Bombay: D.B. Taraporewale, 1929), 60.

50 NCC *Proceedings*, 17-20 December 1930, 26; CMAI, *Ministry of Healing*, 18; and Jeffrey, *Politics of Health Care*, 89-92. The proportion of Christian students declined in the 1930s as more non-Christian women took up the study of medicine.

51 CMAI, *Ministry of Healing*, 18, 69-71; Lazarus, "Sphere of Indian Women," 60. Even in the WMS, Indian women did not receive salaries equivalent to those of their Western counterparts; Geraldine Forbes, *Women in Modern India*, The New Cambridge History of India, IV, 2 (Cambridge: Cambridge University Press, 1996), 166-67.

52 This was perhaps least true of Parsis. In articles and correspondence in the *Indian Social Reformer* in the early 1930s dealing with the subjects of missionaries, Indian Christians, and nationalism, it is noteworthy that the authors, irrespective of their position in the debates, gendered their subjects male.

53 Jeffery, *Politics of Health Care*, 89-92; and Forbes, *Women in Modern India*, 164-65.

54 NCC *Proceedings*, 31 December 1931-4 January 1932, 56-58; and YDL, microfiche of Joint IMC-CBMS Archives, India, NCC records, mf box 395, mf no. 39, J.Z. Hodge to Paton, 22 April 1932, enclosing minutes of joint NCC-CMAI executive meeting.

55 For Hodge's views on these matters, see ibid., mf no. 37, Hodge to Paton 10 October and 24 October 1930, mf no. 38, Hodge to Paton, 6 July 1931, mf no. 39, Hodge to Paton, 30 October 1931. Regarding Datta and the NCC, see Keith Clements, *Faith on the Frontier: A Life of J.H. Oldham* (Edinburgh: T and T Clark, 1999), 195. On the Round Table conferences see Brown, *Modern India*, 261ff.

56 As Baago has noted in his history of the NCC, as a body it "neither identified itself with nor dissociated itself from the struggle for political independence," in part because the Government of India placed sharp restrictions on non-British missionaries regarding political matters, forbidding their own participation and enjoining them to promote loyalty among their mission-school students and even their Indian agents; see K. Baago, *A History of the National Christian Council of India, 1914-1964* (Nagpur: National Christian Council, n.d. [1965]), 37-39 (quotation at 37). In these circumstances, Hodge was circumspect in his public utterances. Thus, in an article entitled "The Christian Approach to Evangelism," he wrote that "the evangelist should make it clear that the Message he is charged to deliver is in no sense hostile to that deep love of country that claims the right to manage its own affairs" (*National Christian Council Review* August 1938, 423). But he evidently felt that he

could not go beyond cautious statements like this one and, therefore, looked to projects like a Christian medical college as an indirect means of providing Indians with opportunities to fulfill personal ambitions.

57 YDL, NCC-CMAI records, mf no. 78, Paton to Oliver, 9 March [1931]; and India-NCC records, mf no. 37, Paton to Hodge, 1 April 1931.

58 "A Problem in India Medical Missions, *Journal* 6, no. 5 (November 1931): 354-58.

59 YDL, India-NCC records, mf no. 40, Hodge to Paton, 22 April 1932, with minutes of joint meeting.

60 Ibid.

61 Ibid., Paton to Hodge, 11 May 1932. Firor, a Johns Hopkins surgery professor who had briefly been attached to Miraj, would be an ongoing enthusiast of the college scheme.

62 YDL, NCC-CMAI records, mf no. 79, Paton to Oliver, 12 March 1935.

63 UCA, Jamieson Fonds, Oliver diaries, entries for 30 and 31 December 1935 and 6 and 14 January 1936; "A Spirited Debate," *Journal* 11, no. 3 (May 1936): 238-39. Although the sanitized report in the *Journal* played down Paton's confrontational approach, his authorized biography acknowledges (citing a close friend) that "there were occasions when he was a little too ruthless and at meetings sometimes a little too compelling"; Eleanor M. Jackson, *Red Tape and the Gospel: A Study of the Significance of the Ecumenical Missionary Struggle of William Paton* (Birmingham: Phlogiston Press and Selly Oak Colleges, 1980), 13.

64 YDL, NCC-CMAI records, mf no. 80, "Informal Group for Consideration of Union Christian Medical College in India," 14 July 1936; Paton to Warnshuis and Paton to Goheen, 31 July 1936 (latter contains "green world"); and Warnshuis to Oliver, 5 October 1936. See also UCA, Jamieson Fonds, Oliver diary, entries for 17 April and 7 July 1936.

65 Letter to Dr. Forman [editor], *Journal* 9, no. 2 (March 1934): 118.

66 The *Journal* series began in May 1934 and continued to July 1935. The Japan situation was featured in 9, no. 3 (May 1934): 49-59; and PUMC in 10, no. 4 (July 1935): 296-306 (305 for "medical mecca"). For details of the Rockefeller takeover of what became PUMC, see also E. Richard Brown, "Rockefeller Medicine in China: Professionalism and Imperialism," in *Philanthropy and Cultural Imperialism: The Foundations at Home and Abroad*, ed. Robert F. Arnove (Boston: G.K. Hall, 1980), 123-46.

67 While the Lindsay Commission *did* express sympathy with the project in a brief reference to medical education, it also reported hearing from those who favoured only the more basic medical training required by men and women prepared to devote their lives to village medicine; A.D. Lindsay, *Report of the Commission on Christian Higher Education in India: An Enquiry into the Place of the Christian College in Modern India* (London: Oxford University Press, 1931), 272-73. This was, of course, similar to the message that would come to the forefront decades later among advocates of "barefoot doctors" and critics of "high-tech" medicine in development work.

68 YDL, NCC-CMAI records, mf no. 79, copy of Oliver to Arthur J. Lacy, 3 May 1934. The custodians of the Rackham Estate later decided that despite Rackham's expressed interest in "mankind everywhere," they would concentrate on the state of Michigan!

69 "Our Secretary: An Appreciation," *Journal* 7, no. 2 (March 1932): 100-101, and "The Secretary," 9, no. 4 (July 1934).

70 For example, YDL, NCC-CMAI records, Paton to Oliver, 12 March 1935.

71 "Possible Ancillary Functions of the Projected Medical College," *Journal* 7, no. 3 (May 1932): 159. Forman identified postgraduate training and benefits to the Indian medical profession at large as examples.

72 YDL, NCC-CMAI records, mf no. 77, Joseph to Dr. Firor, 19 March 1931.

73 Ibid., Oliver to Paton, 10 April 1930; interview with Dr. V. (Dassen) Benjamin, Bangalore, India, 10 November 1999.

74 Charles E. Harvey, "Speer versus Rockefeller and Mott, 1910-1945," *Journal of Presbyterian History* 60, no. 4 (1982): 283-99; Brown, "Rockefeller Medicine," especially 127, 123-24. Dr. Forman's early interview with the head of the Rockefeller Foundation evidently bore no fruit; YDL, NCC-CMAI records, mf no. 77, Oliver to Paton, 10 April 1930. Indeed, even before the Depression, a Foundation official had written to Ida S. Scudder that "he [Rockefeller] cannot undertake to go into the needs of individual institutions, no matter

how appealing the circumstances"; YDL, John R. Mott Papers, RG45, Series 1, General Correspondence, box 78, folder 146, Arthur Packard to Scudder, 31 December 1941, quoting from 6 June 1929 correspondence.

75 As IMC secretary, Paton never achieved Oldham's level of influence at the Colonial Office. However, by 1934 Oldham's involvement in IMC matters was largely nominal, and, in any case, Africa, not India, had been his main field of interest.

76 In his otherwise supportive letter of March 1931, Paton had warned Oliver that the project should avoid any hint of being "'put across' by a group of partisans." Later that year Hodge sought to reassure him that Forman's action in investigating land sites was wholly tentative and not self-serving. See YDL, NCC-CMAI records, mf no. 78, Paton to Oliver, 9 March, and Oliver to "The Editor of the Pioneer, Allahabad," 19 August 1931, regarding the premature press report; YDL, India-NCC records, mf no. 38, Hodge to "My dear Chief," 6 July 1931, contains Hodge's reassurance.

77 The assessment of Paton's concerns in this paragraph reflects Jackson's *Red Tape and the Gospel* as well as my own research.

78 See *National Christian Council Review* 66, no. 7 (July 1942): 299, and Clements, *Oldham*, 67, 177, for biographical information on Datta; YDL, NCC-CMAI records, mf no. 79, Oliver to Paton, 22 January 1935, for his opposition to the medical college scheme; and mf no. 77, Paton to Oliver, 13 March 1930, regarding a possible Christian university.

79 Harper, *Azariah*, chap. 9. Regarding Azariah's own education and his reservations about the value of higher academic and professional training as aids in village ministry, see 34, 201-202, 293.

80 YDL, India-NCC records, mf no. 38, Hodge to Paton, 10 April 1931, and fiche no. 39, Minutes accompanying Hodge to Paton, 22 April 1932; YDL, NCC-CMAI records, mf no. 77, Oliver to Paton, 17 April 1931, 5.

81 See, for instance, ibid., mf no. 79, Paton to Oliver, 12 March 1935.

82 Testimonial from Dr. Goheen with "For the Christian Medical College" [n.d.], in YDL, NCC-CMAI records, 1934, mf no. 79; and ibid., Oliver to Paton, 22 January 1935, for her correction of his reference to the "American College." For an example of Paton's concern about Americanization in the movement see YDL, India-NCC records, mf no. 39, Paton to Hodge, 2 February 1932. Cf. Lesslie Newbigin, *Unfinished Agenda: An Autobiography* (London: SPCK, 1985), 118-19.

83 LFMI, *Commission of Appraisal*, chap. 6, especially 176, 189, and LFMI, *Fact-Finders' Reports*, 415-59 *passim*; review of *Re-Thinking Missions* in *Journal* 8, no. 3 (May 1933): 155-66.

84 Letter of K.M. Harbord endorsing Dr. Brown's objections to the *Journal's* sympathetic response to *Re-Thinking Missions*, in *Journal* 9, no. 1 (January 1934): 37; also UCA, Jamieson Fonds, Oliver diary, entry for 10 June 1934.

85 LFMI, *Commission of Appraisal*, 194-96, and Hocking, *Re-Thinking Missions*, 209-10; Oliver, "Our Special Mission in the Light of Furlough Experiences," *Journal* 9, no. 3 (May 1934), 149-59 (quotation at 150 from the China Council on Medical Missions).

86 LFMI, *Commission of Appraisal*, xvii.

87 See, for example, her review essay on a volume entitled *Emotions and Bodily Changes*, in *Journal* 15, no. 3 (May 1940): 134-46, and no. 4 (July 1940): 207-17.

88 UCA, Jamieson Fonds, Oliver diary, entries for 29 March and 1 April, 1935.

89 Ibid., diary entries for 2 February and 25 September 1934; 27 January, 2 April, and 23 May 1935; 10 October and 11 January 1938; and box/file 001-2, "Oliver," 340. Canadian mission nurse Margaret Colthart was Oliver's closest friend for the last three decades of her life, albeit often at long distance. In Nagpur, Dr. Anna Martin, CMAI treasurer from 1934, acted as her physician as well as her confidant; regarding Coltart see Brouwer, *New Women*, 183-84, and for Martin, "In Memorium [sic]: Dr. Anna Martin," *Journal* 23, no. 3 (May 1948): 144-45.

90 YDL, NCC-CMAI records, mf no. 79, Oliver to Paton, 22 January and 15 May 1935, and mf no. 80, Oliver to Paton, 28 August 1936.

91 "Progress of Plans for a Union Christian Medical College," *Journal* 10, no. 5 (September 1935): 369-75, and 10, no. 6 (November 1935): 469-75.

92 On missions and leprosy see Sanjiv Kakar, "Leprosy in British India, 1860-1940: Colonial Politics and Missionary Medicine," *Medical History* 40 (1996): 215-30.

93 "Progress of Plans for a Union Christian Medical College," in YDL, NCC-CMAI records, mf no. 79 (quotations at 13).

94 NCC *Proceedings*, executive committee meeting, 10-13 January 1936, 1, and 1 and 2 December 1936, 8; "Meeting of the College and Executive Committee," *Journal* 11, no. 4 (July 1936): 320, 328. See also UCA, Jamieson Fonds, Oliver diary, entries for 24 April and 8 May 1936.

95 YDL, NCC-CMAI records, mf no. 80, "Informal Group for Consideration of Union Christian Medical College in India," 14 July 1936, and A.L. Warnshuis to Hodge, 16 July 1936.

96 "Our Affairs at the National Christian Council," *Journal* 12, no. 2 (March 1937): 117-18, and "College Affairs," 121; UCA, Jamieson Fonds, Oliver diaries, entries for 11 April, 26 October, 27 November 1936, 1 January 1937, and 11 January 1937; NCC *Proceedings*, minutes of executive meeting, 1 and 2 December 1936, 8, and minutes of Council meeting, 29 December 1936-1 January 1937, 51-52.

97 James A. Scherer, "Hume, Edward H[icks]," in *Biographical Dictionary*, 309; Lian Xi, *The Conversion of Missionaries: Liberalism in American Protestant Missions in China, 1907-32* (University Park: Pennsylvania University Press, 1997), chap. 1.

98 Hume, "A Report to the College Committee of the Christian Medical Association of India, Burma and Ceylon," *Journal* 13, no. 2 (March 1938): 108-23 (quotations at 112, 116).

99 YDL, NCC-CMAI records, mf no. 77, "Meeting of the College Committee," 6 and 7 April 1931, accompanying Oliver to Paton, 17 April 1931, and mf no. 79, Oliver to Paton, 15 May 1935; "Resolution Expressing the Will of Executive," *Journal* 13, no. 2 (March 1938): 132.

100 Information regarding Forman's role with Hume and the Nehrus comes from letter of Amy Forman [his wife] to their children, 30 December 1937. I am grateful to their son Douglas Forman for copied extracts from this letter. Regarding the Mott visit to Nehru, see UCA, Jamieson Fonds, Oliver diary, entry for 30 January 1937.

101 Ibid., diary entries for 24 July and 5 and 11 November 1937; see also entry for 5 January 1938 regarding further meetings with Madras officials.

102 YDL, NCC-CMAI records, mf no. 80, Oliver to Dr. Somervell, 23 April 1936, and Oliver to Paton, 28 August 1936; mf no. 81, Oliver to Paton, 25 February 1938, enclosing copy of C.R. Wierenga to Oliver, 22 February 1938.

103 Dorothy Jealous Scudder, *A Thousand Years in Thy Sight: The Story of the Scudder Missionaries of India* (New York: Vantage Press for the Scudder Association, 1984).

104 Earl C. Kaylor Jr., "Peabody, Lucy Whitehead McGill Waterbury," in *Notable American Women*, vol. 3 (Cambridge: Harvard University Press, 1971), 36-38. Vellore's governance was complex. Routine administration was managed by a senate, on which permanent staff members served, overseen by the local Vellore Council, which met at least annually. Decisions about senior staff appointments, expansion, and reorganization also involved the American and British sections of the Vellore Governing Board. Because the American section provided most of the funds, in practice it had an effective veto over non-routine decision making. See CMAI, *Ministry of Healing*, 106-107, and YDL, Pamphlet Collection, box no. HR441, FGS7414: Records of the Vellore Christian Medical Center, 1929-1960, 7-8, containing "Missionary Medical College for Women, Vellore, Incorporated," n.d., 3-4.

105 Valentin Rabe, "Scudder, Ida Sophia," in *Notable American Women: The Modern Period* (Cambridge: Harvard University Press, 1980), 634-36; Jeffery, *Dr. Ida*; and Dorothy Clarke Wilson, *Dr. Ida: The Story of Dr. Ida Scudder of Vellore* (New York: McGraw-Hill, 1959). Both Jeffrey's and Wilson's are hagiographic accounts that leave little room for other actors in the Vellore story. See also Jayawardena, *White Woman's Other Burden*, 78-79, and Maina Chawla Singh, "Missionary Legacies and Christ-Filled Doctors: Gender, Religion and Professionalisation in the History of Christian Medical College, Vellore," in *Knowledge, Power and Politics: Educational Institutions in India*, ed. Mushirul Hasan (New Delhi: Roli Books, 1998), 430-63. Perhaps the most telling illustration of Scudder's fame was a Ripley's "Believe It or Not" item (n.d.) reporting that a letter had reached her addressed only "Dr. Ida, India"; Radcliffe College, Schlesinger Library, Ida Sophia Scudder Papers, MC205, Unprocessed Addenda, 84-M159, box 1, vol. 1.

106 Singh, "Missionary Legacies," 447.
107 Schlesinger Library, Ida Sophia Scudder Papers, box 1, vol. 44, Scudder diary, entries for 23 January, 10 February, 27-28 March, 18 April, 1935; Vellore Christian Medical College Library, Archives Library, Minutes of the American Section of the Governing Board of the Missionary Medical College for Women, July 1934-October 1942 (hereafter Vellore Archives Library, Governing Board, American Section), "Report of the Campaign for Vellore Medical College, India, March 14 to April 30, 1936," by Mrs. Peabody, (quotation at 4).
108 YDL, NCC-CMAI records, mf no. 80, Oliver to Paton, 2 May 1936.
109 Schlesinger Library, Ida Sophia Scudder Papers, Unprocessed Addenda, 84-M159, box 1, vol. 2, form letter of 20 October 1937.
110 Quoted in Xi, *Conversion of Missionaries*, 114.
111 For example, "Report of the All-India Women's Conference Meeting," *ISR*, 25 August 1934, 821; and Lindsay Commission, *Report*, 253-54.
112 YDL, NCC-CMAI records, mf no. 81, C.R. Wierenga to Oliver, 22 February 1938, accompanying Oliver to Paton, 25 February 1938. Wierenga gave several reasons for the Council's decision: Vellore's constitution might not allow funds raised for a women's institution to be used for coeducation; those who had raised the funds might object; a majority of Council members objected to coeducation at Vellore; and the CMAI's proposal did not come accompanied by any funds of its own.
113 Ibid.; UCA, Jamieson Fonds, Oliver diary, entries for 8 and 9 February, and 13 March and 15 April 1938; "Re the Proposed Union Christian Medical College," *Journal* 13, no. 3 (May 1938): 217-18; "Sir H.T. Holland's Closing Address at the Delhi Conference," *Journal* 13, no. 4 (July 1938): 295-96; and "N.C.C. Action on Union Christian Medical College Scheme," *Journal* 13, no. 5 (September 1938): 381.
114 UCA, Jamieson Fonds, Oliver diary, entry for 20-22 April 1938; YDL, NCC-CMAI records, mf no. 81, Oliver to S.H. Dixon, 24 May 1938.
115 YDL, NCC-CMAI records, mf no. 82, "Minutes of the College Committee," 10 December 1938. Interestingly, the CBMS secretary suggested that the Vellore Council's negative response to the previous proposal may have been partly a matter of hurt feelings and implicitly called for more delicacy in a future approach (5).
116 Wilson, *Dr. Ida*, 279.
117 UCA, Jamieson Fonds, Oliver diary, entry for 1 June 1941.
118 Oliver, "At Tambaram," *Journal* 14, no. 2 (March 1939): 110-12; UCA, Jamieson Fonds, Notebooks and Diaries, diary entries for 12 December 1938 to 1 January 1939, and 8 and 28 January 1940.
119 Editorial, *Journal* 15, no. 4 (July 1940): 220.
120 See, for example, College Committee report to CMAI general conference in *Journal* 16, no. 2 (March 1941): 101-103; YDL, NCC-CMAI records, mf no. 83, "Extract from Dr. Oliver's Survey of Christian Medical Work in India, 1941."
121 Ibid., and Oliver to Paton, 22 March 1943. The problem of recruiting teaching staff was exacerbated by India's retaliatory response to the unwillingness of the US to recognize its medical degrees. Given this situation, some American medical missionaries went briefly to Canada to obtain certification there. See also J.C. McGilivray, "The Union Christian Medical College, Vellore," *IRM* 34 (1945): 319.
122 Minutes of Eighth General Conference of CMAI at Miraj, *Journal* 16, no. 2 (March 1941): 82-83; UCA, Jamieson Fonds, Oliver diary, entries for 28 June, 5-7 July, 14 and 17 August, and 9 and 12 October 1943.
123 UCA, Jamieson Fonds, Oliver diary, entries for 6 and 10 June 1941, and 6 August 1941.
124 Association Notes/Statement, *Journal* 17, no. 5 (September 1942): 281.
125 Vellore Archives Library, records of British Section of the Governing Board, Minutes of 8 October 1942, containing paraphrase of letter of J.C. McGilivray.
126 Vellore Archives Library, records of American Section of the Governing Board, Minutes, twelfth meeting of the corporation, 16 May 1941, 3. See also "Vellore Medical College," *National Christian Council Review* 62, no. 11 (November 1942): 483.
127 Wilson, *Dr. Ida*, 299; UCA, Jamieson Fonds, Notebooks and Diaries, diary entry for 31 January 1943. In her discussion of the transformation of Vellore from a women's medical

college to a coeducational institution, Maina Singh does not deal with Scudder's protracted resistance to the change or the role of the CMAI in initiating it; see Maina Chalwa Singh, *Gender, Religion, and "Heathen Lands": American Missionary Women in South Asia (1860s-1940s)* (New York: Garland, 2000), chap. 8, especially 297-302.

128   For a glowing tribute to Lazarus, obviously timed to establish her suitability as the first Indian principal of Vellore, see *Journal* 16, no. 6 (November 1942): 332-33, and, for Oliver's invitation, UCA, Jamieson Fonds, Oliver diary, entry for 18 February 1943. Like Oliver, Ida S. Scudder had long been eager to secure Lazarus for Vellore.

129   Association Notes/Statement, *Journal* 17, no. 5 (September 1942): 281-82; YDL, NCC-CMAI records, mf no. 83, Oliver to Paton, 22 March 1943. See also "In Loving Memory," *Journal* 22, nos. 4 and 5 (July-September 1947): 187-89.

130   "The Christian Medical College," and "Farewell Message from Dr. Oliver," *Journal* 19, no. 4 (July 1944): 157 and 170-71; "Reactions of the West to Christian Medical Work in India," *Journal* 22, no. 1 (January 1946): 40-41; interview with Dr. Jacob Chandy, Kottayam, India, 27 November 1999, and Dr. Jacob Chandy, *Reminiscences and Reflections: The Story of the Development of the Christian Medical College and Hospital, Vellore in the Healing Ministry of the Indian Churches* (Kottayam: CMS Press, 1988), chap. 5.

131   See, for example, "Appreciation[s]," by Sir Henry Holland and P.V. Benjamin, *Journal* 19, no. 4 (July 1944): 163-64; "In Loving Memory," *Journal* 22, nos. 4-5 (July-September 1947): 187-89. Oliver had briefly come back to India as temporary CMAI secretary in 1945 following the sudden death in office of her successor, but she herself was soon fatally ill with Hodgkin's Disease and returned home to die.

132   UCA, Jamieson Fonds, Oliver diary, entry for 19 June 1943; *Autobiography of Hilda Mary Lazarus* (Visakhapatnam: SFS Printing [n.d.]), 7; "Dr. Hilda Lazarus," typescript, n.p., n.d. Lazarus had been recruited in 1943 to serve as chief medical officer of the Women's Medical Service. She was also appointed to the Government of India's Health Survey and Development Committee (the Bhore Committee), whose 1946 report set out a blueprint for future medical developments in India. I am grateful to Professors Geraldine Forbes and John Paul for providing copies of Lazarus's autobiographical writings.

133   "Report of the Christian Medical College, Vellore," and "The Golden Anniversay of Dr. Ida S. Scudder," *Journal* 25, no. 1 (January 1950): 69-72, and no. 2 (March 1950): 91-92.

134   Unless, like Jacob Chandy (the young neurosurgeon referred to above), they had been recruited by Oliver or had benefited later from the Oliver Fund. Established at the time of her retirement, it was anticipated that part of the fund would go towards a professor's house and the rest for medical scholarships. No residence – or any other building – in her name was ever established at Vellore, although Oliver House was later built in Nagpur as a residence for the CMAI secretary. "Commemoration of Dr. B.C. Oliver," *Journal* 19, no. 4 (July 1944): 164-65; interview with Mrs. Ancilla D'Costa and Ms. Najoo Dungore, Nagpur, 3 November 1999 and visit to Oliver House.

135   YDL, NCC-CMAI records, mf no. 81, Oliver to S.H. Dixon, 24 May 1938.

136   Regarding the Bhore Committee, see note 132 above and Sir Henry Holland, "The Bhore Report," *Journal* 21, no. 5 (September 1946): 218-21.

137   "In Loving Memory," *Journal* 22, nos. 4-5 (July-September 1947): 188; YDL, NCC-CMAI records, mf no. 80, Paton to Goheen, 31 July 1936.

138   Regarding Frimodt-Möller, see p. 62 above; see also UCA, Jamieson Fonds, Oliver diary, entry for 26 July 1941, where she noted that in speaking about some matter, Hodge had referred to her as a man: "I think that meant a feeling of comradeship." For the borrowed phrase, see "In Loving Memory," *Journal* 22, nos. 4-5 (July-September 1947): 188.

139   Nancy F. Cott, *The Grounding of Modern Feminism* (New Haven: Yale University Press, 1987); Ellen S. More, *Restoring the Balance: Women Physicians and the Profession of Medicine,1850-1995* (Cambridge: Harvard University Press, 1999); Rosalind Rosenberg, *Beyond Separate Spheres: Intellectual Roots of Modern Feminism* (New Haven: Yale University Press, 1982). Also Deborah Gorham, *Vera Brittain: A Feminist Life* (Cambridge, MA: Blackwell, 1996) and Marion Shaw, *The Clear Stream: A Life of Winifred Holtby* (London: Virago Press, 1999). These two biographies have been chosen for purposes of illustration because they deal with two women (successful authors and each other's closest companions even after Brittain's marriage)

whose equal-rights feminism led them into diverse, ungendered causes; whose values bore marks of Victorianism even as they struggled to be "modern"; and who were conscious of themselves as women living in a transitional period. As well, books by Brittain were part of Oliver's eclectic diet of reading.

Chapter 3: The Triumph of "Standards" over "Sisterhood"

1 UCA, UCC, WMS, Overseas Missions, Korea Correspondence, box 83, file 51a, Murray to Ruth Taylor, 4 January 1947 (hereafter Korea Correspondence).

2 An earlier version of the main part of this chapter was published as "Beyond 'Women's Work for Women': Dr. Florence Murray and the Practice and Teaching of Western Medicine in Korea, 1921-1942," in *Challenging Professions: Historical and Contemporary Perspectives on Women's Professional Work* (Toronto: University of Toronto Press, 1999), ed. Elizabeth Smyth Sandra Acker, Paula Bourne, and Alison Prenctice, 65-95. Some of the material on Murray's postwar career was published in "Standards versus Sisterhood: Dr. Murray, President Kim, and the Introduction of Medical Education at Ewha Womans University, Seoul, 1947-1950," in *Nation, Ideas, Identities: Essays in Honour of Ramsay Cook*, ed. Michael D. Behiels and Marcel Martel (Toronto: Oxford University Press, 2000), 161-79.

3 The emergence of a new model of scientific medical education in early twentieth-century Canada following late nineteenth-century changes has been the subject of a number of articles focusing on specific settings. See, for example, R.D. Gidney and W.P.J. Millar, "The Reorientation of Medical Education in Late Nineteenth-Century Ontario: The Proprietary Medical Schools and the Founding of the Faculty of Medicine at the University of Toronto," *Journal of the History of Medicine and Allied Sciences* 49 (January 1994): 52-78; and Colin Howell, "Medical Professionalization and the Social Transformation of the Maritimes, 1850-1950," *Journal of Canadian Studies* 27, no. 1 (1992). A.B. McKillop's "The Healing Science" in his *Matters of Mind: The University in Ontario, 1791-1951* (Toronto: University of Toronto Press, 1994), 347-61, captures essential changes in the interwar period. For the United States see Kenneth M. Ludmerer, *Learning to Heal: The Development of American Medical Education* (New York: Basic Books, 1985).

4 For example, Ruth Compton Brouwer, *New Women for God: Canadian Presbyterian Women and India Missions, 1876-1914* (Toronto: University of Toronto Press, 1990), and Rosemary R. Gagan, *A Sensitive Independence: Canadian Methodist Women Missionaries in Canada and the Orient, 1881-1925* (Montreal and Kingston: McGill-Queen's University Press, 1992); and, in the United States, Jane Hunter, *The Gospel of Gentility: American Women Missionaries in Turn-of-the-Century China* (New Haven: Yale University Press, 1984), and Leslie A. Flemming, ed., *Women's Work for Women: Missionaries and Social Change in Asia* (Boulder: Westview Press, 1989). Even these books give only limited attention to medical missionaries, with the exception of one article in *Women's Work for Women*, mentioned below, in note 6.

5 For example, Dagmar Engels and Shula Marks, eds., *Contesting Colonial Hegemony: State and Society in Africa and India* (London: British Academic Press, 1994), part 3, and introduction, 11, for the quoted phrase; Geraldine Forbes, "Medical Careers and Health Care for Indian Women: Patterns of Control," *Women's History Review* 3, no. 4 (1994): 515-30; Louise White, "'They Could Make Their Victims Dull': Genders and Genres, Fantasies and Cures in Colonial Southern Uganda," *American Historical Review* 100, no. 5 (1995): 1379-1402; Megan Vaughan, *Curing Their Ills: Colonial Power and African Illness* (Stanford: Stanford University Press, 1991), chap. 3.

6 Roy Porter's *The Greatest Benefit to Mankind: A Medical History of Humanity* (New York: W.W. Norton, 1998) has few references to missionary medicine and Ellen S. More's *Restoring the Balance: Women Physicians and the Profession of Medicine, 1850-1995* (Cambridge: Harvard University Press, 1999) none at all. Karen Minden's *Bamboo Stone: The Evolution of a Chinese Medical Elite* (Toronto: University of Toronto Press, 1994) deals with the role of Canadian missionary medicine in "the process of technology transfer over time and between cultures," (3-4) but women doctors do not figure largely in her account or in Yuet-wah Cheung's brief sociological study, *Missionary Medicine in China: A Study of Two Canadian Protestant Missions in China before 1937* (Lanham, MD: University Press of America, 1988). Sara W. Tucker's "A Mission for Change in China: The Hackett Women's Medical Center of

Canton, China, 1900-1930," in Flemming, ed., *Women's Work for Women*, 137-57, is one of the few published studies directly related to the issue of the impact of new ideas of professionalism on the work of women who were medical missionaries.

7 Florence J. Murray, *At the Foot of Dragon Hill* (New York: Dutton, 1975), preface; UCA, biographical files for Florence and Alexander Murray; Public Archives of Nova Scotia (PANS), Maritime Missionaries to Korea Collection, MG 1, vol. 2276, file 1 (hereafter MMKC, with volume and file number); UCA, UCC, *Record of Proceedings, Thirty-Second Annual Meeting of the Maritime Conference*, 5-10 June 1956, 43, for obituary for Robert Murray; Robert Murray Personal Notebooks (RMPN), vol. 8, "Family Records." I am grateful to Heather Murray for making her grandfather's notebooks available to me and for providing information on her father, Charlie. For Charlie, see also William Repka and Kathleen Repka, *Dangerous Patriots: Canada's Unknown Prisoners of War* (Vancouver: New Star Press, 1982). For more information on Florence's early years, see my "Home Lessons, Foreign Tests: The Background and First Missionary Term of Florence Murray, Maritime Doctor in Korea," *Journal of the Canadian Historical Association*, n.s., 6, (1996): 103-28.

8 Murray, *At the Foot of Dragon Hill*, preface. See also Brouwer, "Home Lessons," 112-13. On early Maritime Presbyterian missions, see John S. Moir, *Enduring Witness: A History of the Presbyterian Church in Canada*, new ed. (n.p.: Eagle Press Printers, 1987), chap. 8. On the founding of the Korea mission see UCA, William Scott, "Canadians in Korea: A Brief Historical Sketch of Canadian Mission Work in Korea," typescript, 1975, and A. Hamish Ion, *The Cross and the Rising Sun, Volume 1: The Canadian Protestant Missionary Movement in the Japanese Empire, 1872-1931* (Waterloo: Wilfrid Laurier University Press, 1990), 31-33. In 1925 the mission passed under the control of the newly formed United Church of Canada.

9 Murray, *At the Foot of Dragon Hill*, ix-xii, and Dalhousie University Archives (DUA), Robert Murray and Family Papers, MS-2/535 (hereafter MFP), A-10, Murray to "Dear Papa," 3 March 1916; A-12, Murray to Father, 27 October 1918; A-13, Murray to Father, 23 July 1919; Enid Johnson MacLeod, *Petticoat Doctors: The First Forty Years of Women in Medicine at Dalhousie University* (Lawrencetown Beach, NS: Pottersfield Press, 1990), 60-68.

10 MacLeod, *Petticoat Doctors*, 62.

11 Minden, *Bamboo Stone*, 93; Gagan, *Sensitive Independence*, 42.

12 Abraham Flexner, *Medical Education in the United States and Canada: A Report to the Carnegie Foundation for the Advancement of Teaching* (New York: Carnegie Foundation, 1910), 320-21, 325; Charles Vevier, ed., *Flexner 75 Years Later* (Lanham, MD: University Press of America, 1987), 3-4.

13 T.J. Murray, "The Visit of Abraham Flexner to Halifax Medical College," *Nova Scotia Medical Bulletin* 64 (June 1985): 34-41; Sheila M. Penny, "'Marked for Slaughter': The Halifax Medical College and the Wrong Kind of Reform," *Acadiensis* 19 (Fall 1989): 27-51; P.B. Waite, *The Lives of Dalhousie University*, vol. 1: 1818-1925, *Lord Dalhousie's College* (Montreal and Kingston: McGill-Queen's University Press, 1994), 202-203, 245-48; Marianne P. Stevens, "The Rockefeller Foundation and Canadian Medical Education," *Research Reports from the Rockefeller Archive Center*, Spring 1999, 15.

14 Penny, "'Marked for Slaughter'"; Gidney and Millar, "Reorientation"; William G. Rothstein, *American Medical Schools and the Practice of Medicine: A History* (New York: Oxford University Press, 1987), 144-50.

15 Ludmerer, *Learning to Heal*, chap. 9 (quotation at 167).

16 The argument that Murray's religious upbringing strengthened rather than attenuated her concern for medical professionalism is developed in Brouwer, "Home Lessons."

17 Veronica Strong-Boag, "Canada's Women Doctors: Feminism Constrained," in *A Not Unreasonable Claim: Women and Reform in Canada, 1880s-1920s* (Toronto: Women's Press, 1979), 109-29; Ellen J. Smith, "Medical Missionaries, 'Ourselves Your Servants for Jesus' Sake,'" in *"Send Us a Lady Physician": Women Doctors in America, 1835-1920* (New York: W.W. Norton, 1985), 199; Steven J. Peitzman, *A New and Untried Course: Woman's Medical College and Medical College of Pennsylvania, 1850-1998* (New Brunswick, NJ: Rutgers University Press, 2000), 3, 66.

18 Carlotta Hacker, *The Indomitable Lady Doctors* (1974; reprint, Halifax: Formac Publishers, 1984), chap. 6; Brouwer, *New Women* 58; Patricia R. Hill, *The World Their Household: The*

American Woman's Foreign Mission Movement and Cultural Transformation, 1870-1920 (Ann Arbor: University of Michigan Press, 1985), 44, 129; Regina Markell Morantz-Sanchez, *Sympathy and Science: Women Physicians in American Medicine* (New York: Oxford University Press, 1985), 98-99; Peitzman, *Untried Course*, 3.

19 Morantz-Sanchez, *Sympathy and Science*, chap. 7.

20 Michael Bliss, *William Osler: A Life in Medicine* (Toronto: University of Toronto Press, 1999), 199-206.

21 Morantz-Sanchez, *Sympathy and Science*, especially 144 (for quoted phrase), chap. 7, and 242ff; Thomas Neville Bonner, *To the Ends of the Earth: Women's Search for Education in Medicine* (Cambridge: Harvard University Press, 1992), especially chap. 7; More, *Restoring the Balance*, 5. In Canada in 1921, only 1.7 percent of doctors were women; see Mary Kinnear, *In Subordination: Professional Women, 1870-1970* (Montreal and Kingston: McGill-Queen's University Press, 1995), 76 and 178.

22 Stewart Lone and Gavan McCormack, *Korea since 1850* (New York: St Martin's Press, 1993), chap. 1; Wi Jo Kang, "The Presbyterians and the Japanese in Korea," *Journal of Presbyterian History* 62, no. 1 (1984): 35-50; Allen D. Clark, *A History of the Church in Korea*, rev. ed. (Seoul: Christian Literature Society, 1971).

23 Carter J. Eckert, Ki-baik Lee, Young Ick Lew, Michael Robinson, and Edward W. Wagner, *Korea Old and New: A History* (Seoul: Ilchokak Publishers for Korea Institute, Harvard University, 1990), 254-69.

24 Chong-Sik Lee, *The Politics of Korean Nationalism* (Berkeley: University of California Press, 1963), part 3.

25 Lone and McCormack, *Korea*, 55; Donald N. Clark, *Christianity in Modern Korea* (Lanham, MD: University Press of America, 1986), xi.

26 Lone and McCormack, *Korea*, 78-82; Bruce Cumings, *Korea's Place in the Sun: A Modern History* (New York: W.W. Norton, 1997), 154-55.

27 James Dale Van Buskirk, *Korea: Land of the Dawn* (Toronto: Missionary Education Movement of the United States and Canada, 1931), 56; Scott, "Canadians," 87-95; Helen Fraser MacRae, *A Tiger on Dragon Mountain: The Life of Rev. Duncan M. MacRae, D.D.* (Charlottetown: Williams and Crue, 1993), 169-70.

28 For the autobiography of one such young man with connections to Canadian Presbyterian missionaries, see Younghill Kang, *The Grass Roof* (New York: Scribner's, 1931). As Van Buskirk acknowledges, the best (and best-off) students sought places in the government schools, given the greater prestige and profitability of such an education (*Korea*, chap. 5).

29 Kenneth M. Wells, *New God, New Nation: Protestants and Self-Reconstruction Nationalism in Korea, 1896-1937* (North Sydney, Australia: Allen and Unwin, 1990), quotations at 16.

30 Wells, *New God*, 8, 18, 161ff; Lone and McCormack, *Korea*, 80-81.

31 PANS, MMKC, MG1, vol. 2270, file 3, Robert Grierson, "Episodes on a Long, Long Trail," manuscript, n.d.; Scott, "Canadians," 66; Florence J. Murray, "Medical Work in the Canadian Mission," *The Korea Mission Field* (hereafter *KMF*) (May 1941): 78. Copies of this and other articles cited from *KMF* may be found in PANS, MMKC, MG1, vol. 2287, various files. See also Laura MacDonald, "'Minister of the Gospel and Doctor of Medicine': The Canadian Presbyterian Medical Mission to Korea, 1898-1923" (master's thesis, Queen's University, Kingston, ON, 2000).

32 Murray, *At the Foot of Dragon Hill*, 4; italics added.

33 PANS, MMKC, MG1, vol. 2276, file 1, 21 September 1921.

34 Ibid., Murray to Mother, 3 November 1921. She seems to have been referring to the journal of the Canadian Medical Association.

35 Ibid., file 3, Murray to "Dear People," 15 August 1922. In *Technology in the Hospital: Transforming Patient Care in the Early Twentieth Century* (Baltimore: Johns Hopkins University Press, 1995), Joel D. Howell identifies blood tests and x-rays (as well as urine samples) as procedures that went from being unusual to purely routine in the period between 1900 and 1925 in US hospitals.

36 PANS, MMKC, vol. 2276, file 3, Murray to "Dear Folks," 2 October 1922.

37 Sherwood Hall, *With Stethoscope in Asia* (McLean, VA.: MCL Associates 1978), chap. 1.

38 PANS, MMKC, vol. 2276, file 3, Murray to "Dear Father," 27 December 1922. Surgery was a speciality that was gaining status in North America by 1900, by which time "a handful of women" in the US had begun to demonstrate proficiency in it; Morantz-Sanchez, *Sympathy and Science*, 233.

39 Allen DeGray Clark, *Avison of Korea: The Life of Oliver R. Avison, M.D.* (Seoul: Yonsei University Press [1979]), chap. 7.

40 O.R. Avison, "Some High Spots in Medical Mission Work in Korea/Part 4 – A Medical School," in *KMF* 35 (July 1939), copy in PANS, MMKC, vol. 2287, file 7. Avison was himself a graduate of the University of Toronto Medical School and had briefly taught pharmacology there.

41 Clark, *Avison*, 112-15.

42 William Ernest Hocking, comp., *Re-Thinking Missions: A Laymen's Inquiry after One Hundred Years* (New York: Harper and Brothers, 1932), 199ff and 267 (for quotations). For a brief overview of the controversies created by the efforts of John D. Rockefeller Jr. to impose a corporate model on foreign missions through the wedding of ecumenism and US big business techniques see Charles E. Harvey, "Speer versus Rockefeller and Mott, 1910-1935," *Journal of Presbyterian History* 60, no. 4 (1982): 283-99.

43 See, for example, Yung-chung Kim, "Women's Movement in Modern Korea," in Sei-wha Chung, ed., *Challenges for Women: Women's Studies in Korea* (Seoul: Ewha Womans University Press, 1986), 75-102.

44 Hall, *Stethoscope*, 42; Martha Huntley, "Presbyterian Women's Work and Rights in the Korean Mission," *American Presbyterians* 65, no. 1 (1987): 40, 42-43. See also Yung-Chung Kim, ed. and trans., *Women of Korea: A History from Ancient Times to 1945* (Seoul: Ewha Womans University Press, 1976), chap. 18, especially 204.

45 Grant S. Lee, "The Growth of Medicine and Protestantism under Persecution: The Korean Experience," *Korea Journal* 29, no. 1 (1980): 40-41.

46 "The Canadian Mission Number," *KMF* (May 1941): 67, photocopy in PANS, MMKC, vol. 2287, file 228. See also Kang, *Grass Roof*, 174-75, 310-11.

47 Nor, clearly, had Dr. McMillan done so during her years of practice there; see Murray, *At the Foot of Dragon Hill*, 1.

48 PANS, MMKC, vol. 2276, file 8, Murray to Father, 24 August 1925.

49 Ibid., file 22, Murray to Alex, 15 March 1939.

50 Ibid., file 36, Annual Report for Hamhung Mission Hospital and Nurses' Training School, 1930, 2-3.

51 Ibid., 1, 15-18.

52 See, for example, Murray, *At the Foot of Dragon Hill*, 50, 184-85.

53 In Seoul, for instance, Professor Horace G. Underwood recalls that in the church his missionary family attended in 1923 "the curtains to divide the men and women were still there but were left open"; letter to author, 3 June 1997. Regarding the impact of the March First movement see Chung-yang Chung, "Women's Organizations and Their Activities," *Korea Journal* 4, no. 2 (1964): 14-17; and Sangduk Kim, "Chung-Hee Kil," in *Notable Women in the Life Sciences: A Biographical Dictionary*, eds., Benjamin F. Shearer and Barbara S. Shearer (Westport: Greenwood Press, 1996), 227-28.

54 Nancy F. Cott, *The Grounding of Modern Feminism* (New Haven: Yale University Press, 1987), especially 37 and chap. 7.

55 Rosalind Rosenberg, *Beyond Separate Spheres: Intellectual Roots of Modern Feminism* (New Haven: Yale University Press, 1982), quotation at 209.

56 More, *Restoring the Balance*, chap. 5, quoted phrase at 125.

57 UCA, Presbyterian Church in Canada, Board of Foreign Missions, Korea Mission Correspondence (KMC), box 8, file 118, William Scott to A.E. Armstrong, 19 January 1924; Brouwer, "Home Lessons," 121-23.

58 PANS, MMKC, vol. 2276, file 6, Murray to Alex, 20 January and to Mother, 9 February, 1924.

59 Ibid., file 7, Murray to Foster, 11 December 1924; file 8, to Father, 19 January, to Foster, 21 January, and to Mother 22 February, 1925.

60 I am grateful to Professor Horace G. Underwood of Yonsei University, Seoul, for reminding me of the fact that the kinds of frustrations Murray experienced were common to many

first-term missionaries and that their criticisms routinely targeted senior missionaries as well as local people; letter of 3 June 1997. What was perhaps unusual in Murray's case was the extent to which her frustrations were related to her professional work.

61 PANS, MMKC, vol. 2276, file 12, Murray to Alex, 27 October 1929; file 13, to Alex, 5 June 1930, and to "Dear Friends," 15 September 1930; "Our Korean Hospital," *The United Church-man*, 22 April 1931, 14.

62 PANS, MMKC, vol. 2276, file 13, Murray to "Dear Friends," 15 September 1930.

63 Murray, *At the Foot of Dragon Hill*, 97-102, 186-90; Murray, "The Tiger Year in Hamheung Hospital," *KMF* (September 1939): 184-86, and "Skirmishes With Tuberculosis," *KMF* (October 1940): 147-49, 154; copies in PANS, MMKC, vol. 2287, files 190 and 191. The *Canadian Medical Association Journal* featured a significant number of articles dealing with surgical treatment of tuberculosis during the decades that Murray was practising in northern Korea. See also Thomas Dormandy, *The White Death: A History of Tuberculosis* (London: Hambledon Press, 1999), chap. 22, "Collapse Therapy."

64 PANS, MMKC, vol. 2276, file 22, Murray to Alex, 2 August 1939; "Personal Report of 1938," *United Churchman*, 22 February 1939, 12.

65 PANS, MMKC, vol. 2276, file 17, Murray to Alex, 10 April 1934.

66 Kathryn McPherson, *Bedside Matters: The Transformation of Canadian Nursing, 1900-1990* (Toronto: Oxford University Press, 1996), especially chap. 2.

67 Murray, *At the Foot of Dragon Hill*, 161-63 (quotation at 163).

68 Ibid., 164; McPherson, *Bedside Matters*, 35-39.

69 PANS, MMKC, vol. 2276, file 12, Murray to "Dear Folks All," 12 May 1929; Murray, *At the Foot of Dragon Hill*, 162-65.

70 Murray, *At the Foot of Dragon Hill*, 163-64, and 169 (for quotation). Prior to the establishment of the nurses' training program at Hamhung, there appears to have been only one such program run by Protestant missions in Korea; see Institute of Social and Religious Research, *World Missionary Atlas* (New York: Institute of Social and Religious Research, 1925), 150.

71 Rhoda Kim Pak, "Medical Women in Korea," *Journal of the American Medical Women's Association* 5 no. 3 (1950): 116-17; Kim, "Chung-Hee Kil," in *Notable Women*, 226-30; Hall, *Stethoscope*, 332. I am most grateful to Dr. Bong Hak Hyun for providing copies of the articles by Pak and Kim.

72 "Personal Report of 1938" in *United Churchman*, 22 February 1939, 12; Murray, *At the Foot of the Dragon Hill*, 214.

73 PANS, MMKC, vol. 2276, file 8, Murray to Father, 24 August 1925. Dr. Hall had arranged in the 1890s for the American medical education of Dr. Esther Kim Pak, reportedly the first Korean physician to practise Western medicine in her country.

74 Murray's assumption was wide of the mark: many North American women doctors of her own and earlier generations continued to practise medicine after marriage. See Morantz-Sanchez, *Sympathy and Science*, 135-37, and Kinnear, *In Subordination*, 60, 61, 71. When she learned in 1930 that her sister Anna, a recent medical school graduate, was planning to marry, Murray was horrified, commenting twice in the same letter that it would be "her own funeral"; see PANS, MMKC, vol. 2276, file 13, Murray to Alexander, 26 April 1930.

75 Marriage in Korea *was* a near-universal phenomenon (Laurel Kendall, *Getting Married in Korea: Of Gender, Morality, and Modernity* [Berkeley: University of California Press, 1996]), but here, too, Murray was mistaken in assuming that women doctors who married entirely gave up practice; see, e.g., Sangduk Kim, "Chung-Hee Kil," in *Notable Women*, and autobiographical entries for Moon Gyung Chang and Duck-Heung Bang in *Women Physicians of the World: Autobiographies of Medical Pioneers*, ed. Leone McGregor Hellstedt (Washington: Hemisphere Publishing, 1978), 267-69 and 361-63.

76 Murray, *At the Foot of Dragon Hill*, 165, 168; McPherson, *Bedside Matters*, 191.

77 PANS, MMKC, vol. 2276, file 9, Murray to Mother, 4 April 1926; file 11, Murray to Alexander, 4 October 1928, and to "Dear Friend," 10 November 1928.

78 Ibid, file 9, Murray to Mother, 4 April 1926; Jung-Gun Kim, "'To God's Country': Canadian Missionaries in Korea and the Beginnings of Korean Migration to Canada" (Ed.D. thesis, University of Toronto, 1983), chap. 2.

79   See also PANS, MMKC, vol. 2276, file 19, Murray to "Dear People All," 12 November 1936. Here Murray explained that although Dr. Ahn, a valued former associate, now had his own private practice, she and he continued to consult each other and remained friends. During the 1930s Murray also lost the men whom she had trained as the hospital's druggist, business manager, and x-ray technician as each one left for other opportunities. While she found these losses inconvenient, she accepted them with little complaint; see ibid., file 20, to "Dear People," 11 October 1937; file 22, to Alex 15 March, and to Father and Mother, 20 April, 1939.

80   Ibid., file 23, Murray to Alex, 25 March 1940.

81   See, for example, ibid., file 15, Murray to "Dear Alex," 31 July 1932; file 17, Murray to Alexander, 1 June 1934; file 20, Murray to "Dearest People," 6 April, 1937; file 22, Murray to Alexander, 9 April 1939. Since, as the last of these letters indicates, it was not unusual for students in government-run medical schools in Korea to graduate without any hospital experience, Murray's concern for her teaching function was understandable.

82   Huntley, "Presbyterian Women's Work," 41.

83   PANS, MMKC, vol. 2276, file 7, Murray to her father, 28 August 1924.

84   See, for example, ibid., file 4, Murray to Alex, 16 June 1923, p. 8; and file 9, Murray to Mother, 24 March 1926. Murray's racialist discourse prior to and during her first term is discussed more fully in Brouwer, "Home Lessons."

85   For an example of her "positive orientalism," see PANS, MMKC, vol. 2276, file 19, Murray to "Dear People All," 12 November 1936. A tendency to "positive" orientalism sometimes developed as missionaries gained a better understanding of "their" people and took pride in their accomplishments, especially in the face of adversity. As Nicholas Thomas has observed, while depictions of the cultural differences of an "other" were (and are) almost invariably reductionist, they are not invariably hostile; see *Colonialism's Culture: Anthropology, Travel and Government* (Cambridge: Polity Press, 1994), 26.

86   After she returned from her first furlough, Murray's letters to family members tended to be freer of criticism generally, not just of Korean co-workers but also of her siblings and fellow missionaries.

87   PANS, MMKC, vol. 2276, file 12, Murray to "Dear Ones All," 14 February 1929; Personals column, *United Churchman*, 28 April 1930, 261.

88   PANS, MMKC, vol. 2276, file 11, D.M. MacRae to Murray, 24 February 1928; and ibid., Murray to "Dear Friend," 10 November 1928. The initiative had come from Dr. Hong himself, who had asked ordained missionary D.M. MacRae to write to Murray in Canada and ask her to make the necessary arrangements.

89   Ibid., file 22, Murray to Alexander, 9 April 1939; Murray, *At the Foot of Dragon Hill*, 146-47.

90   Ibid., file 12, Murray to Alexander, 5 September 1929; file 15, to Alexander, 27 April 1932; and file 23, to Father and Mother, 4 January 1940.

91   Murray, "Personal Report of 1938," *United Churchman*, 15 February 1939, 12. PANS, MMKC, vol. 2276, file 13, Murray to Alex, 27 January 1930 (second quotation).

92   Ibid., file 12, Murray to "Dear Folks All," 12 May 1929 (for quoted phrase), and 16 June 1929. In the 16 June letter, Murray noted that the local population was impressed by the significance of the fine house. The stark difference between the quality of missionaries' housing and that provided for indigenous mission workers had been a subject of reproach upon early missions in Korea, as elsewhere.

93   See, for example, ibid., file 9, Murray to Alex, 16 October 1926; file 12, to "Dear Folks," 12 July 1929; file 17, to Alex, 10 April 1934; Murray, *At the Foot of Dragon Hill*, 98-99.

94   PANS, MMKC, vol. 2276, file 20, Murray to "Dear Everybody," 22 January 1937 (first quotation); and ibid., 2 June 1937 (second quotation).

95   Telephone interview with Isabelle Johnston (Murray's niece), Toronto, 23 February 1996. The phrase originated with Mrs. Johnston's late husband.

96   PANS, MMKC, vol. 2276, file 20, Hamheung [sic] Station Report 1937-38, 7.

97   Florence J. Murray, "Medical Work in the Canadian Mission," *KMF* (May 1941): 79; copy preserved in PANS, MMKC, vol. 2287, file 228.

98   Ibid., also containing P.K. Koh, "Korean Doctor Takes Over Mission Hospital," *KMF* (May 1941): 79, 80; see also ibid., vol. 2276, file 24, Murray to "Dear Korea Folks at Home," 1 May 1941, and Murray, *At the Foot of Dragon Hill*, 228.

99   PANS, MMKC, vol. 2276, file 23, Murray to parents from Komahura, Japan, 14 January 1940.
100 Ibid., file 37, "Report of the Interim Committee of the Korea Mission of the United Church of Canada," August 1942, 1, 2, 12.
101 UCA, UCC, WMS, Korea Correspondence, 1933-45, box 3, file 51b, Murray to WMS, 13 March 1941; PANS, MMKC, vol. 2276, file 24, Murray to parents, 15 May 1941.
102 Ibid., file 37, "Report of the Interim Committee," 12; Murray, "Medical Work," *KMF* (May 1941), containing photograph of medical staff; copy in PANS, MMKC, vol. 2287, file 228.
103 Ibid., vol. 2276, file 37, "Report of the Interim Committee," 4.
104 Ibid., 4-5; Murray, *At the Foot of Dragon Hill*, 238-40.
105 According to Murray there were some three million refugees from the north in 1947; see her posthumously published *Return to Korea* (Belleville: Essence Publishing, 1999), 43. Christians were over-represented in the refugee population.
106 Scott, "Canadians in Korea," 171-80 (quotations at 180).
107 DUA, MFP, A-18, Murray to family, 7 and 17 August 1947, and A-19, 2 January 1948; Murray, *Return*, chap. 3. The bonds with Koreans from Hamhung remained strong even years later. Writing during the Korean War about encountering patients from there, Murray observed, "It is just about the same to meet someone from Hamheung [sic] as from Canada in a foreign land"; DUA, MFP, A-23, Murray to Father, 20 July 1952. Social gatherings with former Hamhung hospital staff continued into the late 1960s, although by then key figures like Dr. Koh had died; see ibid., G-2, Murray to "Dear Folks," 17 February 1967.
108 On the requests for the women missionaries and particularly Murray, see UCA, UCC, WMS, Korea Correspondence, box 83, file 51a, Mrs. Hugh Taylor to Murray, 16 May 1946; and Yale University Divinity School Library and Archives (YDL), RG11A, United Board for Christian Higher Education in Asia (UBCHEA), box 148A, file 1961, Ewha Co-operating Board (ECB), minutes of 18 May 1946. On Kim see *Grace Sufficient: The Story of Helen Kim by Herself*, ed. J. Manning Potts (Nashville: Upper Room, 1964), and Ewha Womans University Library (EWUL), Helen Kim Collection, Helen Kim, Personal History (curriculum vitae).
109 UCA, UCC, WMS, Korea Correspondence, box 83, file 51a, copy of Murray to Mr. Thomas Hobbs, 28 November 1946.
110 For Murray's unease about non-clinical teaching see ibid., box 83, file 51a, Murray to Mrs. Taylor, 21 May 1946, and regarding her tuberculosis work, file 51b, Murray to Mrs. Taylor, 10 October 1945, and Murray to Edith McKenzie, 15 April 1946. Regarding the Trudeau sanatorium see Dormandy, *White Death*, 176-86, and, for its most famous Canadian patient, Dr. Norman Bethune, who attempted thoracic surgery on himself while there, Ted Allen and Sydney Gordon, *The Scalpel, the Sword* (Toronto: McClelland and Stewart, 1978).
111 UCA, UCC, WMS, Korea Correspondence, box 2, file 25, Murray to Mrs. Taylor, 20 August 1947, and "Report on Medical Education by Florence J. Murray," September 1947; Murray, *Return*, chaps. 2, 5; DUA, MFP, A-18, Murray to parents, 7 and 17 August 1947. In her letter to Mrs. Taylor, the WMS secretary for overseas missions, Murray acknowledged that other members of the mission staff had thought her draft report on the situation at Ewha was "unduly pessimistic," but she pointed out that it was a personal, rather than a mission, report, one for which she had been asked by the Ewha Co-operating Board in New York (a mainly Methodist board on which the United Church had been represented since it had begun sharing in support for Ewha College in 1929). In the report itself, she stated that she was not seeking "to emulate the scale at which medical education is carried on in the west," but that there was nonetheless "a minimum of basal necessities that must be attained or the work is not worth doing" (1-2). During the war years, already overstretched medical schools and hospitals in Korea had deteriorated further, the schools experiencing double and even triple enrolment as the colonial government sought to meet wartime needs. Murray was concerned that if Ewha made a premature beginning in medical education, it would merely perpetuate the low standards established by wartime pressures. She also suggested that Korea could safely follow the pattern being adopted in India and China and move to coeducation in medical schools.
112 YDL, RG11A, UBCHEA, box 148A, file 1961, ECB executive committee meeting, 13 and 14 December 1947, and ECB, full board, 12 May 1948.

113   UCA, UCC, WMS, Korea Correspondence, box 83, file 51a, Murray, "1949 Annual Report" (quotation at 1). I have written more fully about Murray's Ewha interval in Brouwer, "Standards versus Sisterhood."

114   UCA, UCC, WMS, Korea Correspondence, box 83, file 51a, Murray, "1949 Annual Report"; Murray, *Return*, chaps. 5-8; DUA, MFP, A-20, Murray to Alexander and Esther, 27 July 1949.

115   For instance, YDL, RG11A, UBCHEA, 181A-2576, College Files, Yonsei, Murray, Florence J., 1949-53: Murray to Dr. R. Morris Paty, 14 April 1949; a note attached to this letter described Murray as "sane and judicious" in her recommendations. See also Murray, *Return*, 81.

116   UCA, UCC, WMS, Korea Correspondence, box 2, file 25, Murray to Mrs. Taylor, 20 August 1947; box 83, file 51a, "1949 Annual Report" (for quotation).

117   She had been prepared to go back to do relief work a year earlier and had asked the WMS about serving with a Red Cross medical team if no mission appointment could be arranged; see UCA, UCC, WMS, Korea Correspondence, box 83, file 51a, Murray to Mrs. Taylor, 9 October 1950, and 13 February 1951.

118   UCA, *Annual Report of The Woman's Missionary Society of the United Church of Canada*, 1951-52, 176ff, and 1952-53, 198ff; Murray, *Return*, chaps. 9, 10, 12, 14-16; PANS, MMKC, vol. 2276, file 29, Murray to "Dear Friends," (circular letter), 3 May 1952; "Story of the Years/Dr. Florence J. Murray," *Missionary Monthly*, August 1961; YDL, RG11A, UBCHEA, file 181A-2577, Murray, "Severance Hospital" [June 1954].

119   DUA, MFP, file A-23, Murray to father, 1 February 1952: "The Severance staff want Beulah and me to be there and help get them started on a modern basis as they want to get away from the old Japanese ways."

120   For example, DUA, MFP, A-23, Murray to father, 9 March and 13 April 1952 (April letter contains quotation).

121   DUA, MFP, A-23, Murray to father, 22 June and 20 July 1952.

122   DUA, MFP, A-23, Murray to father, 20 July; 17 and 20 August; and 23 November 1952 (quotation from July letter).

123   DUA, MFP, A-23, Murray to father, 27 July 1952.

124   DUA, MFP, A-23, Murray to father, 9 March and 26 October 1952, and A-24, Murray to father, 17, 24, 31 May, and 7 June 1953, and A-25, to father, 7 March 1954. What did trouble Murray greatly was the problems created by the birth of mixed-race children as a result of relationships between Korean women and soldiers, since such children, especially those of black fathers, were doomed to be social outcasts. She used extreme language to condemn irresponsible fathers, although the possibility that "Canadian boys" were among them seems not to have occurred to her, and she was full of sympathy for the women who had been their partners; see Murray, *Return*, 145-47.

125   PANS, MMKC, vol. 2276, file 29, Murray to "Dear Friends" (circular letter), 3 May 1952; DUA, MFP, A-23, Murray to father, 9 November 1952.

126   YDL, RG11A, UBCHEA, Yonsei, College Files, Murray to Douglas Forman, 23 August 1953; Forman to Murray, 29 March 1954; Murray to William Fenn, 1 April 1954 (regarding Dr. Moon) and 28 April; Fenn to Murray, 21 April 1954; Murray to Forman, 24 April 1954 (for "indifferent training"); and Murray, "Severance Hospital" (n.d., received by Board 7 June 1954). For Murray's recollection of these years, see her *Return*, chaps. 18, 19.

127   There is extensive discussion of this subject in YDL, RG11A, UBCHEA correspondence with Murray in files 181A-2578 and 181A-2579 for 1954-55. See, for example, Murray to Miss Mary Ferguson, 27 November 1954 and 30 March 1955, and to Prof. Bockholtz, 4 February 1955; and Ferguson to Murray, 2 February 1955 .

128   YDL, RG11A, UBCHEA, Yonsei, file 181A-2580, Murray to Frank Cartwright, 27 May 1958; to William Fenn, 28 May 1958; to Mary Ferguson, 23 June 1959; Murray, *Return*, chap. 21; "Story of the Years," *Missionary Monthly*, August 1961.

129   See DUA, MFP, A-25, Murray to father, 22 February 1954, for details of various birthday celebrations.

130   YDL, RG11A, UBCHEA, file 181A-2580, Murray to "Dear Friends of Korea" (circular letter), April 1959; Murray, *Return*, chaps. 22-29; DUA, MFP, G-3, Murray to "Dear Family Folks," 16 September 1968.

131 Florence Murray, "After 48 years in Korea," *United Church Observer*, July 1970, 21. See page 80 for a photo of the monument at "Murray Village."

132 DUA, MFP, file G-2, Murray to "Dear Folks," 19 June 1967 and to Norman MacKenzie, 11 May 1968; file M-4, newsletter from Murray, 7 May 1969; and Murray, "Biographical Notes"; YDL, RG11A, UBCHEA, file 181A-2581, Murray to "Dear Friends" (circular letter), n.d. [probably 1968]; interview with Rev. Frederick M. Bayliss, Toronto, 22 September 1995. In 1970, medical records librarian Rita Steeds arrived from Canada to initiate a professional training program. Mrs. Suhn-Hei Kim took over in 1973; Rita B. Steeds, *Woman Not Alone* (Chilliwack, BC: privately published, 1992), 145, 153, 177, 198.

133 DUA, MFP, file A-23, Murray to father, 1 June 1952, and G-2, Murray to "Dear Folks," 17 March 1967.

134 Interview with Dr. Anna Murray Dike Musgrave, Clarkesburg, ON, 25 June 1990; PANS, MMKC, vol. 2276, file 6, letter to Alex, 17 February 1924; file 8, to father, 24 August 1925; and file 12, to "Dear People," 5 August 1929, especially 2-3.

135 YDL, RG11A, UBCHEA, file 181A-2577, Murray to Dr. Fenn, 1 April 1954.

136 Murray, *Return*, 79 and chaps. 19, 21.

137 YDL, RG11A, UBCHEA, file 181A-2578, Murray to Dr. Fenn, 19 August 1954.

138 Regarding Dr. Kim see Murray, *At the Foot of Dragon Hill*, 232-33; DUA, MFP, file A-25, Murray to father 22 February 1954 and A-26, Murray to father, 1 May 1955; UCA, UCC, Florence Jessie Murray Papers, box 1, diaries, file 4, entries for 15 February and 2 April 1966, and file 8, entry for 19 February 1970. Information about Dr. Lee comes from her letter to the author, 20 August 1997, and from letter of Dr. Helen Mackenzie to author, 9 July 1997; also letter from Murray in *United Churchman*, 23 June 1965, 12.

139 UCA, UCC, WMS, Korea Correspondence, box 83, file 51a, Murray, "1949 Annual Report"; Murray, *Return*, 84-85; author's conversation with Dr. Jung-Jai Park, Seoul, 15 May 1997; DUA, MFP, file A-23, Murray to father, 4 May 1952, and A-26, to father, 3 January 1955.

140 UCA, tapes collection, tapes 303, 304, interview with Dr. Florence Murray; Murray, *At the Foot of Dragon Hill*, xiii.

141 PANS, MMKC, vol. 2276, file 16, Murray to Alex, 7 and 23 January 1933.

142 "Medical Work in the Canadian Mission," *United Churchman*, 16 July 1941, 15-16; ibid., for Murray letter of 6 March 1929, 13, and 30 December 1936, 12; Murray, *At the Foot of Dragon Hill*, 98-99, 157-59, 192-94.

143 See, for example, DUA, MFP, A-23, Murray to father, 15 June 1952, and A-24, to father, 12 and 24 May 1953.

144 UCA, UCC, Murray Diary, box 1, file 2, entries for 25 and 26 November 1964. See also DUA, MFP, A-24, Murray to father, 22 February and 4 March 1953, for Murray's reference to surgery and other hospital work as "my own work" and various church-related functions as "extras."

145 DUA, MFP, G-2, Murray to family, 18 May 1967.

146 DUA, MFP, file G-2 Murray to "Dear Folks," 4 August 1967.

147 Murray, "After Forty-Eight Years in Korea," *United Church Observer* (July 1970): 21.

148 UCA, UCC, Murray Diary, box 1, file 8, entries for 26 April and 26 June 1970; author's interview with Rev. Yu-Rak Kim, Hamilton, ON, 25 February 1997.

149 DUA, MFP, file G-2, Murray to family, 1 January 1967, and M-4, Murray newsletter of January 1967; PANS, MMKC, vol. 2276, file labelled "Florence Murray correspondence" but containing newspaper clippings related to retirement activities; UCA, taped interview with Murray.

150 Ibid., article entitled "Present Situation in Korea Alarms Former Missionary," from *Halifax Chronicle-Herald*, 3 February 1973.

151 UCA, taped interview with Murray for the quotation, and also Gretchen Pierce, "'The Whole World Is Waiting,'" *Mail Star* (Halifax), 21 January 1970. Cf. Stephen Lewis, "Lend a Hand," *Globe and Mail*, 25 May 2000, A15, adapted from his convocation address to graduates of the University of Prince Edward Island.

152 Pierce, "'The Whole World Is Waiting.'"

153 Donald Jones, "Deep from Seoul's Soul," *Toronto Star*, 1 March 1986, M3; and untitled article on the pagoda in *Vic Report* 16, no. 2 (1985-86), 11. The two men honoured were University of Toronto graduate Oliver Avison, the effective founder of Severance, and Newfoundlander Stanley Martin, who worked there in the interwar era.

Chapter 4: Books for Africa

1 "Miss Margaret Wrong," *Times* (London), 6 May 1949; Modupe Oduyoye, "The Role of Christian Publishing Houses in Africa Today," in *Publishing in Africa in the Seventies: Proceedings of an International Conference on Publishing and Book Development Held at the University of Ife, Ile-Ife, Nigeria, 16-20 December 1973*, ed. Edwina Oluwasanmi, Eva McLean, and Hans Zell (Ile-Ife: University of Ife Press, 1975), 229. An earlier version of this chapter was published in *International Journal of African Historical Studies* 31, no. 1 (1998): 53-71. The introductory paragraph is adapted from my article "Margaret Wrong's Literacy Work and the 'Remaking of Woman' in Africa, 1929-48," *Journal of Imperial and Commonwealth History* 23, no. 3 (1995): 427-52.

2 *Books for Africa: The Quarterly Bulletin of the International Committee on Christian Literature for Africa* (hereafter *BFA*), January 1931, 1.

3 UNESCO data for 1985 showed adult female illiteracy at 64.5 percent compared to 43.3 percent for males; H.S. Bhola, "An Overview of Literacy in Sub-Sahara Africa – Images in the Making," *African Studies Review* 33, no. 3 (1990): 12. Karin A.L. Hyde's "Sub-Saharan Africa," in *Women's Education in Developing Countries: Barriers, Benefits, and Policies*, ed. Elizabeth M. King and M. Anne Hill (Baltimore: Johns Hopkins University Press for the World Bank, 1993), 100-35, provides detailed national breakdowns.

4 School of Oriental and African Studies, University of London, International Missionary Council (hereafter SOAS/IMC), box 221, Advisory Committee on Education in the Colonies (ACEC), file on Training of Educationalists containing extract from letter to Miss Gibson, 21 April 1926, and box 213, Africa General/Education, file on Training of Teachers, 1929-30, containing Wrong's "Some Notes on African Elementary Education and the Training of Staff," 11-15; SOAS/ICCLA, box 512/10, file on Broadcast Talks, 1934-47, Wrong to Miss [Mary] Sheepshanks, 2 February 1934; written response to author's questionnaire from Mrs. Agnes Adesegbin, Nigeria, 17 January 1994, 5; letters to author from Rosalind Wrong Mitchison, 30 September and 11 October 1991.

5 For Margaret Read (1889-1991), see *Who's Who 1974*, 2713, obituaries in the *Independent*, 31 May 1991, and *Times*, 19 June 1991, 16, and Henrika Kuklick, *The Savage Within: The Social History of British Anthropology, 1885-1945* (Cambridge: Cambridge University Press, 1991), 213, 268, 269. Formerly a YWCA secretary in India, Read was a student of Malinowski in the 1930s at the London School of Economics and did field work in Northern Rhodesia and Nyasaland (Zambia and Malawi). From 1940 to 1955, she taught at the University of London Institute of Education and was head of its Department of Education in Tropical Areas. Her publications included *Education and Social Change in Tropical Areas* (1955) and *Children of Their Fathers: Growing up among the Ngoni of Nyasaland* (1959).

6 Nupur Chaudhuri and Margaret Strobel, eds., *Western Women and Imperialism: Complicity and Resistance* (Bloomington: Indiana University Press, 1992), introduction.

7 Great Britain, Colonial Office, *Report of a Sub-Committee on the Education of Women and Girls in Africa* (Africa no. 1169, February 1943). Wrong was part of the subcommittee. See also her "The Education of African Women in a Changing World," *Yearbook of Education* (London: University of London Institute of Education, 1940), 497-520, and Brouwer, "Margaret Wrong's Literacy Work."

8 For instance, the use of offensive terminology in the BBC's *The Listener* and Africans' lack of access to commissions in the wartime armed forces. Regarding the former see SOAS/ICCLA, box 512/10, file on Broadcast Talks 1934-47, for Wrong to Mr. Lambert, 8 March 1934. The reference to wartime commissions is in Wrong, "Book 1" [Journal], sequence for 27 September-20 October 1939, 31-32, in the Margaret Wrong segment of uncatalogued family papers held (at the time of this research) by Agnes Wrong Armstrong, Toronto, now deceased (hereafter Armstrong Collection).

9 These personal priorities and the broad range of Wrong's work are discussed more fully in Brouwer, "Margaret Wrong's Literacy Work."

10 Such men seem to exemplify Homi Bhabha's concept of colonial hybridity. Bhabha is not attentive to gender in developing the concept; in practice, his exemplars are typically male. See, for example, "Signs Taken for Wonders: Questions of Ambivalence and Authority under a Tree outside Delhi, May 1817," in Bhaba's *The Location of Culture* (London: Routledge, 1994), 102-22.

11 Michael Wade, *Peter Abrahams* (London: Faber and Faber, 1972); Peter Abrahams, *The View from Coyaba* (London: Faber and Faber, 1985). One could add the much better known case of Ngugi wa Thiong'o; see Carol Sicherman, "Ngugi's Colonial Education: 'The Subversion ... of the African Mind,'" *African Studies Review* 38, no. 3 (1995): 11-41.

12 See Florence Stratton, *Contemporary African Literature and the Politics of Gender* (London: Routledge, 1994), 7-8, where she points out that the problem of "assimilation through education," which modernizing African men would eventually come to resent, was one that women in colonial Africa seldom had to face; but it was a problem they escaped at considerable long-term cost to themselves.

13 Margaret Wrong, *Africa and the Making of Books* (London: ICCLA, 1934), chap. 1. Wrong identified three "stages of demand" (9) among African readers: Christian literature, particularly the Bible; textbooks and instructional works; and, well behind these, "general literature" for personal entertainment or development, read mainly by urban people. On the continuing small market for creative literature in Africa, see Chinua Achebe, "What Do African Intellectuals Read?" in his *Morning Yet on Creation Day* (London: Heinemann, 1975), 61-67, and Jan Raath, "Africa Finding Its Place in Crowded Literary World," *Globe and Mail*, 6 August 1994, Review section, C15.

14 O.R. Dathorne, *African Literature in the Twentieth Century* (London: Heinemann, 1974), 2-3; Ngugi wa Thiong'o, *Decolonising the Mind: The Politics of Language in African Literature* (London: James Currey, 1986), especially 69-70; T. Jack Thompson, "Speaking for Ourselves: The African Writers of Livingstonia," *Bulletin of the Scottish Institute of Missionary Studies*, n.s., no. 10 (1994): 24-35; Jeff Opland, "The Drumbeat and the Cross: Christianity and Literature," in *Christianity and South Africa: A Political, Social, and Cultural History*, ed. Richard Elphick and Rodney Davenport (Oxford: James Currey, 1997), 297-315.

15 On market literature see Peter Hogg and Ilse Sternberg, eds., *Market Literature from Nigeria: A Checklist* (London: British Library, 1990); Achebe, "Onitsha, Gift of the Niger," in *Morning Yet*, 153-9; entry on Cyprian Ekwensi in Hans Zell and Helene Silver, eds., *A Reader's Guide to African Literature* (London: Heinemann, 1972), 142-44. Ekwensi, an eventual recipient of the Margaret Wrong prize, contributed to this genre early in his career.

16 Wole Soyinka, for instance, is the great-great grandson of an ordained Yoruba clergyman, one of many African agents of the Church Missionary Society who served their "literary apprenticeship" writing for its publications; see J.D.Y. Peel, "Problems and Opportunities in an Anthropologist's Use of a Missionary Archive," in *Missionary Encounters: Sources and Issues*, ed. Robert A. Bickers and Rosemary Seton (Richmond, UK: Curzon Press, 1996), 70-94 and especially 74-78. Soyinka's own father was an Anglican headmaster, while Chinua Achebe's father was a catechist; see Soyinka, *Aké: The Years of Childhood* (London: Rex Collings, 1981), and Ezenwa Ohaeto, *Chinua Achebe: A Biography* (Oxford: James Currey, 1997).

17 For the International Institute of African Languages and Cultures (later called the International African Institute – the IAI), established in 1924 by missionary bureaucrats, scholars, and colonial officials, see Andrew Roberts, "The Imperial Mind," in *The Colonial Moment in Africa*, ed. Andrew Roberts (Cambridge: Cambridge University Press, 1986), 58, and Keith Clements, *Faith on the Frontier: A Life of J.H. Oldham* (Edinburgh: T and T Clark, 1999), 230. For the emphasis on vernaculars see, for instance, *BFA*, January 1931, and October 1941. The 1941 issue contained Ida Ward's "African Languages and Literature" (49-52). This emphasis reflected the belief of English-speaking missionaries and many British colonial reformers that early schooling should be conducted in indigenous rather than colonial languages.

18 "Wrong, George MacKinnon," *Dictionary of National Biography, 1941-50*, ed. L.G. Wickman Legg (London: Oxford University Press, 1959), 979-80; Armstrong Collection, Agnes Wrong

Armstrong, "A Canadian Family," manuscript, chap. 1; Carl Berger, *The Writing of Canadian History* (Toronto: Oxford University Press, 1976), 8-13. See also Richard Symonds, *Oxford: The Last Lost Cause?* (London: Macmillan, 1986), 243, 244, 277-78. Of the five Wrong children, four – Marga, Murray, Harold, and Hume – studied at Oxford.

19 Wrong obtained an MA in history in 1920. She had earlier become head of the University College Women's Union and in that role was involved in struggles to get new residential and recreational facilities for women roughly equivalent to Hart House, the resource-rich new centre for men's extracurricular activities. Her frustrations over controversies and delays in that matter, and perhaps a desire not to be locked into permanent responsibilities in her parents' household, made her well disposed to an offer of interesting overseas work in 1920. Armstrong Collection, Margaret Wrong to Murray Wrong, 15 April 1916, to Harry Gerrans, 7 September and 10 October 1920, and George Wrong to Gerrans, 15 August 1920; author's conversations with Mrs. Agnes Wrong Armstrong, 5 June and 18 December 1990; University of Toronto Archives, Vincent Massey Personal Records, box 140, files regarding U of T Memorial, Margaret Wrong to Massey, 1 December [1918], and Massey to Wrong, 6 December 1918.

20 Agnes Wrong Armstrong, "There's Too Much Waiting to Be Done," *Food for Thought* 16 (March 1956): 258-63, and Brouwer, "Margaret Wrong's Literacy Work," 429-31. On Carney see Richard Glotzer, "The Career of Mabel Carney: The Study of Race and Rural Development in the United States and South Africa," *International Journal of African Historical Studies* 29, no. 2 (1996): 309-36.

21 On these restructuring efforts see chap. 1, pp. 26-27. Recommendations for what became the ICCLA emerged from an international conference on the Christian mission in Africa at Le Zoute, Belgium, in 1926, but it was officially established at an IMC committee meeting in the US in the summer of 1929; William Richey Hogg, *Ecumenical Foundations: A History of the International Missionary Council and Its Nineteenth-Century Background* (New York: Harper and Brothers, 1952), 277-78. On Wrong's adaptability, Canadian identity, and "many years [of] international work" as qualities favouring her appointment, see Yale Divinity School Library (YDL), microfilm collection of IMC/ICCLA records, fiche 7, "M. Wrong's Appointment," unsigned copy of letter [probably from J.H. Oldham] to A.L. Warnshuis, 19 March 1929.

22 On Smith see Kuklick, *Savage Within*, 208, 313, and W. John Young, "The Legacy of Edwin W. Smith," *International Bulletin of Missionary Research* 25, no. 3 (2001): 126-30. Smith was the only missionary ever to become president of the Royal Anthropological Society.

23 Armstrong Collection, Wrong to parents, 12 August [1928]. On Achimota see Edwin W. Smith, *Aggrey of Africa: A Study in Black and White* (New York: Friendship Press for the Phelps-Stokes Fund, 1929), chap. 14.

24 Armstrong Collection, Wrong to parents, 6 September 1928 (includes "interracial work"); Wrong to Mother, 11 December [1928], and 11 January, 22 February, 8 March and 19 March 1929; and Wrong to Father, n.d. (latter two for "co-operative" and "pioneering" work). Wrong's WSCF position had involved her in work with ethnically and religiously diverse, sometimes mutually hostile, student groups in Europe, and with African American as well as white students when she did fundraising and promotional work in the US.

25 See "An Unknown and Yet Well-Known/in Memoriam Margaret Christian Wrong," 2, in Armstrong Collection for the quotation, and for more on their friendship, E.C. Graham, *Nothing Is Here for Tears: A Memoir of S.H. Hooke* (Oxford: Blackwell, 1969), 16-20. Family members likewise do not remember Wrong as especially devout; interviews with Agnes Wrong Armstrong, Toronto, 5 June 1990, and with June Wrong Rogers, Ottawa, 2 October 1992.

26 Armstrong Collection, Wrong to Mother, 9 April 1930. "He has invited me to Bagdad," she continued, "and says if I'll go in no other capacity I may go as a missionary."

27 Armstrong Collection, "An Unknown and Yet Well-Known," 2; and ibid., Carney, "First Tour of Africa (1926) /Personal Notes for the Memoir of Margaret Wrong," April 1948.

28 See, for instance, Armstrong Collection, Wrong to Mother, 11 December 1927, to Father, 12 October [1928], and to Mother, 29 November 1928. Wrong's interracial work extended to sending some of her non-white contacts on to her father in Toronto and to her diplomat brother, Hume, in Washington, when they were visitors to North America. That her elderly

father got into the spirit of this activity in a manner expressive of goodwill but also class and race consciousness is illustrated in the following excerpt from a letter describing his reception of "your coloured friend, Mr King": "I told Burgy [his second wife] that I was going to treat him as I do my more eminent friends, so we had sherry in the drawing room and a light wine at table. You cannot persuade me that the negro is not capable of rising as high as the white man, time and opportunity being equal" (Armstrong Collection, George Wrong to Marga, 19 June 1938).

29 J.W.C. Dougall, quoted in *BFA*, July 1948, tribute issue.

30 Address by John Read on the late Margaret Read in *Institute of Education Society Newsletter* 6, no. 2 (1991): 13-14; copy kindly supplied by Kate Hallett, archivist, University of London.

31 For public references to the intersecting private and public aspects of Wrong's career see, for instance, B.D.G. [Betty Gibson], "Margaret Wrong," *International Review of Missions (IRM)* 37 (July 1948): 292-94; Armstrong Collection, untitled posthumous tributes to Wrong by W.J. McAndrew, 25 May 1948, by Rev. J.O. Dobson, n.d., and by S.H. Hooke from the *Times*, 24 April 1948. For family perspectives I am grateful for letters from Oliver Wrong, 30 September and 28 October 1991; from Rosalind Wrong Mitchison, 30 September and 11 October 1991; from Charles Wrong, 31 October 1991; and from Jill Wrong Cant, 29 September 1999. As the unmarried daughter in the family, Wrong was also expected to take on particular responsibilities for her ailing mother despite living abroad. In seeking her parents' approval for the ICCLA job offer, she described it as providing an ideal opportunity to visit them regularly when on North American tours. Following her mother's death in 1931, she continued to correspond with Hume and her father about Murray's children and to involve them in her professional life by having them receive visitors such as Gandhi's associate C.F. Andrews and Read's mentor Bronislaw Malinowski as well as the non-white visitors mentioned in note 28. She took it for granted that George and Hume Wrong would willingly facilitate the North American itineraries of these visitors. See, for instance, Armstrong Collection, Hume Wrong letters, Hume to Marga, 20 January 1929, 2 April, 1933, and 26 November 1934; Margaret Wrong letters, Marga to father, 29 October 1928, and 20 January 1929; George Wrong letters, George to Marga, 20 and 27 October 1940.

32 J.T. Hardyman and R.K. Orchard, *Two Minutes from Sloane Square: A Brief History of the Conference of Missionary Societies in Great Britain and Ireland, 1912-1977* (London: Conference of British Missionary Societies, 1977), 13, 28-29.

33 The ICCLA was initially financed by mission boards belonging to its British and North American sections and by Bible societies, some publishers, and the Phelps-Stokes Fund. Later, as the ICCLA's work expanded, Wrong became adept at obtaining additional funding from the Carnegie and Rockefeller foundations and other agencies for specific projects undertaken by or linked to the ICCLA. See *BFA*, 1 January 1931, 1; Hogg, *Ecumenical Foundations*, 278, 332; Armstrong Collection, Wrong, "Memorandum on the Expansion of the Work of the International Committee on Christian Literature for Africa," 1 November 1934, and "International Committee on Christian Literature for Africa," November 1935.

34 Articles in *Listen* attributed to African women and girls included "From a Teacher's Diary" and "Washing Baby," January-February 1934; and "Mothers and Milk," September-October 1938. For calls for contributions see "A Page for Women," March-April 1940, and "Notes for Women," May-June 1942. *Listen's* efforts to encourage contributions by Africans came to include prizes for brief book reviews. The flood of correspondence from would-be contributors that Wrong described near the end of the period probably came mainly from men; servicemen had become an important new constituency during the war. See SOAS/ ICCLA, box 512/10, Circular Letters 1941-47, for her 16 March 1947 letter (4), also Hogg, *Ecumenical Foundations*, 332.

35 *BFA*, January 1931, 4-7.

36 Ibid., 14.

37 Thomas Mofolo, *Chaka* (London: Oxford University Press for IAI, 1931); *BFA*, January 1932; Nadine Gordimer, "English-Language Literature and Politics," in *Aspects of South African Literature*, ed. Christopher Heywood (London: Heinemann, 1976), 106-107.

38 She had briefly visited Egypt for the ICCLA in 1930 before proceeding to Germany and Switzerland for meetings with IAI and mission officials ("Secretary's Report," Armstrong Collection, ICCLA, April-May 1930). For a list of colonies/countries visited by Margaret Wrong, see Appendix 2 of this book.

39 Memoirs by Africans educated in the early twentieth century tell of learning and accepting "things that had nothing to do with our own lives, our history, or our languages"; see Monica Wilson, *Freedom for My People – The Autobiography of Z.K. Matthews: Southern Africa 1901 to 1968* (London: Rex Collings, 1981), 17, and also Phyllis Ntantala, *A Life's Mosaic: The Autobiography of Phyllis Ntantala* (Berkeley: University of California Press, 1993), 30.

40 Wrong, *Africa and the Making of Books: Being a Survey of Africa's Need of Literature* (London: ICCLA, 1934).

41 Armstrong Collection, Wrong, Letter 2, 5 August 1936, from Ekwendeni, 6; J.D. Rheinallt Jones, "African Authors' Conference/A Unique Gathering," *The Bantu World*, 14 November 1936, 17. On Shepherd's early role in promoting South African writing, see G.C. Oosthuizen, *Shepherd of Lovedale* (Johannesburg: Hugh Keartland, n.d.), chap. 18, and, for a more critical perspective, Jeffrey Peires, "The Lovedale Press: Literature for the Bantu Revisited," *History in Africa* 6 (1979): 155-75. The numbered letters that Wrong wrote during the tour were marked "Confidential/Not to be printed" and evidently intended to keep close colleagues informed of the progress of her work rather than to be grist for publication.

42 Rheinallt Jones, "African Authors' Conference."

43 Ibid. See also Tim Couzens, *The New African: A Study of the Life and Work of H.I.E. Dhlomo* (Johannesburg: Revan Press, 1985) and Catherine Higgs, *The Ghost of Equality: The Public Lives of D.D.T. Jabavu of South Africa, 1885-1959* (Athens, OH: Ohio University Press). Couzens discusses the conference (104-105) but Higgs does not.

44 Couzens, *New Africa;* Higgs, *Ghost of Equality;* Gordimer, "English-Language Literature," 108-109, and Tim Couzens, "The Social Ethos of Black Writing in South Africa 1920-50," 78, both in Heywood, ed., *Aspects*; Peter Abrahams, *Return to Goli* (London: Faber and Faber, 1953), 142-43, and *Tell Freedom: Memories of Africa* (New York: Knopf, 1954), 272-73.

45 Armstrong Collection, Letter no. 2, 6-7; Letter no.1, 1 June 1936, from Johannesburg, 12.

46 Ibid., Letter no. 2, 10-11.

47 Ibid., Letter no. 3, 2, 3.

48 Ibid., Letter no. 4, 30 October 1936, from Cape Town, 5, 8.

49 Regarding the Literature Bureau, see SOAS/ICCLA, box 512/10, Margaret Wrong Memorial Fund, file on "Prize Competition," list for 1958, Appendix B; C.P. Groves, *The Planting of Christianity in Africa*, vol. 4, *1914-1954* (London: Lutterworth Press, 1958), 134, 290-91; Oduyoye, "Christian Publishing," 229.

50 Armstrong Collection, Wrong, "Report on Tours in Africa 1936 and 1939," 8 April 1940, prepared for the Carnegie Corporation.

51 Ibid., Letter no. 1: Kenya and Uganda, 31 January 1939, from Juba, 6.

52 Hogg, *Ecumenical Foundations*, 332; W.E.F. Ward, *Educating Young Nations* (London: George Allen and Unwin, 1959), chap. 11; SOAS/ICCLA, file 509, 1944 West Africa Tour, containing Margaret Wrong Circular Letter, 29 December 1944.

53 J.D. Hargreaves, *Decolonization in Africa* (London: Longman, 1988), 61-62; Patricia Pugh, *Educate, Agitate, Organize: 100 Years of Fabian Socialism* (London: Methuen, 1984), chap. 18. Wrong identified herself as a member of the Fabian Colonial Bureau in promotional material and contributed a chapter to Rita Hinden, ed., *Fabian Colonial Essays* (London: Allen and Unwin, 1945).

54 See SOAS/ICCLA, box 512/10, file on Colonial Development, 1940-45, especially for her "The Future of British African Colonies," 5 January 1942; and Wrong, "Colonial Development and Welfare," *IRM* 29 (October 1940): 470-76.

55 University of Lagos Library, S.I. Kale Collection, Correspondence file, March 1933-December 1948, Wrong to Kale, 13 August 1941.

56 Ibid.; SOAS/ICCLA, box 501/2, Minutes (British Section), 23 February 1940; communication of 13 February 1992 from Trevor White, enquiry assistant, BBC, to Brouwer.

57 Advisory Committee on Education in the Colonies (ACEC), *Mass Education in African Society* (London, 1944, reprinted 1945), Appendix 2; *BFA*, January 1943: 10-13; National Archives of Ghana (NAG), RG3/1/206, "Report on Mass Education ... Distribution of," 30, 34.

58 SOAS/ICCLA, box 512/10, file of Circular Letters, 14 February 1944 and Easter Monday, 1945; NAG, RG3/1/323, Margaret Wrong, "Report on Literacy and Adult Education in the Gold Coast" [1945].

59 NAG, RG3/1/323, Miss Margaret Wrong/ Report/Literacy and Adult Education in Ghana: Wrong to Mr. Barton, 12 June 1945 (1), and "Mss. in the hands of Publishers." Included for proposed translation were a book about Abe Lincoln and stories based on Grimms' fairy tales; indigenous work included Ewe proverbs and "Infant Singing in African Schools" in Ga. See also RG3/1/37, Arrangements for Publication of Manuscripts (1943 to 1970), especially Wrong to Barton, 22 October 1946, and Barton to Wrong, 30 November 1946; and J.B. Danquah, to Director of Education, 29 May 1957. Danquah, one of the earliest Gold Coast men to obtain a doctorate in England and, later, an ardent nationalist and an authority on his country's legal history, was seeking publication assistance.

60 M.M. Green, "Ward, Ida Caroline," *Dictionary of National Biography, 1941-1950*, ed. L.G. Wickman Legg (London: Oxford University Press, 1959), 925-26; Ward, "African Languages and Literature," *BFA*, October 1941. Here Ward wrote: "The African should not make the mistake of thinking this [writing instructional literature] is an elementary and simple task, unworthy of a trained mind." The concern that well-educated Africans *did* hold this view was something of a refrain among colonial reformers like Ward and Wrong, one which seemed not to take account of the fact that this elite might have no interest in writing about subjects such as improving soil productivity and Christian family life, however worthwhile they might be. Clearly, it was one thing to encourage and assist indigenous writers; it was quite another to refrain from trying to shape their agendas.

61 SOAS/ICCLA, box 511/9, Articles, 1940-45. In the absence of a central collection of African publications in England, the ICCLA itself sometimes tried to meet specific requests; see University of Lagos Library, Chief Ladipo Solanke Papers, Wrong to Solanke, 4 November 1943, in response to his enquiry about Nigerian newspapers. My thanks to Nina Mba for this reference.

62 SOAS/ICCLA, "Importance of Literature," 14.

63 SOAS/IMC: Africa General/ box 204, IIALC/ File: IAI-Memoranda, 1943-47, DF [Darryl Forde], "Notes on the Position and Prospects of the IAI," n.d. [probably 1946]; File: IAI/ Correspondence, Vischer, 1926-44, letters to Miss Betty Gibson, 20 February 1941 and 30 June 1943; "Obituary/Miss Margaret Wrong," *Africa* 13 (July 1948): 207.

64 Several sets of documents in the Rockefeller Archive Center (RAC) provide information on Wrong's professional and personal links with Davis and his growing interest in African affairs. See GEB, series 1, box 288, folder 3008, Margaret Wrong, 1942-1945, and, in particular, Wrong to Davis, "confidential," 20 December 1943, urging him to join a survey team to West Africa. For the evolution of his plans to tour Africa and the decision to link up with Wrong, see Jackson Davis, Diaries [interviews and memoranda], series 12, vols. 6 and 7. Regarding meetings about the IAI see vol. 8, 22 June and 1 August 1945, and vol. 10, 1 and 22 March, and 5 and 21 November 1946 (latter contains quotations). Wrong's sister, Agnes Wrong Armstrong, alerted me to the personal relationship (she recalled a proposal of marriage) during an interview in Toronto, 16 September 1991. Further evidence exists in correspondence from Wrong following Davis's sudden death in April 1947. See RAC, GEB, RG1, subseries 642, box 291, folder 3038, Wrong to Miss Scheiffer, 16 April 1947; telegram from Wrong to F. McCuiston and letter to McCuiston, 19 April 1947; Wrong to Raymond Fosdick, 21 April 1947. Wrong's influence on Davis notwithstanding, his cautiously liberal views on decolonization were in keeping with those of what Basil Davidson calls "official America" and "academic America"; see *The Black Man's Burden: Africa and the Crisis of the Nation-State* (London: James Currey, 1992), 193.

65 PRO, CO 1045/128, Sir Christopher Cox papers, ACEC, Missions/Christian Literature for Africa/International Committee on, Wrong to Cox, 4 May 1944; SOAS/ICCLA, box 512/10, file on Wrong's estate, containing "A Tribute to Margaret Wrong," 1; Kenya National Ar-

chives, Christian Church Educational Association, 481, for "Christian Council of Kenya Literature Committee," and "Advisory Committee on Literature," Minutes, 25 May [1948]. The minutes described recent arrangements whereby the newly created East African Literature Bureau would produce non-religious literature, while the Advisory Committee would continue to produce Christian literature. See also *BFA*, July 1949, 38-40; and Oduyoye, "Christian Publishing Houses," 229.

66 Margaret Wrong, "The Education of African Women in a Changing World," 497-520. In the Gold Coast, an educationally advanced colony, only 43,448 girls out of a total of 184,520 children were reported to be receiving primary schooling in 1945, while only 12 of the colony's 136 students then studying in Britain were female; see NAG, "Report of the Education Department," 1945-46, 8, 9.

67 The interviews and meetings recorded in the Jackson Davis diaries are valuable sources of information on the cooperative efforts of these groups. See note 63 above.

68 SOAS/ICCLA, Wrong, "Gold Coast," 14-15; Ward, "African Languages."

69 Foreign-educated South African women with whom Wrong had contacts included Sibusisiwe (Violet) Makhanya and Mrs. Z.K. (Frieda) Matthews. Regarding Makhanya, see Armstrong Collection, Wrong, Letter 1, 1 June 1936, 11-12, and Shula Marks, *Not Either an Experimental Doll: The Separate Worlds of Three South African Women* (Bloomington: Indiana University Press, 1987), especially 30-39. Regarding Mrs. Matthews, a Xhosa musician and teacher, see her "African Music in South Africa," *BFA*, October 1938, 52-56, and, for background, Wilson, *Freedom*, 68-71, 89-91, 103-104. Although Wrong had links with many members of Nigeria's male Christian elite, she seems not to have worked with even as high-profile a female Christian social activist as Mrs. Funmilayo Ransome-Kuti, whose reform interests included literacy work among market women and whose husband was a prominent Anglican churchman and educator. By the 1940s Mrs. Ransome-Kuti's growing radicalism on matters of gender and colonial rule would perhaps have made her uninclined to collaborate with a moderate like Wrong in spite of their overlapping interest in women and literacy. See Cheryl Johnson-Odim and Nina Emma Mba, *For Women and the Nation: Funmilayo Ransome-Kuti of Nigeria* (Urbana: University of Chicago Press, 1997). Similarly, I have found no evidence of collaborative work by Wrong with Gold Coast women. Ghanaian theologian and historian C.G. Baëta, who as a young man knew Wrong in London as well as in the Gold Coast, recalled that her concern was to encourage African writing and education generally, rather than to focus on the needs of women and girls; personal interview, Accra, Ghana, 10 June 1993.

70 Wrong, *Africa and the Making of Books* 39; Dorothy L. Njeuma, "An Overview of Women's Education in Africa," in *The Politics of Women's Education: Perspectives from Asia, Africa, and Latin America*, ed. Jill Ker Conway and Susan C. Bourque (Ann Arbor: University of Michigan Press, 1993). Rural women in southern and eastern Africa were often actively discouraged from following their male partners to urban centres and mine sites.

71 Abrahams, *Tell Freedom*, 192, 197. See also Tim Couzens' "The Social Ethos," 73, on the importance of the Social Centre as a meeting place for white liberals and black intellectuals.

72 Wrong, *Africa and the Making of Books*, 7.

73 For instance, ibid., 7-9.

74 G.A. Gollock, *Daughters of Africa* (1932; reprint, New York: Negro Universities Press,1969), quotation at 172. Despite the condescension in this book, Gollock was a popular writer and editor who served for years on the British Section of the ICCLA. She published articles in African-edited West African newspapers. In 1938 her *Lives of Eminent Africans* was the most popular of the 200 books in the library of Alliance High School, Kikuyu, Kenya Colony, the school that produced over half of independent Kenya's first cabinet; Armstrong Collection, Wrong, "Christian Literature in Africa," [1936] 4; "List of Forty Popular Books" and "Report, 1940," in *BFA*, April 1938, 21-22, and January 1941, 1; T.A. Beetham, *Christianity and the New Africa* (New York: Praeger, 1967), 57. Cf. Flora Nwapa, *Women Are Different* (Enugu: Tana Press, 1986). In this somewhat autobiographical novel, the students at Nigeria's first Anglican secondary school for girls maintain their regard for their English headmistress even though she forbids them to read the nationalistic *West African Pilot* and urges them to be dutiful, patient Christian women in the political unrest ahead.

75 Wrong, "The African Woman's Work and Education," no. 4 of "West Africa ... The Next Fifty Years?" *West Africa*, 26 October 1935, 1250-51; copy located in SOAS/ICCLA, box 511/9, file of "Articles on Education." Mrs. Agnes Ayodele Taylor Adesegibin, one of the first Nigerian women to go to the US for advanced education (a Teachers College MA in 1937) and herself a writer and educator, remembered Wrong's views on women's education as consistent with those expressed in this piece: "Margaret Wrong's whole work showed the necessity and importance of Education for women and the desirability of developing good reading habits amongst them – but like most of the missionary theories of the time it was felt [by Wrong that] women should be trained for the home, the Church, to teach or nurse. And not for the professions"; responses to "Questionnaire on Margaret Wrong, 1887-1948," completed 17 January 1994. (Again, my thanks to Nina Mba for providing this contact.) It is important to note that non-white women who came to England for advanced education received support and sympathy from Wrong. See, for instance, Armstrong Collection, Wrong to Mother, 11 December 1927, and Rhodes House Library, Perham Papers, MSS-Perham 691/1, Wrong to Miss [Margery] Perham, 28 June 1938.

76 Mariama Bâ, *So Long a Letter* (1980; reprint, Oxford: Heinemann, 1989); Buchi Emecheta, *The Joys of Motherhood* (New York: George Braziller, 1979).

77 In *So Long a Letter*, the letter-writer reminds her friend Aissatou – like herself a Muslim woman who has experienced pain over her husband's decision to take a second wife – of the solace as well as the opportunities they have both been able to draw from literature as a result of their advanced (French colonial) education: "books saved you. Having become your refuge, they sustained you ... They enabled you to better yourself. What society refused you, they granted" (32). This kind of empowerment through literature was, of course, a highly unusual experience for real-life African women. See Edward Said's comment on the important role of representation in "keeping the subordinate subordinate, the inferior inferior" (*Culture and Imperialism* [New York: Knopf, 1993], 80).

78 Bâ, *Letter*, 14.

79 Emecheta, *Head above Water* (London: Fontana, 1986), 23-24. See also Obioma Nnaemeka, "From Orality to Writing: African Women Writers and the (Re)Inscription of Womanhood," *Research in African Literature* 25 (Winter 1994): 139-40, regarding the rejection of Grace Ogot's short stories by the East African Literature Bureau on the grounds that they were not what was expected of a Christian woman.

80 Regarding this reluctance, see Tsitsi Dangarembga's novel *Nervous Conditions* (London: Women's Press, 1988). In this book, Tambudzai's uncle, a mission-school headmaster who appears to be fully assimilated into Western, middle-class values, persuades her parents to allow her to come and live with his family and attend his school following the death of her brother. But later even this uncle hesitates about allowing Tambudzai to continue her education at an elite multiracial school in urban Rhodesia. His concern that young girls who "associate too much with these white people ... [and] have too much freedom ... do not develop into decent women" (180) is overcome only after his wife persuades him that he is being influenced by an old and invalid stereotype.

81 With the notable exception of Ngugi wa Thiong'o, most of Africa's best-known writers have continued to write in a "colonial" language, believing, with Achebe, that they can do so while still writing authentically on African subject matter. Ngugi, *Decolonizing the Mind*; Achebe, "The African Writer and the English Language" in *Morning Yet*. See also Oyekan Owomoyela, "The Question of Language in African Literatures," in *A History of Twentieth-Century African Literature*, ed. Oyekan Owomoyela (Lincoln: University of Nebraska Press, 1993), 347-68.

82 Chinua Achebe, *Things Fall Apart* (London: Heinemann, 1958). Kofi Awoonor's term "clash of cultures" novels is cited in Stratton, *Literature*, 22.

83 Stratton, *Literature*, 29. Interestingly, although its central character is female rather than male, and anything but "shadowy," *The Joys of Motherhood* echoes *Things Fall Apart* in providing a fictional illustration of women's delayed and less direct experience of colonialism.

84 The transfer took place in stages but was finalized in the early 1960s with the last issue of *Books for Africa*; see *BFA*, January 1963. Regarding de Mestral see his *Mémoires d'un Homme Libre* (Montreal: Méridien, 1986).

85 Claude de Mestral, "Christian Literature for Africa," *IRM* 43 (October 1954): 437.
86 The East African Literature Bureau, for instance, planned in its first year for "[a] series of new fiction by African writers, an attempt to provide something more stimulating than folk stories, which many Africans are beginning to tire of reading"; see "East African Literature Bureau," *BFA*, July 1949, 38-40. On the role of Christian publishing generally in facilitating African authorship, see Oduyoye, "Christian Publishing," and Dathorne, *African Literature*, 2-3. Bernth Linfors, *Mazungumzo: Interviews with East African Writers, Publishers, Editors and Scholars* (Athens: Ohio University Center for International Studies, 1980) provides fascinating illustrations of both encouragement and censorship.
87 Winners of the prize were announced in *Books for Africa*, and, irregularly, in other periodicals published in England and Africa. Fragmentary information about nominees and the decision-making process may be found in SOAS/ICCLA, box 512/10, files on Margaret Wrong Memorial Fund, 1953-65, and Margaret Wrong Memorial: Minutes, 1949-63; and in PRO, CO, 1045/1379 and 1380, Christopher Cox papers, Margaret Wrong Memorial Fund Committee. In 1972, decision making about awards was transferred to Africa; see Oduyoye, "Christian Publishing," 229. Alfa I. Sow and Mohamed H. Abdulaziz err in claiming that "works written in African languages or in Arabic could not be awarded the prize unless they had already been published in Afrikaans, French, English or Portuguese" (though for some years works in vernaculars were awarded a medal rather than a cash prize); see their "Language and Social Change," in Ali A. Mazrui, ed., *General History of Africa*, vol. 8 *Africa since 1935* (Paris: UNESCO, 1993), 527. Achebe won the prize in 1959 for *Things Fall Apart*. Soyinka won second prize for "Oji River" in 1957 while still a student at Leeds University; in 1962 he won again "for the originality of his literary contributions as a playwright" (*BFA* [July 1963], 66). Information about Tutola's attempt to win the prize comes from Ezenwa Ohaeto, *Achebe*, 69.
88 Abrahams, *Tell Freedom*, 296; Edem Kodjo and David Chanaiwa, "Pan-Africanism and Liberation," in *General History*, vol. 8, 744.
89 SOAS/ICCLA, box 512/10, file marked "Death; Estate; Obituaries; Tributes etc" for "ICCLA/ 25th Anniversary/A Tribute to Margaret Wrong," 8 October 1954; PRO, CO 1045/1379, Cox papers, minutes of meeting of Margaret Wrong Memorial Fund Committee, 1 June 1955, Peter Abrahams, "The Margaret Wrong Award for 1954," and Una Snow to committee members, 17 October 1955.
90 This information is drawn from primary sources cited in note 87.
91 Susan Gardner, "The World of Flora Nwapa," *The Women's Review of Books* 11, no. 6 (1994): 9-10.
92 The first class to include women graduated from Makerere College in East Africa in 1947, and from 1946 the English Department included a woman professor with a strong interest in creative writing; Makerere University Archives, "Uganda Education Department Report," 1947, 29, and Sicherman, "Ngugi's Colonial Education," especially 27-30.
93 SOAS/ICCLA, box 512/10, files for Margaret Wrong Memorial: Minutes, 1949-63, and for Memorial Fund, 1953-65. One trustee, for instance, anticipating that the award "might become the Nobel Prize in Literature for Africa," argued against considering vernacular writing for it and in justification of his position maintained that it had not been Wrong's intent "to perpetuate the Tower of Babel" (Fund file), thus perversely ignoring her strong desire to encourage literature in vernaculars. Others, including Margaret Read at an 18 June 1963 committee meeting, invoked Wrong's name and catholic interests in support of considering a wider range of literature, including that from Muslim communities (Minutes file).
94 Said, *Culture and Imperialism*, xx.
95 Ali A. Mazrui, "Towards the Year 2000," in *General History of Africa*, vol. 8, 919-20.
96 PRO, CO, Cox Papers, 1045/128, ACEC, Missions; Christian Literature for Africa, International Committee on the (Miss Wrong, Secretary), Wrong to Cox, 22 June 1945, with letter from Jones; "Pan-Africanism and Liberation," in *General History of Africa*, vol. 8, 744, 746; *BFA*, October 1961.
97 RAC, Davis Diaries, Series 12, box 4, vol. 9, Interview with A.K. Nyabonge, 25 March 1946 and vol. 10, Interview with Claude Barnett, 10 December 1946. Sometimes, however, Wrong sought to deter rather than assist educated Africans whose motives or stability she suspected. This was the case with Nnamdi Azikiwe – Zik – a future president of Nigeria, a

journalist, and a graduate of an American university. Wrong had friendly dealings with Zik during her visits to Lagos in 1939 and 1945 despite the nationalist radicalism of his *West African Pilot*. But when he was planning a return visit to the US in 1946, she warned Davis that he was "suffering from a persecution complex." Armstrong Collection, Wrong, "Memorandum 6, Eastern Provinces [sic]," 20 April-16 May 1939; Wrong, *For a Literate West Africa: The Story of a Journey in the Interests of Literacy and Christian Literature* (New York: Friendship Press for the Africa Committee of the Foreign Missions Conference of North America, 1946), 32; RAC, GEB, RG1, subseries 637.1, box 288, folder 3009, Wrong/Davis Correspondence, Wrong to Davis, 17 April 1946.

98 SOAS/ICCLA, box 512/10, file of Wrong's Circular Letters, letter no. 17, 16 March 1947; Wrong, "Memorandum on the activities of the British Council," 23 June 1941, in Rhodes House Library, Perham Papers, MSS. Perham 691/1.

99 The literature on this subject is extensive. See, for instance, Brouwer, "Margaret Wrong's Literacy Work," 433-34, 439-44; Jean Allman, "Making Mothers: Missionaries, Medical Officers and Women's Work in Colonial Asante, 1924-1945," *History Workshop Journal* 38 (1994): 23-47; Diane Barthel, "Women's Educational Experience under Colonialism: Toward a Diachronic Model," *Signs* 11, no. 1 (1985): 137-54; Nancy Rose Hunt, "Domesticity and Colonialism in Belgian Africa: Usumbura's Foyer Social, 1946-1960," *Signs* 15, no. 3 (1990): 447-74; Tabitha Kanogo, "Mission Impact on Women in Colonial Kenya," in *Women and Missions: Past and Present/Anthropological and Historical Perspectives,* ed. Fiona Bowie, Deborah Kirkwood, and Shirley Ardener (Providence and Oxford: Berg, 1993), 165-86. As Kanogo shows, the emotional costs to the first generation of mission-educated girls and their families could be high even if their training was rudimentary and domestic-oriented and their absence from home brief; they often became "misfits in their own societies" (171). It was only after the Second World War that Western education for girls came to be more widely regarded as a desirable route to new opportunities. Even then, however, as Barthel points out, for women who obtained a university education it was often a case of being "all dressed up with no place to go" (151).

100 In 1980, Margaret Read, who outlived Wrong by forty-three years, signed the necessary forms to transfer what little remained in the Margaret Wrong Memorial Fund to a new organization, "Feed the Minds"; Archives of the Institute of Education, University of London, Margaret Read Collection, correspondence between "Feed the Minds" and Trustees of the Margaret Wrong Memorial Fund, 30 January and 7 February 1980.

Chapter 5: Women in a Transitional Era

1 Margaret Wrong segment of uncatalogued family papers held (at the time of this research) in the collection of Agnes Wrong Armstrong, Toronto (now deceased) (hereafter Armstrong Collection): Canon F. Rowling to Professor and Mrs. Wrong, 2 May 1948, and to Hume Wrong, 1 May 1948; Hume Wrong to Rowling, 11 May 1948; S. Moore to "Dear Friends," 12 April 1948.

2 Interview with Mrs. Agnes Wrong Armstrong, Toronto, 18 December 1990.

3 See Armstrong Collection, H.D. Hooper to Hume Wrong, 3 May 1948, regarding the inappropriateness of the proposed reinterment for Marga, given her distaste for being "singled out as a notability."

4 See above, p. 63.

5 Peter Conn, *Pearl S. Buck: A Cultural Biography* (Cambridge: Cambridge University Press, 1996), especially 246-47; Deborah Gorham, *Vera Brittain: A Feminist Life* (Cambridge, MA: Blackwell, 1996). Oliver was familiar with the work of both these writers. Like a number of other Americans, Pearl Buck was directed to Wrong by Jackson Davis when she developed an interest in Africa. Wrong probably knew Brittain as well, through their shared Somerville College connection and possibly through their shared loss of an Oxford brother to the First World War and their active interest in the League of Nations.

6 See SOAS/ICCLA, box 512/10, file on Broadcast Talks 1934-47, for correspondence with Wrong regarding her BBC broadcasts, much of it from women. Lucy Meyer, who identified herself as a "Jewess," was one of a number of correspondents who wanted to help the cause of African literacy by providing reading material for children; see Meyer to Wrong, 9 July 1939.

7 Geraldine Forbes, *Women in Modern India,* The New Cambridge History of India, IV, 2
   3(Cambridge: Cambridge University Press, 1996), 103-105; Oliver, "Secretarial Notes," *The
   Journal of the Christian Medical Association of India, Burma and Ceylon (Journal)* 5, no. 5
   (November 1930): 295. The Association of Medical Women of India brought Western and
   non-Western women together at conferences and allowed them to cooperate on shared
   concerns.

8 Sa-Yeup Kim, comp., *Theses Collection in Commemoration of Dr. Pyung Kan Koh's Sixtieth
   Birthday* (Taegu: Graduate School, Kyungpook University, 1960), personal history; information provided by Dr. Bong Hak Hyun.

9 Armstrong Collection, Wrong to father, 15 January 1927, and to mother, 7 March 1927
   and 17 November 1929. Wrong provided a detailed critique of economic and political
   conditions for native South Africans in a private letter to Joseph Oldham written from
   Cape Province at the time of her 1936 visit; SOAS/ICCLA, box 509, File E, Wrong to "Dear
   Joe," 16 May 1936.

10 Armstrong Collection, C.W. Ransom to Hume Wrong, 20 October 1948: "She saw and
    counselled persons whose views were far apart. Her Fabian connections seldom seemed to
    lessen the weight given by conservatives to her mature judgements."

11 Kwame Nkrumah, *Ghana: The Autobiography of Kwame Nkrumah* (1957; reprint, New York:
    International Publishers, 1970), 16. There are frequent references to Guggisberg in Wrong's
    letters during the late 1920s. See, for instance, Armstrong Collection, Wrong to father, n.d.
    [August 1928] regarding a conference in Scotland to which she had travelled with Dr. S.K.
    Datta and where she had brought him and Guggisberg together, and 18 October 1928,
    regarding a farewell gift from Guggisberg as he prepared to leave for a new posting in
    British Guyana.

12 See Armstrong Collection, Wrong to mother, 19 May 1929, regarding Malinowski's agnos-
    ticism; letter to author from Dr. Andrew Mabyn Read, 1 May 1992, regarding his ribald
    humour.

13 Armstrong Collection, Wrong to parents, 7 October 1928.

14 See Great Britain, Secretary of State for the Colonies, *Correspondence Relating to the Welfare
    of Women in Tropical Africa, 1935-37* (London: His Majesty's Stationery Office, 1938). At-
    tending a conference convened by the British Commonwealth League in London in 1935
    where allegations of women coerced into unwanted marriages were being discussed, Jomo
    [then Johnston] Kenyatta asked why no African women were present to offer their perspec-
    tive and was told that "a number of African women had been invited to attend, but that no
    replies had been received" (5). Kenyatta's fellow Kenyan Dr. L.S.B. Leakey provided a paper
    for the conference in which he joined Kenyatta in defending Kenyan marriage customs
    against the interference of missionaries, feminists, and other critics.

15 Jomo Kenyatta, *Facing Mount Kenya: The Tribal Life of the Gikuyu* (1938; reprint, New York:
    Vantage Press, 1965); Jeremy Murray-Brown, *Kenyatta* (London: George Allen and Unwin,
    1972); Carolyn Martin Shaw, *Colonial Inscriptions: Race, Sex and Class in Kenya* (Minneapolis:
    University of Minnesota Press, 1995), chap. 3.

16 Regarding Haille Selassie's daughter, see Armstrong Collection, Wrong, Circular Letters,
    letter of 26 December 1941. In South Africa, Sibusisiwe (Violet) Makanya, US-educated,
    was prominently involved with liberal missionaries in various social reforms, including
    "purity work." Wrong met her on her 1936 tour. See Shula Marks, *Not Either an Experimental
    Doll: The Separate Worlds of Three South African Women* (Bloomington: Indiana University
    Press, 1987), 30-54; Deborah Gaitskell, "Housewives, Maids or Mothers: Some Contradic-
    tions of Domesticity for Christian Women in Johannesburg, 1903-1939," *Journal of African
    History* 24 (1983): 241-56, especially 242; and Armstrong Collection, Wrong, Letter no. 1, 1
    June 1936, from Transvaal.

17 Regarding Max Yergan see Brenda Gayle Plummer, "Evolution of the Black Foreign Policy
    Constituency," in *The African American Voice in U.S. Foreign Policy since World War II,* ed.
    Michael L. Crenn (New York: Garland, 1998), 89-103, especially 90-91, and Martin Bauml
    Duberman, *Paul Robeson* (New York: Knopf, 1998), 206, 210, 256-57, 331-33, 548. Wrong's
    contacts with Yergan and his wife began with her first visit to Africa, in 1926; see Armstrong
    Collection, Wrong, "South Africa – Some Impressions," 19 May-24 June 1926.

18 The Margaret Wrong segment of the Armstrong Collection contains correspondence, tributes, and obituaries.

19 Ibid., Circular Letters file, for June White to Margaret Read, 17 August 1948, sending a list of people who had received the circular letters. In 1950 Bunche became the first African American to win a Nobel prize. See Robert Harris, "Ralph Bunche and Afro-American Participation in Decolonization," in *U.S. Foreign Policy since World War II*, 163-80.

20 Armstrong Collection, Hume Wrong to H.D. Hooper, 11 May 1948, quoting Norman Robertson, Canadian High Commissioner in London.

21 Armstrong Collection, file of correspondence, tributes, and obituaries regarding Wrong. The *West Africa* tribute appeared 24 April 1948 and that in the *Manchester Guardian*, 19 April 1948. The quoted phrase is taken from the wooden plaque in her memory in the Anglican cathedral in Kampala: "Margaret Wrong: Servant of God, Friend of Africa."

22 The pagoda sent by Yonsei University to the University of Toronto in the mid-1980s to honour Murray and two other Canadian doctors who had served on the staff of Severance Union Medical College is a case in point (see page 95, above). But perhaps the most remarkable of such tributes was that paid to Canadian Dr. Frank Schofield. Following his death in 1970, Schofield was buried in Korea's National Cemetery, one of the few Westerners so honoured. On the staff of Severance in 1919, he had played a supportive role in the March First Movement for Korean independence; see Doretha E. Mortimore, "Dr. Frank W. Schofield and the Korean National Consciousness," *Korea Journal* 17, no. 3 (1977): 37-47.

23 Personal interview with Dr. Tai-Yun Whang, Toronto, 29 December 1998; letters from Dr. Kilchai K. Yim, 25 August 1996, and from Dr. Heung Joo Lee, 20 August 1997 and 18 March 1998; telephone conversation with Dr. Bong Hak Hyun, 14 April 1999, and letter of 7 December 1999. Dr. Whang's links to Murray are described in the preface to this book.

24 Grant Wacker, "Second Thoughts on the Great Commission: Liberal Protestants and Foreign Missions, 1890-1940," in *Earthen Vessels: American Evangelicals and Foreign Missions, 1880-1980*, ed. Joel A. Carpenter and Wilbert R. Shenk (Grand Rapids: William B. Eerdmans, 1990), 297; Rebekah Chevalier, "Where Have All the Missionaries Gone?" in *Fire and Grace: Stories of History and Vision*, ed. Jim Taylor (Toronto: United Church Publishing House, 1999), 37-42. When I visited Indore, India, for research in 1985, the United Church of Canada had just one missionary remaining in that city, which had been the centre of its India work from the 1870s. She and three other United Church missionaries living in the state were all near retirement and not replaced.

25 Wacker, "Second Thoughts," 281-300, especially 296-97; Dana L. Robert, "Shifting Southward: Global Christianity since 1945, *International Bulletin of Missionary Research* 24, no. 2 (2000): 50-58. In his review of Paul Gifford's *African Christianity: Its public Role*, Christopher Fyfe speaks of American religious influence in contemporary Africa as "as all-pervasive as its T-shirts and trainers, and similarly representing an enormous American export industry" ("Born Again in Africa," *Times Literary Supplement*, 25 December 1998).

26 By the 1980s, Wacker claims, "the very idea of moderate, not to mention old-fashioned liberal, foreign missions seemed a bit anachronistic [but] ... one could argue that broad public support for humanitarian programs such as the Marshall Plan, the Peace Corps, and world famine relief marked not the demise but the consummation of the liberal search for a mandate that would respond to the deepest impulses of Christian faith while respecting the integrity of other cultures" ("Second Thoughts," 297). Wacker's argument seems apt for the Canadian parallel to the Peace Corps, CUSO [originally Canadian University Service Overseas], which in 2001 marked the fortieth anniversary of its founding; CBC radio, "Vinyl Café," 13 May 2001, featuring a segment on Keith Spicer and CUSO; Hugh Winsor, "Big Bill McWhinney Towered over Us All," *Globe and Mail*, 4 June 2001, A15.

27 UCA, UCC, Florence Murray Personal Papers, box 2, file 37, "reactions to recent oxfam questionaire," [sic] found with draft of *Return to Korea*. See also Dalhousie University Archives (DUA), Murray Family Papers, File G-2, Murray to "Dear Family Folks," 1 January 1967.

28 Philip Quarles von Ufford and Matthew Schoffeleers, eds., *Religion and Development: Towards an Integrated Approach* (Amsterdam: Free University, 1988), 12. The editors maintain

that the term was coined for United Nations use in 1944 and gained wide currency in the 1950s and 60s.

29 Ian Smillie, *The Alms Bazaar: Altruism under Fire – Non-Profit Organizations and International Development* (London: Intermediate Technology Publications, 1995). As Smillie notes, while religion-based aid organizations are part of the NGO mix and while many secular NGOs have an ancestry in missions, the history of their roots and the nature of the links have not been systematically explored (3, 37).

30 E. Richard Brown, "Rockefeller Medicine in China: Professionalism and Imperialism," in *Philanthropy and Cultural Imperialism: The Foundations at Home and Abroad*, ed. Robert F. Arnove (Boston: G.K. Hall, 1980), 123-46; John Ehrenreich, *The Cultural Crisis of Modern Medicine* (New York: Monthly Review Press, 1978), introduction (quotations at 4, 7), and part 3 for "Medicine and Imperialism."

31 David Arnold, *Colonizing the Body: State Medicine and Epidemic Disease in Nineteenth-Century India* (Berkeley: University of California Press, 1993).

32 Jacob Chandy, *Reminiscences and Reflections: the Story of the Development of the CMC and Hospital, Vellore, in the Healing Ministry of the Indian Churches* (Kottayam: CMS Press, 1988), especially 100; Gillian Paterson, *Whose Ministry? A Ministry of Health Care for the Year 2000* (Geneva: WCC Publications, 1993), especially 10-12, 21, 28, 64 (quotations at 28, 64). Dr. Chandy, the neurosurgeon recruited by Dr. Oliver at the end of her career, initiated the constitutional changes that officially indigenized CMC, Vellore, in the early 1950s.

33 Resolution no. 6 of third biennnial conference as printed in *Journal* 4, no. 2 (March 1929): 44-45. See also CMAI, *The Ministry of Healing in India: Handbook of the Christian Medical Association of India* (Mysore: Wesleyan Mission Press, 1932), chap. 8; Oliver, "Secretary's Report," *Journal* 16, no. 2 (March 1941): 94ff.

34 Interview with Dr. V. (Dassen) Benjamin, Bangalore, India, 10 November 1999. Primary health care continued to suffer from underfunding in former colonies, even in the late twentieth century when its new *cachet* in the West "promised to open NGO and donor agency safes" (John Iliffe, *East African Doctors: A History of the Modern Profession* [Cambridge: Cambridge University Press, 1998], 158).

35 See Paterson, *Whose Ministry?* chap. 4, for Paterson's enthusiastic discussion of holistic medicine. Regarding Oliver's visit to Gandhi, see UCA, Glenna Jamieson Fonds, 3330, 88.002, box/file 003, Oliver Notebooks and Diaries, diary entry for 20 March 1935.

36 Soon Young Yoon, "A Legacy without Heirs: Korean Indigenous Medicine and Primary Health Care," *Social Science and Medicine* 17, no. 19 (1983): 1467-76. When Yoon's article was written, South Korea's government still provided no support for research and training in indigenous medicine, and few medical schools integrated it into their teaching on primary health care. See also David Arnold, "The Rise of Western Medicine in India," *The Lancet* 347, no. 9034 (19 October 1996), especially 1075, and Karen Minden, *Bamboo Stone: The Evolution of a Chinese Medical Elite* (Toronto: University of Toronto Press, 1994), chaps. 6 and 7. As Minden explains, by the 1980s the Chinese government was rehabilitating and redeploying the mission-trained medical elite whom it had persecuted during the era of the Great Leap Forward and the Cultural Revolution, using them, for instance, to re-establish medical contacts with the West.

37 Ester Boserup, *Women's Role in Economic Development* (New York: St. Martin's Press, 1970). Another pioneering overview was "Women: The Neglected Human Resource for African Development," *Canadian Journal of African Studies* 6, no. 2 (1972), 359-70, prepared by the Human Resources Development Division, United Nations Economic Commission for Africa.

38 For instance, Ruth E. Meena, "Foreign Aid and the Question of Women's Liberation," and Marjorie Mbilinyi, "'Women in Development' Ideology: The Promotion of Competition and Exploitation," both in *The African Review* 11, 1 (1984): 1-13, 14-33.

39 Elizabeth M. King and M. Anne Hill, eds., *Women's Education in Developing Countries: Barriers, Benefits, and Policies* (Baltimore: Johns Hopkins University Press for the World Bank, 1993), v; Betty Plewer and Rieky Stuart, "Women and Development Revisited: The Case for a Gender and Development Approach," in *Conflicts of Interest: Canada and the Third World*, ed. Jamie Swift and Brian Tomlinson (Toronto: Between the Lines, 1991), 107-32.

40 Armstrong Collection, Hume Wrong to Marga, 24 November 1935 regarding the St. Hilda's position, and George Wrong to Marga, 23 November 1939; also his letter of 14 February 1939, where he quoted his wife, Burgy: "no wonder she did not want the commonplace life of a college." The Uganda women's college to which George Wrong's letters refer seems never to have materialized, perhaps because of a later decision to make Makerere College coeducational. Hume Wrong supported his sister's decision not to return to Toronto in 1935: "St. Hilda's strikes me as a mouldy job. If you were 60, and partly crippled, it might be all right for you. Stay where you are, my dear, and don't worry about it."

41 Wrong did not, however, necessarily agree with all missionaries on what these particulars should be; Brouwer, "Margaret Wrong's Literacy Work and the 'Remaking of Woman,'" in *Africa, 1929-48," Journal of Imperial and Commonwealth History* 23, no. 3 (1995): 433.

42 Great Britain, Colonial Office, *Report of a Sub-Committee on the Education and Welfare of Women and Girls in Africa* (Africa No. 1169, February 1943), 1 (for "stabilizing element"); Diane Barthel, "Women's Educational Experience under Colonialism: Towards a Diachronic Model," *Signs* 11, no. 1 (1985): 151 (for "all dressed up").

43 Wrong, "The Education of African Women in a Changing World," *Yearbook of Education* (London: University of London Institute of Education, 1940), 497-520 (quotations at 501, 518).

44 For instance, Theodora Foster Carroll, *Women, Religion and Development in the Third World* (New York: Praeger, 1983), chap. 8.

45 Gender specialist Caroline Moser as quoted in Smillie, *Alms Bazaar*, 85.

46 For instance, Karin Hyde, "Sub-Saharan Africa," and Rosemary T. Bellow and Elizabeth M. King, "Educating Women: Lessons from Experience," in *Women's Education in Developing Countries: Barriers, Benefits, and Policies*, ed. Elizabeth M. King and M. Anne Hill (Baltimore: Johns Hopkins University Press for the World Bank, 1993).

47 Regarding Aggrey, see Margaret Wrong, "The African Woman's Work and Education," no. 4 of "West Africa ... The Next Fifty Years?" *West Africa*, 26 October 1935, 1250; copy located in SOAS/ICCLA, box 511/9, file of "Articles on Education"; and for Ransome-Kuti, see Cheryl Johnson-Odim and Nina Emma Mba, *For Women and the Nation: Funmilayo Ransome-Kuti of Nigeria* (Urbana and Chicago: University of Chicago Press, 1997), especially chap. 3. Wrong began her article with a statement by Aggrey frequently quoted as evidence of his interest in women's education: "Educate a man and you educate an individual; educate a woman and you educate a family." See Carroll, *Women, Religion and Development*, 130, for a quoted statement that articulates virtually the same sentiment, but this time from a third-world woman in the 1970s.

48 Kew, Public Record Office, CO 859 83/2, "Report of sub-Committee on Education and Welfare of Women and Girls in Africa [and] Proposed Investigation into Female Education into Selected Areas in Africa (1943-45)." This file includes Margaret Read's notes of August 1945, evidently prepared for Christopher Cox as a follow-up to the report (no. 1169) of a sub-committee on this subject. Read questioned the need for yet another enquiry into the special conditions affecting the education of women and girls. She suggested publicizing work opportunities for girls in teaching, midwifery, etc., as a means of motivating them and their mothers to make use of schooling opportunities, but she recognized that health and work problems were major physical barriers: "The adult women cannot be expected to pay much attention to education and to new ideas, until their daily burden of physical toil is in some way lightened. Fetching water and pounding or grinding corn are two obvious ways of expending energy, which could be lightened by a village well and a village mill."

49 Elizabeth Bumiler, *May You Be the Mother of a Hundred Sons: A Journey among the Women of India* (New York: Fawcett Columbine, 1990).

50 Ruth Compton Brouwer, "Standards versus Sisterhood: Dr. Murray, President Kim, and the Introduction of Medical Education at Ewha Womans University, Seoul, 1947-1950," in *Nation, Ideas, Identities: Essays in Honour of Ramsay Cook*, ed. Michael D. Behiels and Marcel Martel (Toronto: Oxford University Press, 2000), 173.

51 P.G. Okoth, "The Creation of a Dependent Culture: The Imperial School Curriculum in Uganda," in *The Imperial Curriculum: Racial Images and Education in the British Colonial Experience*, ed. J.A. Mangan (London: Routledge, 1993): 135-46 (quotation at 136).

Select Bibliography

The bibliography that follows is confined mainly to sources cited in the Notes. Where historical accounts of missions and other similar studies were written by individuals personally involved in the missionary movement, I have usually listed them as primary sources. Several of the archival and private collections listed were uncatalogued, or only partly catalogued, when this research was undertaken. This will explain some unwieldiness and inconsistency in titles. The numerous articles, pamphlets, etc., written by my three subjects are generally not listed individually, since they are to be found in larger collections that are listed as primary sources. Finally, some of the periodicals, printed records, and executive correspondence of the ecumenical organizations with which the three women were associated are available in more than one location. Where periodicals and executive correspondence of the NCC and the CMAI, held at SOAS as part of the Joint IMC/CBMS Archives, were also available on fiche at the Yale Divinity School Library and Archives, I made use of them at the Yale location. Where Margaret Wrong's articles, printed reports, and letters for the ICCLA were available in the Armstrong Collection as well as in the Joint IMC/CMBS Archives at SOAS, I made use of them in the Armstrong Collection.

Primary Sources

Christian Medical College and Hospital, Vellore
Minutes of the Association and Council of the Missionary Medical College for Women, Vellore
Annual Reports of the Missionary Medical College and Hospital, 1944-45

Dalhousie University Archives, Halifax
Robert Murray and Family Papers

Ewha Womans University Library, Seoul
Helen Kim Collection

Kenya National Archives, Nairobi
Christian Church Educational Association Records
Colony and Protectorate of Kenya. Education Department. *Annual Report[s]*, 1947, 1949

Makerere University Archives, Kampala, Uganda
Uganda Educational Department Reports, 1939-48
Makerere College Magazine, 1948

National Archives of Ghana, Accra
"Arrangements for Publication of Manuscripts"
Gold Coast Gazette

"Report of the Education Department, 1945-46"
"Report on Mass Education in African Society by the Colonial Office Advisory Committee ... Distribution of"
Wrong, Margaret. "Report on Literacy and Adult Education in the Gold Coast" [1945], and related correspondence

National Council of Churches Library, Nagpur
National Christian Council of India. *Proceedings*

New College Library, Edinburgh
Special Collections. J.H. Oldham Papers

Nigeria National Archives, Ibadan
Annual Reports of the Education Department, 1939-48
A Memorandum on the Extension of Adult Education in the Western Region, n.d.

Privately Held Papers
Collection of the late Mrs. Agnes Wrong Armstrong, Toronto
Robert Murray Personal Notebooks, Montreal

Public Archives of Nova Scotia, Halifax
Maritime Missionaries to Korea Collection

Public Record Office, Kew (Colonial Office Records)
Advisory Committee on Education in the Colonies. Minutes of Meetings, 1944-47 (CO 987/2-3)
Sir Christopher Cox Papers (CO 1045/128; CO 1045/1379; CO 1045/1380)
Mass Education and Literacy (CO 859 22/4)
"Report of a Sub-Committee on Education and Welfare of Women and Girls in Africa [and] Proposed Investigation into Female Education in Selected Areas in Africa [1943-45]," (CO 859 83/2). Follow-up files on "Report of a Sub-Committee on the Education of Women and Girls in Africa."

Rhodes House Library, Oxford
Margery Perham Papers

Rockefeller Archive Center, Tarrytown, NY
General Education Board Records
Jackson Davis Diaries

Arthur and Elizabeth Schlesinger Library, Radcliffe College
Ida Sophia Scudder Papers

United Church/Victoria University Archives, Toronto
Biographical Files
Glenna Jamieson Fonds (Oliver Papers)
Florence Jessie Murray Personal Papers
Presbyterian Church in Canada. Board of Foreign Missions. Korean Mission Correspondence
Scott, William. "Canadians in Korea: A Brief Historical Sketch of Canadian Mission Work in Korea." Typescript, 1975
Tapes Collection. Taped interview with Dr. Florence Murray
United Church of Canada. Board of Foreign Missions. General Correspondence, 1925-61
–. Board of World Mission. Correspondence and reports related to United Board for Christian Higher Education in Asia
–. *Record of Proceedings, Thirty-Second Annual Meeting of the Maritime Conference*

Woman's Missionary Society of the United Church of Canada. *Annual Reports*
–. Overseas Missions. India
–. Korea Correspondence

University of Lagos Library
Bishop S.I. Kale Collection
Chief Ladipo Solanke Papers

University of London, School of Oriental and African Studies Library
International Committee on Christian Literature for Africa records
International Missionary Council. Africa: General
National Christian Council of India, and National Christian Council and Christian Medical Association of India records

University of Toronto Archives
Vincent Massey Personal Records
Margaret Christian Wrong student file

Vellore Christian Medical College, Archives Library, Vellore
British Section of the Governing Board. Women's Medical College, Vellore. Minutes, 1934-42
Minutes of the American Section of the Governing Board of the Missionary Medical College for Women, 1934-42

Yale Divinity School Library and Archives
Archives of the United Board for Christian Higher Education in Asia
International Missionary Council. Staff and Officers' Correspondence. William Paton Papers [fiche]
John R. Mott Papers
National Christian Council of India, and National Christian Council and Christian Medical Association of India Records [fiche]
Missions Pamphlet Collection. Records of the Vellore Christian Medical Center

Periodicals
Africa
Books for Africa: The Quarterly Bulletin of the International Committee on Christian Literature for Africa
Canadian Medical Association Journal
International Review of Missions
Indian Social Reformer
Journal of the Christian Medical Association of India, Burma and Ceylon
The Korea Mission Field
Listen: News from Near and Far
Missionary Monthly
National Christian Council [of India] Review
The New Outlook
The United Churchman
United Church Observer
United Church Record and Missionary Review

Books, Booklets, and Articles
Abrahams, Peter. *Return to Goli*. London. Faber and Faber, 1953.
–. *Tell Freedom: Memories of Africa*. New York: Knopf, 1954.
–. *The View from Coyaba*. London: Faber and Faber, 1985.
–. *A Wreath for Idomo*. London: Faber and Faber, 1965.
Achebe, Chinua. *Things Fall Apart*. London: Heinemann, 1958.

Armstrong, Agnes Wrong. "'There's Too Much Waiting to Be Done.'" *Food for Thought* 16 (1956): 258-63.

Arnup, Jessie H. *A New Church Faces a New World*. Toronto: United Church of Canada, 1937.

Azikiwe, Nnamdi. *My Odyssey: An Autobiography*. London: C. Hurst and Co., 1970.

Bâ, Mariama. *So Long a Letter*. 1980. Reprint, Oxford: Heinemann, 1989.

Beetham, T.A. *Christianity and the New Africa*. New York: Praeger, 1967.

Chandy, Jacob. *Reminiscences and Reflections: The Story of the Development of the Christian Medical College and Hospital, Vellore, in the Healing Ministry of the Indian Churches*. Kottayam, India: CMS Press, 1988.

Christian Medical Association of India. *The Ministry of Healing in India: Handbook of the Christian Medical Association of India*. Mysore: Wesleyan Mission Press, 1932.

Dangaremba, Tsitsi. *Nervous Conditions*. London: Women's Press, 1988.

de Mestral, Claude. *Mémoires d'un Homme Libre*. Montreal: Méridien, 1986.

Emecheta, Buchi. *Head above Water*. London: Fontana, 1986.

–. *The Joys of Motherhood*. New York: George Braziller, 1979.

Flexner, Abraham. *Medical Education in the United States and Canada: A Report to the Carnegie Foundation for the Advancement of Teaching*. New York: Carnegie Foundation, 1910.

Gandhi, M.K. *Christian Missions: Their Place in India*. Ahmedabad: Navajivan Publishing, 1941.

Gedge, Evelyn C., and Mithan Chowski, eds. *Women in Modern India*. Bombay: D.B. Taraporewale, 1929.

Gollock, Georgina A. *Daughters of Africa*. 1932. Reprint, New York: Negro Universities Press, 1969.

–. *Lives of Eminent Africans*. 1928. Reprint, New York: Negro Universities Press, 1969.

Great Britain. Colonial Office. *Report of a Sub-Committee on the Education of Women and Girls in Africa*. Africa No. 1169. 1943.

–. Advisory Committee on Education in the Colonies. *Mass Education in African Society*. London, 1944.

–. Secretary of State for the Colonies. *Correspondence Relating to the Welfare of Women in Tropical Africa, 1935-37*. London, 1938

Groves, C.P. *The Planting of Christianity in Africa*. Vol. 4, *1914-1954*. London: Lutterworth Press, 1958.

Hall, Sherwood. *With Stethoscope in Asia*. McLean, VA: MCL Associates, 1978.

Hinden, Rita. *Fabian Colonial Essays*. London: Allen and Unwin, 1945.

Hocking, William Ernest. *Re-Thinking Missions: A Laymen's Inquiry after One Hundred Years*. New York: Harper and Brothers, 1932.

Hogg, William Richey. *Ecumenical Foundations: A History of the International Missionary Council and Its Nineteenth-Century Background*. New York: Harper and Brothers, 1952.

Institute of Social and Religious Research. *World Missionary Atlas*. New York: Institute of Social and Religious Research, 1925.

International Missionary Council. *The Christian Life and Message in Relation to Non-Christian Systems: Report of the Jerusalem Meeting of the International Missionary Council, March 24-April 8, 1928*. Vol. 1. London: International Missionary Council, 1928.

–. Vol. 8, *Addresses on General Subjects*. London: International Missionary Council, 1928.

–. *The World Mission of the Church: Findings and Recommendations of the International Missionary Council, Tambaram, Madras, India, Dec. 12-29, 1938*. London: International Missionary Council [1939].

Jeffery, Mary Pauline. *Dr. Ida: The Life Story of Dr. Ida S. Scudder*. New York: Fleming H. Revell, 1938.

Jones, R.F. "Secular Civilization and the Christian Task." In *The Christian Life and Message in Relation to Non-Christian System: Report of the Jerusalem Meeting of the International Missionary Council, March 24th-April 8th, 1928*. Vol. 1, 284-338. London: International Missionary Council, 1928.

Jones, T.J. *Education in Africa: A Study of West, South and Equatorial Africa*. New York: Phelps-Stokes Fund, 1922.

–. *Education in East Africa*. London: Edinburgh House Press, 1925.

Kang, Younghill. *The Grass Roof.* New York: Scribner's, 1931.

Kenyatta, Jomo. *Facing Mount Kenya: The Tribal Life of the Gikuyu.* 1938. Reprint, New York: Vantage Press, 1965 .

Kim, Helen. *Grace Sufficient: The Story of Helen Kim by Herself,* edited by J. Manning Potts. Nashville: Upper Room, 1964.

Kuriakose, M.K., comp. *History of Christianity in India: Source Materials.* Madras: Christian Literature Society, 1982.

Laymen's Foreign Missions Inquiry. *Fact-Finders Reports.* Vol. 4, *India-Burma,* edited by Orville A. Petty. Supplementary series. New York: Harper and Brothers, 1933.

–. *Regional Reports of the Commission of Appraisal.* Vol. 1, *India-Burma,* edited by Orville A. Petty. Supplementary series. New York: Harper and Brothers, 1933.

Lazarus, Hilda Mary. *Autobiography of Hilda Mary Lazarus.* Visakhapatnam: SFS Printing, n.d.

–. "The Sphere of Indian Women in Medical Work in India." In *Women in Modern India,* edited by Evelyn C. Gedge and Mithan Chowski, 51-62. Bombay: D.B. Taraporewale, 1929.

Leith-Ross, Sylvia. *African Women: A Study of the Ibo of Nigeria.* 1939. Reprint, New York: Praeger, 1965.

Lewis, C.S. *The Screwtape Letters.* London: Geoffrey Bles, 1942.

Lindsay, A.D. *Report of the Commission on Christian Higher Education in India: An Enquiry into the Place of the Christian College in Modern India.* London: Oxford University Press, 1931.

Linfors, Bernth. *Mazungumzo: Interviews with East African Writers, Publishers, Editors and Scholars.* Athens: Ohio University Center for International Studies, 1980.

Mofolo, Thomas, *Chaka.* London: Oxford University Press for IAI, 1931.

Moorshead, R. Fletcher. *The Way of the Doctor: A Study in Medical Missions.* London: Carey Press, n.d. [1926].

Munro, John, comp. *Beyond the Moon Gate: A China Odyssey, 1938-1950. Adapted from the Diaries of Margaret Outerbridge.* Vancouver: Douglas and McIntyre, 1990.

Murray, A. Victor. *The School in the Bush: A Critical Study of the Theory and Practice of Native Education in Africa.* London: Longmans, 1929.

Murray, Florence J. *At the Foot of Dragon Hill.* New York: Dutton, 1975.

–. *Return to Korea.* Belleville, ON: Essence Publishing, 1999.

Newbigin, Lesslie. *Unfinished Agenda: An Autobiography.* London: SPCK, 1985.

Nkrumah, Kwame. *Ghana: The Autobiography of Kwame Nkrumah.* 1957. Reprint, New York: International Publishers, 1970 .

Ntantala, Phyllis. *A Life's Mosaic: The Autobiography of Phyllis Ntantala.* Berkeley: University of California Press, 1993.

Nwapa, Flora. *Women Are Different.* Enugu: Tana Press, 1986.

Oldham, Joseph H. *Christianity and the Race Problem.* London: SCM Press, 1924.

Oldham, J.H., and B.D. Gibson. *The Remaking of Man in Africa.* London: Oxford University Press, 1931.

Oliver, B. Choné, comp. *Tales from the Inns of Healing: Christian Medical Service in India, Burma and Ceylon.* Toronto: Committee on Missionary Education, United Church of Canada, 1944.

Read, Margaret. *Children of Their Fathers: Growing up among the Ngoni of Nyasaland.* London: Methuen, 1959.

–. *Education and Social Change in Tropical Areas.* London: Thomas Nelson, 1955.

Rheinallt Jones, J.D. "African Authors' Conference/A Unique Gathering." *The Bantu World,* 14 November 1936.

Rouse, Ruth, and Stephen Charles Neill, eds. *A History of the Ecumenical Movement, 1517-1948.* London: SPCK, 1954.

Rowell, N.W. "The League of Nations and the Assembly at Geneva." *International Review of Missions* 10, no. 3 (1921): 402-15.

Scudder, Dorothy Jealous. *A Thousand Years in Thy Sight: The Story of the Scudder Missionaries of India.* New York: Vantage Press for the Scudder Association, 1984.

Smith, Edwin W. *Aggrey of Africa: A Study in Black and White.* New York: Friendship Press for the Phelps-Stokes Fund, 1929.

Soyinka, Wole. *Aké: The Years of Childhood.* London: Rex Collings, 1981.

Steeds, Rita B. *Woman Not Alone.* Chilliwack, BC: privately published, 1992.

Tutola, Amos. *The Palm-Wine Drinkard.* New York: Grove Press, 1953.

Van Buskirk, James Dale. *Korea: Land of the Dawn.* Toronto: Missionary Education Movement of the United Church of Canada, 1931.

Wilson, Dorothy Clarke. *Dr. Ida: The Story of Dr. Ida Scudder of Vellore.* New York: McGraw-Hill, 1959.

Wilson, Monica. *Freedom for My People – the Autobiography of Z.K. Matthews: Southern Africa, 1901 to 1968.* London: Rex Collings, 1981.

Wrong, Margaret. *Across Africa.* London: International Committee on Christian Literature for Africa, 1940.

–. *Africa and the Making of Books: Being a Survey of Africa's Need of Literature.* London: ICCLA 1934.

–. "The African Woman's Work and Education." No. 4 of "West Africa ... the Next Fifty Years?" *West Africa,* 26 October 1935, 1250-51.

–. "The Education of African Women in a Changing World." In *Yearbook of Education.* London: University of London Institute of Education, 1940.

–. *Five Points for Africa.* London: Edinburgh House, 1942.

–. *For a Literate West Africa: The Story of a Journey in the Interests of Literacy and Christian Literature.* New York: Friendship Press for the Africa Committee of the Foreign Missions Conference of North America, 1945.

–. "Is Literacy Necessary in Africa?" In *Fabian Colonial Essays,* edited by Rita Hinden. London: Allen and Unwin, 1945.

Secondary Sources

Achebe, Chinua. *Morning Yet on Creation Day.* London: Heinemann, 1975.

Ackroyd, Peter. *T.S. Eliot.* London: Hamish Hamilton, 1984.

Allen, Ted, and Sydney Gordon. *The Scalpel, the Sword.* Toronto: McClelland and Stewart, 1978.

Allman, Jean. "Making Mothers: Missionaries, Medical Officers and Women's Work in Colonial Asante, 1924-1945." *History Workshop Journal* 38 (1994): 23-47.

Alter, Joseph S. "Gandhi's Body, Gandhi's Truth: Nonviolence and the Biomoral Imperative of Public Health." *Journal of Asian Studies* 55, no. 2 (1996): 301-22.

Arnold, David. *Colonizing the Body: State Medicine and Epidemic Disease in Nineteenth-Century India.* Berkeley: University of California Press, 1993.

–. "The Rise of Western Medicine in India." *The Lancet* 347, no. 9034 (19 October 1996): 1075-78.

Baago, K. *A History of the National Christian Council of India, 1914-1964.* Nagpur: National Christian Council, n.d. [1965].

Barkan, Elazar. *The Retreat of Scientific Racism.* Cambridge: Cambridge University Press, 1992.

Barthel, Diane. "Women's Educational Experience under Colonialism: Toward a Diachronic Model." *Signs* 11, no. 1 (1985): 137-54.

Bays, Daniel H. "The Growth of Independent Christianity in China, 1900-1937." In *Christianity in China from the Eighteeenth Century to the Present,* edited by Daniel H. Bays, 307-16. Stanford: Stanford University Press, 1996.

Bebbington, D.W. *Evangelicalism in Modern Britain: A History from the 1730s to the 1980s.* London: Unwin Hyman, 1989.

Beidelman, T.O. "Social Theory and the Study of Christian Missions in Africa." *Africa* 44, no. 3 (1974): 235-49.

Bellow, Rosemary T., and Elizabeth M. King. "Educating Women: Lessons from Experience." In *Women's Education in Developing Countries: Barriers, Benefits, and Policies,* edited by Elizabeth M. King and M. Anne Hill, 285-322. Baltimore: Johns Hopkins University Press for the World Bank, 1993.

Berger, Carl. *The Writing of Canadian History.* Toronto: Oxford University Press, 1976.

Berman, Edward H. "Educational Colonialism in Africa: The Role of American Foundations, 1910-1945." In *Philanthropy and Cultural Imperialism: The Foundations at Home and Abroad,* edited by Robert F. Arnove, 179-201. Boston: G.K. Hall, 1980.

Bhabha, Homi K. *The Location of Culture*. London: Routledge, 1994.

Bhola, H.S. "An Overview of Literacy in Sub-Sahara Africa – Images in the Making." *African Studies Review* 33, no. 3 (1990): 5-20.

Bliss, Kathleen. "J.H. Oldham/1874-1969: From 'Edinburgh 1910' to the World Council of Churches." In *Mission Legacies: Biographical Studies of Leaders of the Missionary Movement*, edited by Gerald H. Anderson, Robert T. Coote, Norman A. Horner, and James M. Phillips, 577-78. Maryknoll: Orbis Books, 1994.

Bliss, Michael. *William Osler: A Life in Medicine*. Toronto: University of Toronto Press, 1999.

Blumhofer, Edith. *Aimee Semple McPherson, Everybody's Sister*. Grand Rapids: William B. Eerdmans, 1993.

Boahen, A. Adu, ed. *General History of Africa*. Abridged ed. Vol. 7, *Africa under Colonial Domination, 1880-1935*. Berkeley: University of California Press, 1990.

Bonner, Thomas Neville. *To the Ends of the Earth: Women's Search for Education in Medicine*. Cambridge: Harvard University Press, 1992.

Boserup, Ester. *Women's Role in Economic Development*. New York: St. Martin's Press, 1970.

Brouwer, Ruth Compton. "Beyond 'Women's Work for Women': Dr. Florence Murray and the Practice and Teaching of Western Medicine in Korea, 1921-1942." In *Challenging Professions: Historical and Contemporary Perspectives on Women's Professional Work*, edited by Elizabeth Smyth, Sandra Acker, Paula Bourne, and Alison Prentice, 65-95. Toronto: University of Toronto Press, 1999.

–. "Books for Africans: Margaret Wrong and the Gendering of African Literature, 1929-1963." *International Journal of African Historical Studies* 31, no. 1 (1998): 53-71.

–. "Home Lessons, Foreign Tests: The Background and First Missionary Term of Florence Murray, Maritime Doctor in Korea." *Journal of the Canadian Historical Association*, n.s., 6 (1996): 103-28.

–. "Margaret Wrong's Literacy Work and the 'Remaking of Woman' in Africa, 1929-48." *Journal of Imperial and Commonwealth History* 23, no. 3 (1995): 427-52.

–. *New Women for God: Canadian Presbyterian Women and India Missions, 1876-1914*. Toronto: University of Toronto Press, 1990.

–. "Standards versus Sisterhood: Dr. Murray, President Kim, and the Introduction of Medical Education at Ewha Womans University, Seoul, 1947-1950." In *Nation, Ideas, Identities: Essays in Honour of Ramsay Cook*, edited by Michael D. Behiels and Marcel Martel, 161-79. Toronto: Oxford University Press, 2000.

Brown, E. Richard. "Rockefeller Medicine in China: Professionalism and Imperialism." In *Philanthropy and Cultural Imperialism: The Foundations at Home and Abroad*, edited by Robert F. Arnove, 123-46. Boston: G.K. Hall, 1980.

Brown, Judith M. *Modern India: The Origins of an Asian Democracy*. Delhi: Oxford University Press, 1985.

–. "Who Is an Indian? Dilemmas of National Identity at the End of the British Raj in India." Paper presented at the "Missions, Nationalism, and the End of Empire" conference, University of Cambridge, 6-9 September 2000.

Bruce, Steve, ed. *Religion and Modernization*. Oxford: Clarendon Press, 1992.

Bumiler, Elizabeth. *May You Be the Mother of a Hundred Sons: A Journey among the Women of India*. New York: Fawcett Columbine, 1990.

Burke, Sara Z. *Seeking the Highest Good: Social Service and Gender at the University of Toronto, 1888-1937*. Toronto: University of Toronto Press, 1996.

Burton, Antoinette. *At the Heart of the Empire: Indians and the Colonial Encounter in Late-Victorian Britain*. Berkeley: University of California Press, 1998.

Bush, Barbara. "'Britain's Conscience on Africa': White Women, Race and Imperial Politics in Inter-war Britain." In *Gender and Imperialism*, edited by Clare Midgley, 200-23. Manchester: Manchester University Press, 1998.

Carroll, Theodora Foster. *Women, Religion and Development in the Third World*. New York: Praeger, 1983.

Cell, John W., ed. *By Kenya Possessed: The Correspondence of Norman Leys and J.H. Oldham, 1918-1926*. Chicago: University of Chicago Press, 1976.

–. "Colonial Rule." In *The Oxford History of the British Empire*. Vol. 4, *The Twentieth Century*, edited by Judith M. Brown and Wm. Roger Louis. Oxford: Oxford University Press, 1999.

Chaudhuri, Nupur, and Margaret Strobel, eds. *Western Women and Imperialism: Complicity and Resistance*. Bloomington: Indiana University Press, 1992.

Cheung, Yuet-Wah. *Missionary Medicine in China: A Study of Two Canadian Protestant Missions in China before 1937*. Lanham, MD: University Press of America, 1988.

Chevalier, Rebekah. "Where Have All the Missionaries Gone?" In *Fire and Grace: Stories of History and Vision*, edited by Jim Taylor, 37-42. Toronto: United Church Publishing House, 1999.

Christie, Nancy, and Michael Gauvreau. *A Full-Orbed Christianity: The Protestant Churches and Social Welfare in Canada, 1900-1940*. Montreal and Kingston: McGill-Queen's University Press, 1996.

Chung-Yang, Chung. "Women's Organizations and Their Activities." *Korea Journal* 4, no. 2 (1964): 14-17.

Clark, Allen DeGray. *Avison of Korea: The Life of Oliver R. Avison, M.D.* Seoul: Yonsei University Press, [1979].

–. *A History of the Church in Korea*. Rev. ed. Seoul: Christian Literature Society, 1971.

Clark, Donald N. *Christianity in Modern Korea*. Lanham, MD: University Press of America, 1986.

Clarke, Brian. "English-Speaking Canada from 1854." In *A Concise History of Christianity in Canada*, edited by Terrence Murphy and Roberto Perin, 341-43. Toronto: Oxford University Press, 1996

Clements, Keith. *Faith on the Frontier: A Life of J.H. Oldham*. Edinburgh: T and T Clark, 1999.

Comaroff, Jean, and John Comaroff. *Ethnography and the Historical Imagination*. Boulder: Westview Press, 1992.

–. *Of Revelation and Revolution: Christianity, Colonialism, and Consciousness in South Africa*. Chicago: University of Chicago Press, 1991.

Conn, Peter. *Pearl S. Buck: A Cultural Biography*. Cambridge: Cambridge University Press, 1996.

Cott, Nancy. *The Grounding of Modern Feminism*. New Haven: Yale University Press, 1987.

Couzens, Tim. "The Social Ethos of Black Writing in South Africa 1920-50." In *Aspects of South African Literature*, edited by Christopher Heywood, 66-81. London: Heinemann, 1976.

–. *The New African: A Study of the Life and Work of H.I.E. Dholomo*. Johannesburg: Ravan Press, 1985.

Cumings, Bruce. *Korea's Place in the Sun: A Modern History*. New York: W.W. Norton, 1997.

Dathorne, O.R. *African Literature in the Twentieth Century*. London: Heinemann, 1974.

Davidson, Basil. *The Black Man's Burden: Africa and the Crisis of the Nation-State*. London: James Currey, 1992.

Dickin, Janice. "Pentecostalism and Professionalism: The Experience and Legacy of Aimee Semple McPherson." In *Challenging Professions: Historical and Contemporary Perspectives on Women's Professional Work*, edited by Elizabeth Smyth, Sandra Acker, Paula Bourne, and Alison Prentice, 25-43. Toronto: University of Toronto Press, 1999.

Dormandy, Thomas. *The White Death: A History of Tuberculosis*. London: Hambledon Press, 1999.

Douglas, Ann. *Terrible Honesty: Mongrel Manhattan in the 1920s*. New York: Farrar, Straus, Giroux, 1995.

Duberman, Martin Bauml. *Paul Robeson*. New York: Knopf, 1998.

"Duck-Heung Bang." In *Women Physicians of the World: Autobiographies of Medical Pioneers*, edited by Leone McGregor Hellstedt, 361-63. Washington, DC: Hemisphere Publishing, 1978.

Eckert, Carter J., Ki-baik Lee, Young Ick Lew, Michael Robinson, and Edward W. Wagner. *Korea Old and New: A History*. Seoul: Ilchokak Publishers for Korea Institute, Harvard University, 1990.

Ehrenreich, John. *The Cultural Crisis of Modern Medicine*. New York: Monthly Review Press, 1978.

Elphick, Richard. "The Benevolent Empire and the Social Gospel: Missionaries and South African Christians in the Age of Segregation." In *Christianity in South Africa: A Political, Social, and Cultural History,* edited by Richard Elphick and Rodney Davenport, 347-69. Berkeley: University of California Press, 1997.

Emery, G.N. "Oliver, Adam." In *Dictionary of Canadian Biography.* Vol. 11, 651-53. Toronto: University of Toronto Press, 1982.

Engels, Dagmar, and Shula Marks, eds. *Contesting Colonial Hegemony: State and Society in Africa and India.* London: British Academic Press, 1994.

Fitzgerald, Rosemary. "A 'Peculiar and Exceptional Measure': The Call for India in the Late Nineteenth Century." In *Missionary Encounters: Sources and Issues,* edited by Robert A. Bickers, and Rosemary Seton, 174-96. Richmond, UK: Curzon Press, 1996.

Flemming, Leslie A., ed. *Women's Work for Women: Missionaries and Social Change in Asia.* Boulder: Westview Press, 1989.

Forbes, Geraldine. "Medical Careers and Health Care for Indian Women: Patterns of Control." *Women's History Review* 3, no. 4 (1994): 515-30.

–. *Women in Modern India.* The New Cambridge History of India, IV, 2. Cambridge: Cambridge University Press, 1996.

Fyfe, Christopher. "Born Again in Africa." Review of *African Christianity: Its Public Role,* by Paul Gifford. *Times Literary Supplement,* 25 December 1998.

Gagan, Rosemary R. *A Sensitive Independence: Canadian Methodist Women Missionaries in Canada and the Orient, 1881-1925.* Montreal and Kingston: McGill-Queen's University Press, 1992.

Gaitskell, Deborah. "Housewives, Maids or Mothers: Some Contradictions of Domesticity for Christian Women in Johannesburg, 1903-1939." *Journal of African History* 24 (1983): 241-56.

Gardner, Susan. "The World of Flora Nwapa." *Women's Review of Books* 11, no. 6 (1994): 9-10.

Gidney, R.D., and W.P.J. Millar. "The Reorientation of Medical Education in Late Nineteenth-Century Ontario: The Proprietary Medical Schools and the Founding of the Faculty of Medicine at the University of Toronto." *Journal of the History of Medicine and Allied Sciences* 49 (1994): 52-78.

Glotzer, Richard. "The Career of Mabel Carney: The Study of Race and Rural Development in the United States and South Africa." *International Journal of African Historical Studies* 29, no. 2 (1996): 309-36.

Gordimer, Nadine. "English-Language Literature and Politics." In *Aspects of South African Literature,* edited by Christopher Heywood, 99-120. London: Heinemann, 1976.

Gorham, Deborah. *Vera Brittain: A Feminist Life.* Cambridge, MA: Blackwell, 1996.

Graham, Carol. "V.S. Azariah, 1874-1945: Exponent of Indigenous Mission and Christian Unity." In *Mission Legacies: Biographical Studies of Leaders of the Missionary Movement,* edited by Gerald H. Anderson, Robert T. Coote, Norman A. Horner, and James M. Phillips, 324-29. Maryknoll: Orbis Books, 1994.

Graham, E.C. *Nothing Is Here for Tears: A Memoir of S.H. Hooke.* Oxford: Blackwell, 1969.

Gray, Richard. *Black Christians and White Missionaries.* New Haven: Yale University Press, 1990.

–. "Christianity." In *The Colonial Moment in Africa: Essays on the Movement of Minds and Materials, 1900-1940,* edited by Andrew Roberts, 140-90. Cambridge: Cambridge University Press, 1986.

Greenlee, James G., and Johnston, Charles M. *Good Citizens: British Missionaries and Imperial States, 1870-1918.* Montreal: McGill-Queen's University Press, 1999.

Grundmann, Christopher H. "Wanless, William J[ames]." In *Biographical Dictionary of Christian Missions,* edited by Gerald Anderson, 717. New York: Simon and Schuster and Prentice Hall, 1998.

Hacker, Carlotta. *The Indomitable Lady Doctors.* Halifax: Formac Publishers, 1984.

Haggis, Jane. "'Good Wives and Mothers' or 'Dedicated Workers': Contradictions of Domesticity in the 'Mission of Sisterhood,' Travancore, South India." In *Maternities and*

Modernities: Colonial and Postcolonial Experiences in Asia and The Pacific, edited by Kalpana Ram and Margaret Jolly, 81-113. Cambridge: Cambridge University Press, 1998.

–. "White Women and Colonialism: Towards a Non-Recuperative History." In *Gender and Imperialism*, edited by Clare Midgley, 45-79. Manchester: Manchester University Press, 1998.

Hardyman, J.T., and R.K. Orchard. *Two Minutes from Sloane Square: A Brief History of the Conference of Missionary Societies in Great Britain and Ireland, 1912-1977*. London: Conference of British Missionary Societies, 1977.

Hargreaves, J.D. *Decolonization in Africa*. London: Longman, 1988.

Harper, Susan Billington. *In the Shadow of the Mahatma: Bishop V.S. Azariah and the Travails of Christianity in British India*. Grand Rapids: William B. Eerdmans, 2000.

Harris, Robert. "Ralph Bunche and Afro-American Participation in Decolonization." In *The African American Voice in U.S. Foreign Policy since World War II*, edited by Michael Krenn, 163-80. New York: Garland, 1998.

Harvey, Charles E. "Speer versus Rockefeller and Mott, 1910-1935." *Journal of Presbyterian History* 60, no. 4 (1982): 283-99.

Hastings, Adrian. *The Church in Africa, 1450-1950*. Oxford: Clarendon Press, 1994.

Higgs, Catherine. *The Ghost of Equality: The Public Lives of D.D.T. Jabavu of South Africa, 1885-1959*. Athens, OH: Ohio University Press, 1997.

Hill, Patricia R. *The World Their Household: The American Woman's Foreign Mission Movement and Cultural Transformation, 1870-1920*. Ann Arbor: University of Michigan Press, 1985.

Hogg, Peter, and Ilse Sternberg, eds. *Market Literature from Nigeria: A Checklist*. London: British Library, 1990.

Hogg, William Richey. *Ecumenical Foundations: A History of the International Missionary Council and Its Nineteenth-Century Background*. New York: Harper and Brothers, 1952.

Howell, Colin. "Medical Professionalization and the Social Transformation of the Maritimes, 1850-1950." *Journal of Canadian Studies* 27, no. 1 (1992): 5-20.

Howell, Joel D. *Technology in the Hospital: Transforming Patient Care in the Early Twentieth Century*. Baltimore: Johns Hopkins University Press, 1995.

Huber, Mary Taylor, and Nancy C. Lutkehaus, eds., *Gendered Missions: Women and Men in Missionary Discourse and Practice*. Ann Arbor: University of Michigan Press, 1999.

Hunt, Nancy Rose. "Domesticity and Colonialism in Belgian Africa: Usumbura's Foyer Social, 1946-1960." *Signs* 15, no. 3 (1990): 447-74.

Hunter, Jane. *The Gospel of Gentility: American Women Missionaries in Turn-of-the-Century China*. New Haven: Yale University Press, 1984.

Huntley, Martha. "Presbyterian Women's Work and Rights in the Korean Mission." *American Presbyterians* 65, no. 1 (1987): 37-48.

Hurd-Mead, Kate Campbell. *Medical Women of America: A Short History of the Pioneer Women of America and a Few of Their Colleagues in England*. New York: Froben Press, 1933.

Hutchison, William R. *Errand to the World: American Protestant Thought and Foreign Missions*. Chicago: University of Chicago Press, 1987.

Hyde, Karin A.L. "'Sub-Saharan Africa." In *Women's Education in Developing Countries: Barriers, Benefits, and Policies*, edited by Elizabeth M. King and M. Anne Hill, 100-35. Baltimore: Johns Hopkins University Press for the World Bank, 1993.

Iacovetta, Franca. "'A Respectable Feminist': The Political Career of Senator Cairine Wilson, 1921-1962." In *Beyond the Vote: Canadian Women and Politics*, edited by Linda Kealey and Joan Sangster, 63-85. Toronto: University of Toronto Press, 1989.

Iliffe, John. *East African Doctors: A History of the Modern Profession*. Cambridge: Cambridge University Press, 1998.

Ion, A. Hamish. *The Cross in the Dark Valley: The Canadian Protestant Missionary Movement in the Japanese Empire, 1931-1945*. Waterloo: Wilfrid Laurier University Press, 1999.

–. *The Cross and the Rising Sun, Volume 1: The Canadian Protestant Missionary Movement in the Japanese Empire, 1872-1931*. Waterloo: Wilfrid Laurier University Press, 1990.

Jackson, Eleanor M. *Red Tape and the Gospel: A Study of the Significance of the Ecumenical Missionary Struggle of William Paton (1886-1943)*. Birmingham: Phlogiston Press and Selly Oak Colleges, 1980.

Jayawardena, Kumari. *The White Woman's Other Burden: Western Women and South Asia during British Rule.* New York: Routledge, 1995.

Jeffery, Roger. "Doctors and Congress: The Role of Medical Men and Medical Politics in Indian Nationalism." In *The Indian National Congress and the Political Economy of India, 1885-1985,* edited by Mike Shepperdson and Colin Simmons, 160-73. Aldershot: Avebury, 1988.

–. *The Politics of Health Care in India.* Berkeley: University of California Press, 1988.

–. "Recognizing India's Doctors: The Institutionalization of Medical Dependency, 1918-1939." *Modern Asian Studies* 13, no. 2 (1979): 301-26.

Johnson-Odim, Cheryl, and Nina Emma Mba. *For Women and the Nation: Funmilayo Ransome-Kuti of Nigeria.* Urbana and Chicago: University of Chicago Press, 1997.

Jones, Donald. "Deep from Seoul's Soul." *Toronto Star,* 1 March 1986, M3.

Kakar, Sanjiv. "Leprosy in British India, 1860-1940: Colonial Politics and Missionary Medicine." *Medical History* 40 (1996): 215-230.

Kang, Wi Jo. "The Presbyterians and the Japanese in Korea." *Journal of Presbyterian History* 62, no. 1 (1984): 35-50.

Kanogo, Tabitha. "Mission Impact on Women in Colonial Kenya." In *Women and Missions: Past and Present/Anthropological and Historical Perspectives,* edited by Fiona Bowie, Deborah Kirkwood, and Shirley Ardener, 165-87. Providence and Oxford: Berg, 1993.

Kaylor, Earl C. Jr. "Peabody, Lucy Whitehead McGill Waterbury." In *Notable American Women.* Vol. 3, *1607-1950,* 36-37. Cambridge: Harvard University Press, 1971.

Kelm, Mary-Ellen. *Colonizing Bodies: Aboriginal Health and Healing in British Columbia, 1900-1950.* Vancouver: UBC Press, 1998.

Kendall, Laurel. *Getting Married in Korea: Of Gender, Morality, and Modernity.* Berkeley: University of California Press, 1996.

Kennedy, Dane. "Imperial History and Post-Colonial Theory." *Journal of Imperial and Commonwealth History* 24, no. 3 (1996): 345-63.

Kenyatta, Jomo. *Facing Mount Kenya: The Tribal Life of the Gikuyu.* 1938. Reprint, New York: Vantage Press, 1965.

Kim, Jung-Gun. "'To God's Country': Canadian Missionaries in Korea and the Beginnings of Korean Migration to Canada." Ed.D. thesis, University of Toronto, 1983.

Kim, Sangduk. "Chung-Hee Kil." In *Notable Women in the Life Sciences: A Biographical Dictionary,* edited by Benjamin F. Shearer and Barbara S. Shearer, 227-28. Westport: Greenwood Press, 1996.

Kim, Sa-Yeup, comp. *Theses Collection in Commemoration of Dr. Pyung Kan Koh's Sixtieth Birthday.* Taegu: Graduate School, Kyungpook University, 1960.

Kim, Yung-Chung. "Women's Movement in Modern Korea." In *Challenges for Women: Women's Studies in Korea,* edited by Sei-Wha Chung, 75-102. Seoul: Ewha Womans University Press, 1986.

–, ed. and trans. *Women of Korea: A History from Ancient Times to 1945.* Seoul: Ewha Womans University Press, 1976.

King, Elizabeth M., and M. Anne Hill, eds. *Women's Education in Developing Countries: Barriers, Benefits, and Policies.* Baltimore: Johns Hopkins University Press for the World Bank, 1993.

King, Kenneth James. *Pan-Africanism and Education: A Study of Race Philanthropy and Education in the Southern States of America and East Africa.* Oxford: Clarendon Press, 1971.

Kinnear, Mary. *In Subordination: Professional Women, 1870-1970.* Montreal and Kingston: McGill-Queen's University Press, 1995.

Kodjo, Edem, and David Chanaiwa. "Pan-Africanism and Liberation." In *General History of Africa.* Vol. 8, *Africa since 1935,* edited by Ali A. Mazrui, 744-66. Paris: UNESCO, 1993.

Kuklick, Henrika. *The Savage Within: The Social History of British Anthropology, 1885-1945.* Cambridge: Cambridge University Press, 1991.

Lal, Maneesha. "The Politics of Gender and Medicine in Colonial India: The Countess of Dufferin's Fund, 1885-1888." *Bulletin of the History of Medicine* 68 (1994): 29-66.

Lee, Chong-Sik. *The Politics of Korean Nationalism.* Berkeley: University of California Press, 1963.

Lee, Grant S. "The Growth of Medicine and Protestantism under Persecution: The Korean Experience." *Korea Journal* 29, no. 1 (1980): 36-53.

Lewis, Stephen. "Lend a Hand." *Globe and Mail*, 25 May 2000, A15.

Lind, Mary Ann. *The Compassionate Memsahibs: Welfare Activities of British Women in India, 1902-1947.* New York: Greenwood Press, 1988.

Little, Angela. "Professor Margaret Read." *Independent*, 31 May 1991.

Lone, Stewart, and Gavan McCormack. *Korea since 1850.* New York: St. Martin's Press, 1993.

Ludmerer, Kenneth M. *Learning to Heal: The Development of American Medical Education.* New York: Basic Books, 1985.

Lutz, Jessie Gregory. *China and the Christian Colleges, 1850-1950.* Ithaca: Cornell University Press, 1971.

Macdonald, Laura. "'Minister of the Gospel and Doctor of Medicine': The Canadian Presbyterian Medical Mission to Korea, 1898-1923." Master's thesis, Queen's University, Kingston, ON, 2000.

McGregor Hellstedt, Leone, ed. *Women Physicians of the World: Autobiographies of Medical Pioneers.* Washington: Hemisphere Publishing, 1978.

McKillop, A.B. *Matters of Mind: The University in Ontario, 1791-1951.* Toronto: University of Toronto Press, 1994.

MacLeod, Enid Johnson. *Petticoat Doctors: The First Forty Years of Women in Medicine at Dalhousie University.* Lawrencetown Beach, NS: Pottersfield Press, 1990.

McPherson, Kathryn. *Bedside Matters: The Transformation of Canadian Nursing, 1900-1990.* Toronto: Oxford University Press, 1996.

MacRae, Helen Fraser. *A Tiger on Dragon Mountain: The Life of Rev. Duncan M. MacRae, D.D.* Charlottetown: Williams and Crue, 1993.

Mangan, J.A., ed. *Making Imperial Mentalities: Socialisation and British Imperialism.* Manchester: Manchester University Press, 1990.

"Margaret Read." *Times* (London), 19 June 1991, 16.

Marks, Shula. *Not Either an Experimental Doll: The Separate Worlds of Three South African Women.* Bloomington: Indiana University Press, 1987.

Marsden, George M. *Fundamentalism and American Culture: The Shaping of Twentieth-Century Evangelicalism.* New York: Oxford University Press, 1980.

Marshall, David B. *Secularizing the Faith: Canadian Protestant Clergy and the Crisis of Belief, 1850-1940.* Toronto: University of Toronto Press, 1992.

Maxwell, David. "New Perspectives on the History of African Christianity." *Journal of Southern African Studies* 23, no. 1 (1997): 141-48.

Mazrui, Ali A. "Towards the Year 2000." In *General History of Africa.* Vol. 8, *Africa since 1935,* edited by Ali A. Mazrui, 905-34. Paris: UNESCO, 1993

-, ed. *General History of Africa.* Vol. 8, *Africa since 1935.* Paris: UNESCO, 1993.

Mbilinyi, Marjorie. "'Women in Development' Ideology: The Promotion of Competition and Exploitation." *The African Review* 11, no. 1 (1984): 14-33.

Meena, Ruth E. "Foreign Aid and the Question of Women's Liberation." *The African Review* 11, no. 1 (1984): 1-13.

Minden, Karen. *Bamboo Stone: The Evolution of a Chinese Medical Elite.* Toronto: University of Toronto Press, 1994.

Mishra, Pankaj. "The Other India." *New York Review of Books*, 16 December 1999, 98, 100.

Moir, John S. *Enduring Witness: A History of the Presbyterian Church in Canada.* New ed. N.p.: Eagle Press Printers, 1987.

"Moon Gyung Chang." In *Women Physicians of the World: Autobiographies of Medical Pioneers,* edited by Leone McGregor Hellstedt, 267-69. Washington, DC: Hemisphere Publishing, 1978.

Moore, R. Laurence. "Secularization: Religion and the Social Sciences." In *Between the Times: The Travail of the Protestant Establishment in America, 1900-1960,* edited by William R. Hutchison, 233-52. Cambridge: Cambridge University Press, 1989.

Morantz-Sanchez, Regina Markell. *Sympathy and Science: Women Physicians in American Medicine.* New York: Oxford University Press, 1985.

More, Ellen S. *Restoring the Balance: Women Physicians and the Profession of Medicine, 1950-1995*. Cambridge: Harvard University Press, 1999.

Mortimore, Doretha E. "Dr. Frank W. Schofield and the Korean National Consciousness." *Korea Journal* 17, no. 3 (1977): 37-47

Murray, T.J. "The Visit of Abraham Flexner to Halifax Medical College." *Nova Scotia Medical Bulletin* 64 (1985): 34-41.

Murray-Brown, Jeremy. *Kenyatta*. London: George Allen and Unwin, 1972.

Ngugi wa Thiong'o. *Decolonising the Mind: The Politics of Language in African Literature*. London: James Currey, 1986.

Njeuma, Dorothy. "An Overview of Women's Education in Africa." In *The Politics of Women's Education: Perspectives from Asia, Africa, and Latin America*, edited by Jill Ker Conway and Susan C. Bourque, 123-31. Ann Arbor: University of Michigan Press, 1993.

Nkrumah, Kwame. *Ghana: The Autobiography of Kwame Nkrumah*. 1957. Reprint, New York: International Publishers, 1970.

Nnaemeka, Obioma. "From Orality to Writing: African Women Writers and the (Re)Inscription of Womanhood." *Research in African Literature* 25 (1994): 137-57.

Oddie, Geoffrey A. "'Orientalism' and British Protestant Missionary Constructions of India in the Nineteenth Century." *South Asia* 17, no. 2 (1994): 27-42.

Oduyoye, Modupe. "The Role of Christian Publishing Houses in Africa Today." In *Publishing in Africa in the Seventies: Proceedings of an International Conference on Publishing and Book Development Held at the University of Ife, Ife-Ife, Nigeria, 16-20 December 1973*, ed. Edwina Oluwasanmi, Eva McLean, and Hans Zell, 209-32. Ile-Ife, Nigeria: University of Ife Press, 1975.

Ohaeto, Ezenwa. *Chinua Achebe: A Biography*. Oxford: James Currey, 1997.

Okoth, P.G. "The Creation of a Dependent Culture: The Imperial School Curriculum in Uganda." In *The Imperial Curriculum: Racial Images and Education in the British Colonial Experience*, edited by J.A. Mangan, 135-46. London: Routledge, 1993.

Oosthuizen, G.C. *Shepherd of Lovedale*. Johannesburg: Hugh Keartland, n.d.

Opland, Jeff. "The Drumbeat and the Cross: Christianity and Literature." In *Christianity and South Africa: A Political, Social, and Cultural History*, edited by Richard Elphick and Rodney Davenport, 297-315. Oxford: James Currey, 1997.

Owomoyela, Oyekan. "The Question of Language in African Literatures." In *A History of Twentieth-Century African Literature*, edited by Oyekan Owomoyela, 347-68. Lincoln: University of Nebraska Press, 1993.

Pak, Rhoda Kim. "Medical Women in Korea." *Journal of the American Medical Women's Association* 5, no. 3 (1950): 116-17.

Paterson, Gillian. *Whose Ministry? A Ministry of Health Care for the Year 2000*. Geneva: WCC Publications, 1993.

Peel, J.D.Y. "Problems and Opportunities in an Anthropologist's Use of a Missionary Archive." In *Missionary Encounters: Sources and Issues*, edited by Robert A. Bickers and Rosemary Seton, 70-94. Richmond, UK : Curzon Press, 1996.

Peires, Jeffrey. "The Lovedale Press: Literature for the Bantu Revisited." *History in Africa* 6 (1979): 155-75.

Peitzman, Steven J. *A New and Untried Course: Woman's Medical College and Medical College of Pennsylvania*. New Brunswick, NJ: Rutgers University Press, 2000.

Penny, Sheila M. "'Marked for Slaughter': The Halifax Medical College and the Wrong Kind of Reform." *Acadiensis* 19 (1989): 27-51.

Phillips, Clifton J. "Changing Attitudes in the Student Volunteer Movement of Great Britain and North America, 1886-1928." In *Missionary Ideologies in the Imperialist Era: 1880-1920*, edited by Torben Christensen and William R. Hutchison, 131-45. Aarhuis, Denmark: Farlaget Aros, 1982.

[Pillay, K.K.]. *History of Higher Education in India*. Vol. 2, *University of Madras, 1857-1957, Affiliated Institutions*. Madras: Associated Printers, 1957.

Pierce, Gretchen. "'The Whole World Is Waiting.'" *Mail Star* (Halifax), 21 January 1970.

Plummer, Brenda Gayle. "Evolution of the Black Foreign Policy Constituency." In *The African American Voice in U.S. Foreign Policy since World War II*, edited by Michael L. Crenn, 89-103. New York: Garland, 1998.

Pobee, J.S., ed. *Religion in a Pluralistic Society: Essays Presented to Professor C.G. Baëta*. Leiden: Brill, 1976.

Porter, Andrew. "'Cultural Imperialism' and Protestant Missionary Enterprise, 1780-1914." *Journal of Imperial and Commonwealth History* 25, no. 3 (1997): 367-91.

Porter, Roy. *The Greatest Benefit to Mankind: A Medical History of Humanity*. New York: W.W. Norton, 1998.

Prang, Margaret. *A Heart at Leisure from Itself: Caroline Macdonald of Japan*. Vancouver: UBC Press, 1995.

"Professor Margaret Read." *Times* (London), 19 June 1991, 16.

Pugh, Patricia. *Educate, Agitate, Organize: 100 Years of Fabian Socialism*. London: Methuen, 1984.

Raath, Jan. "Africa Finding Its Place in Crowded Literary World." *Globe and Mail*, 6 August 1994, Review Section, C15.

Rabe, Valentin. "Scudder, Ida Sophia." In *Notable American Women: The Modern Period*. 634-36. Cambridge: Cambridge University Press, 1980.

Ranger, Terence O. *Are We Not Also Men? The Samkange Family and African Politics in Zimbabwe, 1920-64*. Harare: Baobab, 1995.

–. "Godly Medicine: The Ambiguities of Medical Mission in Southeastern Tanzania, 1900-1945." In *The Social Basis of Health and Healing in Africa*, edited by Steven Feierman and John M. Janzen, 256-82. Berkeley: University of California Press, 1992.

–. "The Invention of Tradition in Colonial Africa." In *The Invention of Tradition*, edited by Eric Hobsbawm and Terence Ranger, 211-62. Cambridge: Cambridge University Press, 1983.

Read, John. Untitled address on the late Margaret Read. *Institute of Education Society Newsletter* 6, no. 2 (1991): 13-14.

Repka, William, and Kathleen Repka. *Dangerous Patriots: Canada's Unknown Prisoners of War*. Vancouver: New Star Press, 1982.

Robert, Dana L. *American Women in Missions: A Social History of Their Thought and Practice*. Macon: Mercer University Press, 1996.

–. "Shifting Southward: Global Christianity since 1945." *International Bulletin of Missionary Research* 24, no. 2 (April 2000): 50-58.

Roberts, Andrew, ed. *The Colonial Moment in Africa*. Cambridge: Cambridge University Press, 1986.

–. "The Imperial Mind." In *The Colonial Moment in Africa*, edited by Andrew Roberts, 24-76. Cambridge: Cambridge University Press, 1986.

Rosenberg, Rosalind. *Beyond Separate Spheres: Intellectual Roots of Modern Feminism*. New Haven: Yale University Press, 1982.

Rothstein, William G. *American Medical Schools and the Practice of Medicine: A History*. New York: Oxford University Press, 1987.

Said, Edward W. *Culture and Imperialism*. New York: Knopf, 1993.

–. *Out of Place: A Memoir*. New York: Knopf, 1999.

Sanneh, Lammin. *Translating the Message: The Missionary Impact on Culture*. Maryknoll: Orbis Books, 1989.

–. *West African Christianity: The Religious Impact*. Maryknoll: Orbis Books, 1995.

Scherer, James A. "Hume, Edward H[icks]." In *Biographical Dictionary of Christian Missions*, edited by Gerald Anderson, 309. New York: Simon and Schuster and Prentice Hall, 1998.

Shaw, Carolyn Martin. *Colonial Inscriptions: Race, Sex and Class in Kenya*. Minneapolis: University of Minnesota Press, 1995.

Shaw, Marion. *The Clear Stream: A Life of Winifred Holtby*. London: Virago Press, 1999.

Shore, Marlene. *The Science of Social Redemption: McGill, the Chicago School, and the Origins of Social Research in Canada*. Toronto: University of Toronto Press, 1987.

Sicherman, Carol. "Ngugi's Colonial Education: 'The Subversion ... of the African Mind.'" *African Studies Review* 38, no. 3 (1995): 11-41.

Singh, Maina Chawla. *Gender, Religion, and "Heathen Lands": American Missionary Women in South Asia (1860s-1940s)*. New York: Garland Press, 2000.

–. "Missionary Legacies and Christ-Filled Doctors: Gender, Religion and Professionalisation in the History of Christian Medical College, Vellore." In *Knowledge, Power and Politics:*

Educational Institutions in India, edited by Mushirul Hasan, 430-63. New Delhi: Roli Books, 1998.

Smillie, Ian. *The Alms Bazaar: Altruism Under Fire – Non-Profit Organizations and International Development*. London: Intermediate Technology Publications, 1995.

Smith, Ellen J. "Medical Missionaries: 'Ourselves Your Servants for Jesus' Sake.'" In *"Send Us a Lady Physician": Women Doctors in America, 1835-1920*, edited by Ruth J. Abram, 199-204. New York: W.W. Norton, 1985.

Sow, Alfa I., and Mohamed H. Abdulaziz. "Language and Social Change." In *General History of Africa*. Vol. 8, *Africa since 1935*, edited by Ali A. Mazrui, 522-52. Paris: UNESCO, 1993.

Stanley, Brian. *The Bible and the Flag: Protestant Missions and British Imperialism in the Nineteenth and Twentieth Centuries*. Leicester: Apollo, 1990.

Stevens, Marianne P. "The Rockefeller Foundation and Canadian Medical Education." *Research Reports from the Rockefeller Archive Center*, Spring 1999, 14-17.

Stratton, Florence. *Contemporary African Literature and the Politics of Gender*. London: Routledge, 1994.

Strong-Boag, Veronica. "Canada's Women Doctors: Feminism Constrained." In *A Not Unreasonable Claim: Women and Reform in Canada, 1880s-1920s*, edited by Linda Kealey, 109-29. Toronto: Women's Press, 1979.

Studdert-Kennedy, Gerald. "Christian Imperialists of the Raj: Left, Right and Centre." In *Making Imperial Mentalities: Socialisation and British Imperialisms*, edited by J.A. Mangan, 127-43. Manchester: Manchester University Press, 1990.

Symonds Richard. *Oxford: The Last Lost Cause?* London: Macmillan, 1986.

Taylor, Richard W. "E. Stanley Jones, 1884-1973: Following the Christ of the Indian Road." In *Mission Legacies: Biographical Studies of Leaders in the Modern Missionary Movement*, edited by Gerald H. Anderson, Robert T. Coote, Norman A. Horner, and James M. Phillips, 339-47. Maryknoll: Orbis Books, 1994.

Thane, Pat. "The Women of the British Labour Party and Feminism 1906-1945." In *British Feminism in the Twentieth Century*, edited by Harold Smith, 125-43. Aldershot: Edward Elgar, 1990.

Thomas, Nicholas. *Colonialism's Culture: Anthropology, Travel and Government*. Cambridge: Polity Press, 1994.

Thompson, T. Jack. "Speaking for Ourselves: The African Writers of Livingstonia." *Bulletin of the Scottish Institute of Missionary Studies*, n.s., no. 10 (1994): 24-35.

Thorne, Susan. *Congregational Missions and the Making of an Imperial Culture in Nineteenth-Century England*. Stanford: Stanford University Press, 1999.

Tucker, Sara W. "A Mission for Change in China: The Hackett Women's Medical Center of Canton, China, 1900-1930." In *Women's Work for Women: Missionaries and Social Change in Asia*, edited by Leslie A. Flemming, 137-57. Boulder: Westview Press, 1989.

United Nations. Human Resources Development Division. Economic Commission for Africa. "Women: The Neglected Human Resource for African Development." *Canadian Journal of African Studies* 6, no. 2 (1972): 359-70.

[Untitled article on pagoda from Yonsei University]. *Vic Report* (Victoria University, Toronto ON) 16, no. 2 (1985-86), 11.

Vaughan, Megan. *Curing Their Ills: Colonial Power and African Illness*. Stanford: Stanford University Press, 1991.

Vevier, Charles, ed. *Flexner 75 Years Later*. Lanham, MD: University Press of America, 1987.

Viswanathan, Gauri. "'Coping with (Civil) Death': The Christian Convert's Rights of Passage in Colonial India." In *After Colonialism: Imperial Histories and Postcolonial Displacements*, edited by Gyan Prakash, 183-210. Princeton: Princeton University Press, 1995.

von Ufford, Philip Quarles, and Matthew Schoffeleers, eds. *Religion and Development: Towards an Integrated Approach*. Amsterdam: Free University, 1988.

Wacker, Grant. "Second Thoughts on the Great Commission: Liberal Protestants and Foreign Missions, 1890-1940." In *Earthen Vessels: American Evangelicals and Foreign Missions, 1880-1980*, edited by Joel A. Carpenter and Wilbert R. Shenk, 281-300. Grand Rapids: William B. Eerdmans, 1990.

Wade, Michael. *Peter Abrahams*. London: Faber and Faber, 1972.

Waite, P.B. *The Lives of Dalhousie University.* Vol. 1, 1818-1925, *Lord Dalhousie's College.* Montreal and Kingston: McGill-Queen's University Press, 1994.

Walls, Andrew F. "The American Dimension in the History of the Missionary Movement." In *Earthen Vessels: American Evangelicals and Foreign Missions, 1880-1980,* edited by Joel A. Carpenter and Wilbert R. Shenk, 1-25. Grand Rapids: William B. Eerdmans, 1990.

Ward, W.E.F. *Educating Young Nations.* London: George Allen and Unwin, 1959.

–. *Fraser of Trinity and Achimota.* Accra: Ghana University Press, 1965.

"Ward, Ida Caroline," *Dictionary of National Biography, 1941-50,* edited by L.G. Wickman Legg, 925-26. London: Oxford University Press, 1959.

Weber, Hans-Rudi. *Asia and the Ecumenical Movement, 1895-1961.* London: SCM Press, 1966.

Wells, Kenneth M. *New God, New Nation: Protestants and Self-Reconstruction Nationalism in Korea, 1896-1937.* North Sydney, Australia: Allen and Unwin, 1990.

White, Louise. "'They Could Make Their Victims Dull': Genders and Genres, Fantasies and Cures in Colonial Southern Uganda." *American Historical Review* 100, no. 5 (1995): 1379-1402.

Winter, Ralph D., and Bruce A. Koch. "Finishing the Task: The Unreached Peoples Challenge." *Mission Frontiers* 22, no. 3 (2000): 22-26, 31-33.

Wright, Robert. *A World Mission: Canadian Protestantism and the Quest for a New International Order, 1918-1939.* Montreal and Kingston: McGill-Queen's University Press, 1991.

"Wrong, George MacKinnon." *Dictionary of National Biography, 1941-50,* edited by L.G. Wickman Legg, 979-80. London: Oxford University Press, 1959.

Xi, Lian. *The Conversion of Missionaries: Liberalism in American Protestant Missions in China, 1907-1932.* University Park: Pennsylvania State University Press, 1997.

Yoon, Soon Young. "A Legacy without Heirs: Korean Indigenous Medicine and Primary Health Care." *Social Science and Medicine* 17, no. 19 (1983): 1467-76.

Young, W. John. "The Legacy of Edwin W. Smith." *International Bulletin of Missionary Research* 25, no. 3 (2001): 126-30.

Zell, Hans, and Helene Silver, eds. *A Reader's Guide to African Literature.* London: Heinemann, 1972.

Index

Note: References to illustrations are printed in italics.

Abrahams, Peter, 98, 109, 114, 117
Achebe, Chinua, 116, 117
Adesegibin, Agnes Ayodele Taylor, 170n75
Advisory Committee on Native Education in Tropical Africa, 26
Africa, 14, *102-103;* educational missions, 26-27; indigenous Christians, 21, 22; literacy issues, 110, 111, 113-14, 165n12-13; women's social conditions, 113-16, 118, 119, 128-29, 130, 165n12, 169n66, 173n99, 174n14, 177n48. *See also* African literature; International Committee on Christian Literature for Africa (ICCLA); Wrong, Margaret
Africa (journal), 107-108, 112
African literature, 165n13; in colonial languages, 98-99, 113, 116; gendered as masculine, 97, 98, 113-16, 118-19; ICCLA and, 98, 101, 107-108; Margaret Wrong Prize for African Literature, 96, 116-18, 171n87, 172n93; in vernacular languages, 107, 111-12, 113-14; women writers, 101, 107, 115-16, 118; writers, 98-99, 101, 107, 108-109, 115-16, 117-18, 169n60. *See also* International Committee on Christian Literature for Africa (ICCLA)
Aggrey, James E. Kwegyir, 27, 129, 145n77, 177n47
Allahabad, 44, *46,* 60
American Laymen's Foreign Missions Inquiry, 29, 41, *46,* 55. *See also Re-Thinking Missions: A Laymen's Inquiry after One Hundred Years*
Avison, Oliver (Dr.), 73, 163n153
Azariah, V.S. (Bishop), 22, 24, 53-54
Azikiwe, Nnamdi, 172n97

Bâ, Mariama, 115
Baëta, Christian G. (Dr.), 23, *106,* 170n69
Benjamin, P.V. (Dr.), 24, *47,* 52, 53
Books for Africa, 101, 107
Bourns, Beulah, 89

Brittain, Vera, 121, 154n139, 173n5
Buck, Pearl, 30

Campbell, Thomas, 112
Carruthers, L.B. (Dr.), 62
Cary, Joyce, 117
CBMS. *See* Conference of British Missionary Societies (CBMS)
Chandy, Jacob (Dr.), 63, 176n32
Cheng, C.Y., 22
China, 20, 31, 73-4; Peking Union Medical College, 32, 51, 74
Chosen Women's Medical Training Institute, 82
Christian faith: Choné Oliver, 4-5, 35, 36, 37, 43, 56, 64, 131; Florence Murray, 4-5, 93-94, 131; Margaret Wrong, 5, 100. *See also* evangelism; indigenous Christians; missions; secularism
Christian Medical Association of India (CMAI), 14, 38, *46;* support for a union college, 44, 48, 52-53, 54, 60. *See also* Oliver, (Belle) Choné
Christian Medical College and Hospital, Vellore, 34, 126, 152n104; Missionary Medical School for Women, 58, 59-60, 61-62
Christian medical education in India, 40-1; Christian Medical College and Hospital, Vellore, 34, 126, 152n104; coeducation, 31-2, 48, 60, 61, 62; history, 40-44; improvement of educational standards, 43, 48; Missionary Medical School for Women, 58, 59-60, 61-62; sites considered for new college, 44, 58, 60; training of women, 32, 44, 48. *See also* Oliver, (Belle) Choné
Christian medical education in Korea, 82-83; Ewha Womans University, 87-88, 130, 161n111; Severance Union Medical College and Hospital, 15, 73, 87, 88-93, 94
Church Missionary Society (CMS), 22, 54

CMAI. *See* Christian Medical Association of India (CMAI)
CMS. *See* Church Missionary Society (CMS)
coeducation, 31, 69, 87-88, 145n76; India, 31-32, 48, 60, 61, 62
colonial agendas: medicine and, 125-26; missions and, 5-7, 27, 131, 138n11
Colthart, Margaret, 151n89
Conference of British Missionary Societies (CBMS), 13, 57
Cooperating Board for Christian Higher Education, 88-89, 92
Cox, Christopher, *106*
Crowther, Samuel Ajayi, 22

Dalhousie University Faculty of Medicine, 67-69
Datta, S.K., 50, 53-54
Davis, Jackson, *106*, 112, 169n64
de Mestral, Claude, 116-17
development work, 95, 120-21, 125, 127-30. *See also* International Committee on Christian Literature for Africa (ICCLA)
devolution, 12, 21-23, 42. *See also* indigenous Christians
Dodd, Gertrude, 61

East African Literature Bureau, 112-13, 171
East Gate Hospital for Women (Seoul), 72-3
ecumenical structures, 12-15, 126; NCC, 31, 48, 50, 57, 60, 149n56. *See also* Christian Medical Association of India (CMAI); International Missionary Council (IMC)
Edinburgh Conference (1910), 12-13, 22, 24
education: educational missions, 19-21, 26-28, 31-32; literacy issues in Africa, 110, 111, 113-14, 165n12-13; state assumption of responsibilities, 11-12. *See also* International Committee on Christian Literature for Africa (ICCLA); medical education
Eliot, T.S., 17
Emecheta, Buchi, 115, 116
evangelism: proselytization and social activism, 18, 20-21; role of indigenous Christians, 21-23; role of medicine in, 18, 30-39; social change and, 17, 18
Ewha Womans University, 87-88, 130, 161n111

feminist consciousness: Choné Oliver, 4, 37, 64-65, 121, 146n14; Florence Murray, 4, 92-93, 121; Margaret Wrong, 4, 97, 121
Firor, W.F. (Dr.), 50, 52, 54
Flexner Report, 68-69
FMCNA. *See* Foreign Missions Conference of North America (FMCNA)

Foreign Missions Conference of North America (FMCNA), 13, 57
Forman, Douglas, 52, 59
Frimodt-Möller, Christian, 38-39, *46*; support for an advanced medical college, 50, 52, 59, 62

Gandhi, M.K., 16, 41, 49, 59, 141n17; Choné Oliver and, 37, 126
GEB. *See* General Education Board (GEB)
gender roles: transitions, 7-8, 30-33; views of Choné Oliver, 37-38; views of Florence Murray, 82, 83, 92-93, 121, 159n74-75; views of Margaret Wrong, 97, 114-15, 121, 128-29, 170n75. *See also* coeducation; feminist consciousness; separate-spheres paradigm; women's roles
General Education Board (GEB), 112
Gibson, Betty, 31
Gibson, Paul, 11
Goheen, R.H.H. (Dr.), 38, *47*, 50, 52, 54
Gollock, Georgina, 19, 31, 114, 170n74
Gordon, Elsie, *105*
Guggisberg, Gordon, 122, 123

Halifax Medical College, 68-69
Hall, Rosetta Sherwood (Dr.), 72, 74, 82
Hamhung hospital (Korea), 78, 85, 94, 161n107; conditions on Florence Murray's arrival, 71, 73, 85; gender issues, 74-75; staff, 81-85; upgrading of facilities, 72, 76, 81
healing as ministry, 38-39; views of Choné Oliver, 34, 36-37, 38-40, 43
Hocking, William Ernest, 29, 30. *See also* *Re-Thinking Missions: A Laymen's Inquiry after One Hundred Years*
Hodge, J.Z., 48-49, 60
Holland, Henry (Sir), *47*
Hooke, Samuel Henry, 100
Houghton, Henry S. (Dr.), *46*
Hume, Edward Hicks (Dr.), 57-58

IAI. *See* International African Institute (IAI)
ICCLA. *See* International Committee on Christian Literature for Africa (ICCLA)
IMC. *See* International Missionary Council (IMC)
imperialism. *See* colonial agendas; Western imperialism
independence movements. *See* nationalist movements
India, 14, 37, *45*; educational missions, 19-20, 20-21, 27-28, 31-32; indigenous Christians, 21, 22, 142n41, 148n41-42; nationalist movement, 3, 48, 52, 64, 148n38-41, 149n56; NCC, 31, 48, 50, 57, 60, 149n56; state medicine, 41, 42;

upgraded requirements for medical training, 58, 60. *See also* Christian medical education in India; Oliver, (Belle) Choné

indigenous Christians: friendships with missionaries, 23-26; IMC conference participation, 22-23; India, 21, 22, 142n41, 148n41-42; Korea, 22, 70, 160n92; leadership roles, 22; role in evangelism, 21-23

indigenous nationalism. *See* nationalist movements

International African Institute (IAI), 107-108, 112

International Committee on Christian Literature for Africa (ICCLA), 96, 97-98, 167n33; African women's voices, 101, 128-29; publications, 101, 107-108, 111, 119, 167n34. *See also* African literature; Wrong, Margaret

International Missionary Council (IMC), 13-15, 106; Edinburgh Conference, 12-13, 22, 24; Jerusalem Conference, 11, 14, 22, 38; Lindsay Commission, 27-28, 32, 150n67; Margaret Wrong, 14, 31; membership, 13, 14; Tambaram Conference, 14, 22-23, 24, 25, *47*, 106; Whitby Conference, 14; women's roles, 30-31. *See also* International Committee on Christian Literature for Africa (ICCLA); Paton, William

International Review of Missions (IRM), 13

IRM. *See International Review of Missions (IRM)*

Jacobi, Mary Putnam (Dr.), 69

Japan, 21-22, 51; colonial administration in Korea, 70, 81, 86

Jerusalem Conference (1928), 11, 14, 22, 38

Johnson, Hilda, 21, 142n35

Jones, E. Stanley, 37

Jones, Rufus M., 15

Jones, Thomas Jesse, 26, 27

Joseph, T.J. (Dr.), *46*, 52-53

Kim, Helen (Dr.), *79*, 87, 130

Kim, Hyo-Soon (Dr.), 25, *78*, 82, 85, 93

Kim, Suhn-Hei, 92, 162n132

Koh, P.K. (Dr.), *79*, 84, 85, 122

Korea, 14, 70, *77*; advanced education, 19, 161n111; gender issues, 74-75; indigenous Christians, 22, 70, 160n92; Japanese colonial administration, 70, 81, 86; medical standards, 70-72; nationalist movements, 70; wartime conditions, 89-90, 161n111, 162n124. *See also* Murray, Florence Jessie

Lady Harding Medical College (New Delhi), 44

Laymen's Foreign Missions Inquiry. *See* American Laymen's Foreign Missions Inquiry

Lazarus, Hilda (Dr.), 25, *47*, 63, 154n132

Lee, Joo Lee (Dr.), 93

Lee, T.S. (Dr.), 78

leprosy, 43. *See also* Murray, Florence Jessie, interests in leprosy

Lindsay Commission, 27-28, 32, 150n67

Listen: News from Near and Far, 101, 107, 111, 119, 167n34

Malinowski, Bronislaw, 122-23

Margaret Wrong Prize for African Literature, 96, 116-18, 171n87, 172n93

Martin, Anna (Dr.), *46*, 151n89

Martin, Stanley, 163n153

McCully, Louise, 16

McMillan, Kate (Dr.), 71

medical education: coeducational institutions, 31-32, 48, 60, 61, 62, 69, 87-88, 145n76; fundraising for, 48; North America, 68-69; Peking Union Medical College, 32, 51, 74; training of male doctors by women, 32, 66. *See also* Christian medical education in India; Christian medical education in Korea

Medical Missionary Association (India), 38. *See also* Christian Medical Association of India (CMAI)

medical missions: healing as ministry, 34, 36-37, 38-40, 43. *See also* Christian medical education in India; Christian medical education in Korea; Murray, Florence Jessie; Oliver, (Belle) Choné

medicine: indigenous medicine, 126-27, 176n36; as part of colonial agendas, 125-26; role in mission work, 18-19; state assumption of responsibilities, 11-12, 41-42, 148n38-39. *See also* medical education; medical missions

Ministry of Healing in India, The, 39, 43

Miraj, 41, 45

Miraj Medical School, 41, 62, 150n61

mission paradigms: evaluation of roles and goals, 16-17, 26-30; transition, 5, 7, 11-12, 29-30, 34-35, 120-21, 125

missionaries, 9, 16, 21, 142n37; friendships with indigenous Christians, 23-26. *See also* mission paradigms; Murray, Florence; Oliver, (Belle) Choné; Wrong, Margaret

Missionary Medical School for Women (Vellore), 58, 59-60, 61-62. *See also* Christian Medical College and Hospital, Vellore missions: internationalism of, 9, 121; modernization of, 3, 8, 12, 15, 17, 19, 32, 33, 37, 48, 88; research on, 5-7; and modernizing men, 3, 19, 65, 70, 97, 98, 118, 121, 127, 128, 165n12. *See also* education; medical missions; mission paradigms; missionaries

modernity, 4-5, 64, 137n3

Mofolo, Thomas, 107

Moon, P.K. (Dr.), 90

Moot, the, 17

Mott, John R., 12, 13, 14, 59

Murray, Florence Jessie (Dr.), 3, 4, 8-9, 15, *77-80*, 122; cross-cultural tensions, 83-84, 162n124; death, 95; early career, 68, 70; education, 67-69, 76, 84, 92; Ewha Womans University, 87-88, 130, 161n111; family, 67; feminist consciousness, 4, 92-93, 121; honours, *80*, 84, 89, 91, 95, 123, 124; interests in leprosy, 91; interests in records management, 91-92, 162n132; interests in tuberculosis, 76, 81, 87, 91; in Manchuria, 71-72; nurses' training and, 81-82; private life, 25, 66, 76, 90, 161n107; professional standards, 66-67, 68-69, 71-73, 75-76, 81, 87-88, 90, 92, 93, 161n111; in Pusan, 89; repatriation, 85-86; retirement, 94-95; in Seoul, 25, 86-92, 94; spiritual faith, 4-5, 93-94, 131; views on indigenous medicine, 127; views on marriage, 82, 83, 159n74-75; views on sexual segregation, 67, 74-76; views on women's roles, 82, 83, 92-93, 121; work relationships, 66, 82-85, 89-90, 92-93, 122, 159n79. *See also* Hamhung hospital (Korea)

National Christian Council of India, Burma, and Ceylon (NCC), 31, 48, 50, 57, 60, 149n56

national Christian councils, 14-15, 37. *See also* National Christian Council of India, Burma, and Ceylon (NCC)

nationalist movements, 15; African literature and, 108, 110, 112, 114, 116, 118-19; Christian education and, 28, 64; distrust of mission work, 20, 125-6; India, 3, 48, 52, 64, 148n38-41, 149n56; Korea, 70

NCC. *See* National Christian Council of India, Burma, and Ceylon (NCC)

Nehru, Jawaharlal, 58, 59

Newbigin, Lesslie, 21, 24

Nkrumah, Kwame, 118-19

Northern Rhodesia, 110

nurses, 32; training in Korea, 81-82, 159n70

Nyasaland, *105*, 109

Oldham, Joseph H., 12-13, 14, 31, 38, 99, *106*, 144n60; educational missions in Africa, 26-27, 132n10; *Re-Thinking Missions* and, 30; response to secularism, 16, 17, 140n16

Oliver, (Belle) Choné (Dr.), 3, 8-9, 18, 34-35, *45, 46, 47*, 122; American Laymen's Foreign Missions Inquiry, 55; in Banswara (India), 37, 38; Central India mission, 36; CMAI, 14, 38, 40, 50-51; CMAI *Journal* articles, 51, 55, 56; death, 66, 154n131; early career, 37; education, 35, 36; feminist consciousness, 4, 37, 64-65, 121, 146n14; fundraising activities, 49, 50, 51-52, 53, 55, 56, 57, 60-61; honours, 123; NCC, 14, 31; negotiations to establish an advanced medical college, 49-52, 54-57, 58-63; private life, 56, 64-65, 66; *Re-thinking Missions* and, 55; social service attititude, 126-27; spiritual faith, 4-5, 35, 36, 37, 43, 56, 64, 131; views on gendered roles, 37-38; views on healing as ministry, 34, 36-37, 38-40, 43, 56, 64; views on mind-body relationship, 39, 56, 148n46; views on proselytizing, 36, 39; work relationships, 64-65, 122

Oxford Group Movement, 17, 37, 146n11

Pak, Dr., 71

Pak, Esther Kim (Dr.), 159n73

Pandit, R.S., Mrs., 58

Paton, William, 13, 28, 31, 150n63, 150n75; *Re-Thinking Missions* and, 30, 55; views on establisment of medical college in India, 49-50, 53, 54-57

Peabody, Lucy W., 59-60, 61, 62, 64-65

Peking Union Medical College (China), 32, 51, 76, 84

positive orientalism, 83-84, 160n85

Presbyterian Church of Canada, 30, 36. *See also* Oliver, (Belle) Choné; Murray, Florence Jessie; United Church of Canada

professional standards: role in attitudes to mission, 18, 19, 66-7; role in attitudes to women's work, 64-65, 75-76, 92-93. *See also* medical education; Murray, Florence Jessie

proselytization. *See* evangelism

public health work, 94, 127, 176n34

Rackham estate, 51-52, 150n68

Ransome-Kuti, Funmilayo, 170n69

Re-Thinking Missions: A Laymen's Inquiry after One Hundred Years, 18-19, 29-30, 55, 73-74, 93-94

Read, Margaret, 97, 100, 101, *105*, 109, 129, 164n5

The Remaking of Man in Africa, 31
Report of the Commission on Christian Higher Education in India, 27-28

Said, Edward, 26, 118, 171n77
Samkange, Thompson, 22, 23, 24-25
SCM. *See* Student Christian Movement (SCM)
Scudder, Galen, 52, 62
Scudder, Ida B. (Dr.), 62
Scudder, Ida Sophia (Dr.), 41, 59-60, 61, 62, 63, 126, 130
secularism, 11, 15-17
separate-spheres paradigm, 69, 75; Choné Oliver's reaction to, 64-65; Florence Murray's reaction to, 72-76; traditional attitudes towards, 32-33. *See also* coeducation; gender roles; "women's work for women" paradigm
Severance, L.H., 73
Severance Union Medical College and Hospital (Seoul), 15, 73, 87, 89-90, 92-93; roles of Florence Murray, 88-89, 89-93, 94
Shepherd, R.H.W., 108, 109
Sinclair, Margaret, 31
Smuts, General, 122
social activism: development work, 95, 120-21, 125, 127-30; role in mission work, 17-18. *See also* education; medical missions
social change. *See* mission paradigms; secularism; separate-spheres paradigm
social gospel, 17-18
Soon-Kile, *79*
South Africa, 108-109, 112
Soyinka, Wole, 117, 172n87
Steeds, Rita, 162n132
Stewart, Dr., 72
Struthers, Ernest, 90
Student Christian Movement (SCM), 99
Survey of Medical Missions in India, 38, 41

Tambaram Conference (1938), 14, 22-23, 24, 25, *47*, 106
Toyohiko, Kagawa, 21
tuberculosis, 41, 43, 53. *See also* Murray, Florence Jessie, interests in tuberculosis
Tutola, Amos, 117

union institutions: role in modernization, 19. *See also* ecumenical structures
United Church of Canada, 9, 13, 37; *Re-Thinking Missions* and, 30. *See also* Woman's Missionary Society
University of Madras, 61-62, 63. *See also* Missionary Medical School for Women (Vellore)

Vellore. *See* Christian Medical College and Hospital, Vellore

Wanless, William, 41
Ward, Ida, 111
Warnshuis, A.L., 13, 50
Western imperialism, 15
Whang, T.Y. (Dr.), x-xi, *78*
Whitby Conference (1947), 14
Wierenga, C.R., 61
WMS. *See* Women's Medical Service (WMS)
Woman's Missionary Society, 13, 121, 139n24
Women's Medical Service (WMS), 44, 47, 149n51
women's roles: development work and, 127-30; India, 44, 48, 60; International Missionary Council (IMC), 30-31; Korea, 66, 69, 74-76, 130; social conditions in Africa, 113-16, 118, 119, 128-29, 130, 165n12, 169n66, 173n99, 174n14, 177n48; writers in Africa, 101, 107, 115-16, 118. *See also* gender roles; separate-spheres paradigm
"women's work for women" paradigm, 12, 65, 69, 121, 129-30, 138n20; Korea, 66, 69, 74-76, 130
Wonju Union Christian Hospital Board and Building Committee, 91
World Council of Churches, 14, 126
World Student Christian Federation (WSCF), 99
Wrong, Margaret, 4-5, 8-9, *104-106*, 124; *Africa and the Making of Books,* 108, 114; ambiguous role, 120-21; death, 120, 123-24; early career, 99, 166n24; education, 99, 157n18-19; family, 99, 100-101, *104,* 120, 128, 166n28, 167n31, 169n64; feminist consciousness, 4, 97, 121; honours, 117, 123-24; personal characteristics, 100-101, 128, 131; role in ICCLA, 96, 97, 99, 101, 108-10, 111; role in IMC, 14, 31; spiritual faith, 5, 10; tours of Africa, 108-10, 111; views on indigenous literature, 108-109, 110, 111-13; views on political and social issues, 97, 139n24, 170n69; views on women's roles, 97, 114-15, 121, 128-29, 170n75; work relationships, 122-23, 128. *See also* Margaret Wrong Prize for African Literature
WSCF. *See* World Student Christian Federation (WSCF)

Yergen, Max, 123
Yonsei University, College of Medicine (Seoul), 91. *See also* Severance Union Medical College and Hospital (Seoul)